CW01496891

BLOOMSBURY
TEACHER
GUIDE
FRANKENSTEIN

CW01496906

Fe Brewer,
Mary Hind-Portley and
Gwen Nelson

BLOOMSBURY EDUCATION
LONDON OXFORD NEW YORK NEW DELHI SYDNEY

BLOOMSBURY EDUCATION
Bloomsbury Publishing Plc
50 Bedford Square, London WC1B 3DP, UK
Bloomsbury Publishing Ireland Limited
29 Earlsfort Terrace, Dublin 2, D02 AY28, Ireland

First published in Great Britain, 2025 by Bloomsbury Publishing Plc

This edition published in Great Britain, 2025 by Bloomsbury Publishing Plc

A catalogue record for this book is available from the British Library

ISBN: PB: 978-1-8019-9589-4; ePDF: 978-1-8019-9591-7; ePub: 978-1-8019-9592-4

2 4 6 8 10 9 7 5 3 1 (paperback)

Cover design by James Fraser

Text design by Marcus Duck
Typeset by Marcus Duck

Printed and bound in the UK by CPI Group (UK) Ltd., Croydon, CR0 4YY

To find out more about our authors and books visit www.bloomsbury.com and sign up for our
newsletters

For product safety related questions contact productsafety@bloomsbury.com

CONTENTS

CONTENTS

ACKNOWLEDGEMENTS

Fe

As with many things in life, writing this book took more time, more energy and more biscuits to complete than anticipated! For bearing with me through the process, I thank my husband, Rich, and my wonderful children, Archie and Emma, who have given me many a cuddle while Mummy was at her laptop writing (again). I thank every difficult class who made me a better teacher, and all my colleagues in various schools who have inspired me to be a better teacher. As for my co-authors, I thank them for tolerating my sometimes blunt feedback and rambling WhatsApp voice notes, and for the determination and resilience that they have shown through the writing process. Finally, I thank my parents, who inspired me to love reading and history (my first true loves), and my brother, whose battered, 20-year-old GCSE copy of *Frankenstein* I stole to read many years ago.

An honest review of *Frankenstein*, from Fe's dad: 'Not bad for nineteenth-century literature. A bit wordy, though.' (Dave Jarrett, 2024)

Gwen

It is no exaggeration to state that without Fe, this book would not exist – or, at least, not exist for another decade or so. Her ability to get things done, single-mindedness and drive are what got us over the line. To be frank, Fe should have her name in a larger font on the front cover, and probably more royalties than she's going to get. Mary is an absolute asset to English teacher-kind and should be treasured. She is a clever, knowledgeable and diligent teacher and it's been a real privilege to work alongside her. Together, Mary and Fe have been pragmatic and gracious, while I've battled a fair few demons (depression, anxiety and a very nearly fatal dose of carbon monoxide due to a decrepit gas fire) during this process.

Huge thanks are owed to my other half Andrew, who has shown immense patience and kindness when Franken-work ate into our time together many, many times. I also owe a great deal to every class to whom I ever taught this text – it was never less than a joy. Whether you wanted to or not, you all became geeky about words and language and, rightly, developed a deep loathing for Victor Frankenstein by the end of the novel. Errol the kitten deserves a mention, as his kitten shenanigans kept me going during some dark times. Lastly, thanks to my mum and much-missed dad who, while I was young, prioritised education and reading over pretty much all else. Even though I resented it deeply at the time, all those educational trips in school holidays did me so much good.

Mary

Firstly, to my wonderful co-authors Fe and Gwen, without whom this book would not be the brilliant work that it is. We are united in a detestation of Victor Frankestein but an absolute love of Mary Shelley. Thank you, Fe, for your excellent humour, your ability to plan, your giving of honest feedback and your leadership of the process, which got the best out of Gwen and me. To Gwen, for showing me how to teach A level lang/lit a very long time ago and who then became my friend. Your determination is an inspiration to me. A side nod to Twitter (as it was), through which I met these amazing women and whose wisdom I have benefitted from for many years now.

To all my pupils who inspire me to keep on improving as a teacher and who put up with my tangential comments about writers and texts.

I also want to thank my family: my dad, James 'Jimmy' Portley (1947–2021), who taught me determination and resilience; my mum, Jean Portley, who gave me the gift of reading and a lifelong love of books; and my sister, Annette Thompson, who is always there. My gratitude also goes to my friend Stephanie Laurence, who has endless patience and spent many hours listening to my endless talk about the book.

And finally, James, Will, Tabitha and good dog Barney, who put up with being neglected and ignored during 'The year without a summer' while we brought our 'progeny' to life.

A very big thank you to our editors: Emily Evans, who first gave us the opportunity to write this book, and Lucy Vallance, who has also had much patience and allowed us more time to write and edit so that we could do justice to this complex text.

FOREWORD

As a child in the 1990s, I watched reruns of the 1960s American family sitcom, *The Munsters*. Herman Munster was the well-meaning, slightly dim husband to Lily and father to Eddie. Each family member was based on a classic Gothic creature: Eddie was a werewolf, Lily a vampire, and Herman was a tall, broad, grim-looking Frankenstein's monster. My initial idea of who and what The Creature is was shaped by these Saturday mornings in front of the TV, and added to by various appearances of Lurch in *The Addams Family*, multiple episodes of *Scooby* Doo, and even the depiction of a giant letter 'H' in *Sesame Street*.

When I finally read the original novel at age 17, I was struck by the profound and poignant moment when The Creature reflects on its own misery: *'All men hate the wretched; how, then, must I be hated, who am miserable beyond all living things!'* The Creature is at times a philosopher, at others a critic, but always an intelligent, nuanced character who voices the most challenging ideas in this perplexing novel. The reality of Frankenstein's monster is worlds away from the cartoonish green man with a bolt through his neck.

So, the real *Frankenstein*, Mary Shelley's *Frankenstein*, poses a unique challenge for teachers in the English classroom. They must navigate arcane language; classical allusion; multiple narrators; non-linear structure; abstract philosophical ideas, and a story wrapped in over a century of myth and obfuscation.

How, then, can teachers peel back these layers and find the nuanced, subtle reality of Mary Shelley's work? Teaching literature is very often about plotting a course of discovery through a seemingly impenetrable landscape, but it's also about the experience of a text and personal response to human themes. I would defy anyone not to feel some of the agony of The Creature, or the bleakness of the ice at the end of the novel.

In this book, Fe, Mary and Gwen have provided an astonishing treasure trove of knowledge and practical ideas for teachers. Their combined experience, depth of understanding and expertise is evident in the beautifully sequenced, thoughtful approach to the text. Above all, the focus on questions which are threaded through every part of this guide, is a sure way to support students not just to know, but to think, reflect and respond to this timeless masterpiece.

Jennifer Webb

HOW TO USE THIS BOOK

Why, what and how

This book is designed as a teacher's guide and reference point that can be used at any stage of teaching *Frankenstein*, whether teachers are reading it alongside the text or dipping in and out of it when the need or interest arises. It has been written by teachers, for teachers, to ease the demands of teaching a text (particularly one as meaty as *Frankenstein*!) by addressing the 'why', 'what' and 'how' of Shelley's masterpiece. Alongside this, you'll find contextual gems and critical interpretations to build your subject knowledge, but also to enrich the knowledge that you impart to your pupils.

There are accompanying materials available for each chapter, which can be used in your classroom with learners either as they are or adapted to suit your learners' needs. These include the questions and example answers provided through the text, scaffolds and stems for essay writing, key quotations and example essays. A contextual timeline and map of the novel's locations will also be available for download. You can access these at bloomsbury.pub/BTG-Frankenstein. Other resources available on this site will be flagged in this book by this icon: 🖱 and there will be many more available online.

As *Frankenstein* – perhaps uniquely – is often taught at Key Stage 3 but is also a set text at both GCSE and A level, we aim to provide information and activities that can be adapted to suit learners at each key stage.

The sections

Frankenstein is not the slimmest of novels. It is also one much studied by literary scholars. To help you to navigate this, we have divided the novel into sections of between one and four chapters, each focusing on a period or phase in the lives of the novel's narrators.

At the start of each section, we provide an 'At a glance' overview to aid quick navigation of the text. This comprises:

- **Summary quotation:** This key quotation embodies the key concepts, ideas or emotions of each section.

- **Big Question:** To accompany the summary quotation, we offer a 'Big Question' that functions as a springboard for ideas and explorations with your learners (or for your own interest).

- **Significant plot events:** This provides an outline of the key moments of the chapter to remind readers where they are in the novel.

- **Character focus:** This identifies the key characters in the chapter.
- **Key themes:** Following the characters, we identify the key themes of each section to help you to make connections across those themes and encourage critical analysis.
- **Handle with care:** This is a brief note of any elements of the section that should be considered carefully when teaching, due to their sensitive nature.

The 'Why'

Each chapter begins with a 'why', which provides some key questions to guide reflection and discussion in each section. Whether teaching a novel for the first or the fiftieth time, having a selection of 'why' questions can provide a springboard for explorations.

In our 'why' questions, we aim to provoke different levels of critical thinking about:

- the way in which characters behave or feel
- why themes or concepts are important – sometimes to the characters but also sometimes to the plot or to the reader
- why Shelley might have shaped the novel in the way in which she has, why she includes what she includes and why she has made the characters and their journeys as she has.

In recognition of the key role that dialogue teaching holds in English teaching, we encourage you to use these questions to prompt debate and discussion.

The 'What'

Our 'what' is a list of key questions, which provide insight into the key information of the section that teachers and learners need in order to be able to navigate the text successfully.

In this, we provide:

- a summary of what happens in each chapter in the section
- social, historical, biographical or literary context and/or criticism
- high-leverage (essential) vocabulary in context
- notes on plot and character development.

What happens?

Here, you will find an overview of the chapters in the section, with an emphasis on the high-leverage moments and developments. This varies in its detail, depending on the nature and contents of the chapters at hand.

Social, historical, biographical or literary context and/or criticism

Knowledge of context can open a world of meaning for pupils, but getting to grips with 200-year-old sentiments can be tricky. Here, we offer key contextual information that adds meaning or clarity to various aspects of the text.

Vocabulary in context

As English teachers, we are acutely aware of learners' difficulties when reading heritage texts. This should not, however, prevent young people from engaging with or enjoying them. As such, we have carefully chosen high-leverage vocabulary for each chapter, not only so that you can provide explicit instruction and vocabulary teaching, but also so that the words can be used by learners when discussing or writing about the text. The vocabulary can be pre-taught to help with reading fluency and reduce cognitive load.

Plot and character development

The final area of our 'what' explores plot and character development. These are shaped by key questions that teachers can use to develop both their own understanding of the chapters and their pupils' understanding. Some answers are brief or simple lists; others are more detailed, as they explore questions in greater depth.

The questions can be used in a range of ways: retrieval, comprehension or to guide chunking of reading. Teachers may choose to share questions either before or after reading, or adapt them to further cater for their pupils' needs. They could also be used to facilitate discussion or independent explorations of the text. At times, we provide 'stretch' questions too, to cater for the higher-prior-attaining pupils or A level learners. This section also serves as a foundational base for knowledge quizzes, retrieval practice and independent tasks. The example responses provided support teachers, but can also be used to support pupils. ☁

They could also be used for:

* hinge-points for teachers to check key understanding before moving on
* consolidation or retrieval points when revisiting prior learning
* homework or independent learning tasks.

How we approach the 'How' section

This section is where we embark on a literary, linguistic and structural analysis of carefully selected elements of each section, interrogating the decisions made by Shelley to communicate the key messages and meanings of each section. We also spend time on the key characters in each section.

* **Language:** This analysis ranges from granular explorations of specific words and phrases to patterns of language or grammar across a passage.

- **Character focus:** The key characters of each section are identified for deeper analysis, in order to explore their arc (complete character journey) in that section but also Shelley's use of them as devices.

- **Structure:** Here, we look at key structural choices in the sections and how Shelley uses structure, narrative voice, dialogue and key changes or foci in each section. Occasionally, we include critical analysis by academics, to deepen understanding of Shelley's choices and their impact. As several of Shelley's structural features span across the novel, we also make connections between sections to highlight patterns in the novel's structure overall.

- **Extracts:** At the end of the 'How' section, we provide key extracts for each section and closely inspect their key features to highlight examples of close language analysis (such as that developed in Key Stages 3, 4 and 5).

How we will refer to Victor's creation

There are several ways in which Victor's creation is referred to in critical literature and in typical discussion: monster, being, creation, and so on. It is with careful consideration that we chose the name that we would use.

Monster

This is perhaps the most common term used for Victor's creation, reinforced by interpretations of Frankenstein in popular culture that emphasise the violence of the creation rather than his sentience. As this term creates the impression that Victor's creation is indeed monstrous and focuses (or even limits) Shelley's character, we decided against this term.

Being

Arguably, this term is limiting too, in that it acknowledges Victor's creation as a living creature but neglects the conscious act of creation at Victor's hand. As such, we also decided against this term.

Creature

We felt that this term acknowledged both the sentient life that is Victor's creation but also his existence as a result of Victor's actions, which led directly to the Creature's life and, as a result of this, should have carried with them great responsibility. It is for this reason that we decided to use this term for Victor's creation.

Pit stops

These features are used as pause points throughout the chapters to provide suggested learning and assessment activities to help you to plan, scaffold, deepen and develop your learners' understanding of the text.

Retrieval points

Throughout the book, you will find a series of 'retrieval points' to support you in ensuring that the key high-leverage knowledge for each section is understood by learners. These are designed to be low-stakes, straightforward and quick to both complete and check, so that time can be spent building on prior knowledge rather than repeating it.

Academic writing points

Essential to the disciplinary knowledge of English is analytical writing. For this reason, we have included in the book – *and also in our resources* – a range of prompts, scaffolds, suggestions and ideas to support learners' writing. Learners need explicit preparation and support to enable them to unlock the procedural thinking that goes into academic writing (and which we, as subject specialists, often take for granted).

Writing is cognitively demanding for learners, and the teaching of it is often cognitively demanding for teachers too. In light of this, we have included lots of examples of analytical writing, but also prompts for debates and discussion that can deepen learners' understanding while also building their confidence, so that learners' writing is based on well-considered ideas and a strong understanding of these.

S-T-R-E-T-C-H

Frankenstein is one of the few texts that is taught frequently in Key Stages 3, 4 and 5. This being so, we have ensured that we have considered the need to challenge A level and higher-prior-attaining learners. Throughout the book, we have included tasks that will challenge these learners with more conceptual or critical perspectives and debates. As motivation is so key to learning, we hope that this will enable you to bring curiosity, ambition and scholarship into your classroom.

Dual coding

A principle put forward by Allan Paivio (p. 1969), and supported by cognitive scientists since, posits that the human brain can process information through separate systems – the verbal and the visual – and that the engagement of both can improve comprehension and facilitate a secure grasp of complex concepts. Clark, Lyons and Hoover (p. 2004) worked extensively with cognitive scientists to research dual coding. They found that the way in which visuals align with the learning process can result in six key benefits: direct attention, management of cognitive load, activation of prior knowledge, development of schemas, transference to working memory and motivation. It is unsurprising, therefore, how popular this approach is in pedagogical practice. (Shah & Kurczij, 2024, p. 9)

Disciplinary literacy

The following is a graphic summary of some of the commonly recurring concepts in disciplinary literacy. These are signposted across the text and our *downloadable resources*, to maximise opportunities for impact.

- Analysis:

- Inference:

- Context:

- Summarise:

Retrieval:

Structure:

Tracking the text:

Comparison:

Themes

The following is a graphic organiser for some of the key themes (*included in our downloadable resources*). Shelley explores a number of ideas and themes throughout the novel. To support you in navigating key areas for these, we have included them in the 'at a glance' section but also indicated where they arise through a series of icons, so that you can easily find where Shelley builds on them in order to explore them with your classes.

- Ambition and legacy:

- Betrayal and guilt:

- Crime and justice:

- Death and grief:

- Destiny and fate:

- Family and companionship:

- Isolation and loneliness:

- Knowledge and discovery:

- Narrator and narration: **N**

- Obsession:

- Power and responsibility:

- Prejudice:

- Rejection and its consequences:

- Revenge:

- Society and social class:

INTRODUCTION: THE INCEPTION OF A WORK OF LITERARY SIGNIFICANCE

How did Frankenstein come to be?

In 1815, Mount Tambora erupted in Indonesia. The ash cloud resulted in storms and freak weather across the globe. A year later, during 'the year without a summer', one of the most notorious groups in literature gathered in the Villa Diodati, Switzerland, to entertain themselves and escape the weather. This was the beginning of Frankenstein.

This point of confluence was incredible – not just the summer at the villa, but Mary Shelley's genealogy and her social, political and literary circles. The group at the villa comprised Mary (Godwin), Percy Shelley, Lord Byron, Claire Clairmont and Byron's physician, Dr John Polidori. Well-read, intelligent, vibrant and bored, the group considered how to entertain themselves in such circumstances – thus the telling of ghost stories ensued. This, along with the darkness of the storms, provided fertile ground for the creation of new and terrifying stories, such as Polidori's 'The Vampyre' and *Frankenstein* by Mary Shelley. However, it was to be Mary's *Frankenstein* that had the greatest lasting impact on the literary and cultural Western world and is therefore now set for examination.

A short biography of Mary Shelley

The beginning: Mary the daughter

On 30 August 1797, Mary was born to Mary Wollstonecraft and William Godwin. The couple had only married a handful of months earlier, when Wollstonecraft fell pregnant by Godwin, creating a public scandal. Regardless of this, the pair lived a life at the centre of literary London, with a circle of friends who were influential eighteenth-century writers, thinkers and what we would now call scientists. This life was not to continue, however, as a mere 11 days after Mary's birth, Wollstonecraft died of puerperal fever, a loss that would define Mary's life and influence many of the ideas in *Frankenstein*.

Grieving for his wife, racked with debt and keen to provide young Mary with a mother, Godwin married Mary-Jane Clairmont, who had a daughter, Jane Claire Clairmont (known as Claire). Unfortunately, Mary and her stepmother's relationship was far from that of a happy mother and daughter and the household was often filled with tension.

Despite this, their home was also a place that provided a significant element of Mary's literary education. The house was frequented by many of the names present in Key Stages 3 to 5 curricula: a roll call of the famous poets and writers of the Romantic period, such as Wordsworth, Charles Lamb, Coleridge and, later on, Percy Shelley. Legend has it that Coleridge once read aloud *The Rime of the Ancient Mariner* (1798) at a gathering, prompting an eight-year-old Mary to hide behind the sofa and listen.

Mary also grew up surrounded by the work of her mother, Mary Wollstonecraft, through both her published works and the stories that she had written for her first daughter, Fanny Imlay. From these, Mary was able to keep her mother a constant presence in her life. Wollstonecraft's radical ideas lived on through her major work *A Vindication of the Rights of Women* (1792) and influenced many of Mary's actions – for example, her 'elopement' with Percy and the desire to live unconventionally.

Mary the girl

Much of Mary's childhood was spent in day schools or being educated at home, through the input of her father and stepmother's intellectual circles. However, Mary was often an ill child, which prompted Godwin to send her away from home for the sake of her health. In 1811, Mary was sent to boarding school in Ramsgate and then to live in Scotland. While in Scotland, Mary found a best friend, Izabella, and was granted physical freedom in the Scottish countryside, giving her space and time away from the difficulties of living in the Godwin-Clairmont household and the complex relationships therein. Later, she would write of her time in Scotland:

'I lived principally in the country as a girl, and passed a considerable time in Scotland...; my [...] residence was on the blank and dreary northern shores of the Tay, near Dundee [...] they were not so to me then. They were the eyry of freedom, and the pleasant region where unheeded I could commune with the creatures of my fancy.'

(Shelley, 1831)

The rugged and romantic landscapes of Scotland brought her peace, freedom and a great sense of the restorative power of nature – another idea that features in her novel.

Mary the lover

Aged 16, Mary returned to London and the tensions of the Godwin-Clairmont household. During her time away, Godwin had become friends with Percy Shelley, and was financially indebted to him. Percy was 21, and his intelligence and appearance made him immediately attractive to Mary. Despite Percy already being married, the two quickly began an affair. By October 1814, Percy separated from his wife, Harriet, and regularly met Mary at her mother's grave in St Pancras churchyard. This secluded spot offered Mary a quiet place to study and commune with her mother, but also a place for the two to secretly meet, with the aid of her stepsister, Jane Clairmont (later known as Claire or Clair Clairmont).

Godwin did not approve of the relationship between his daughter and Percy, although the reason for this is unclear. Perhaps Godwin, despite his radical beliefs, disapproved of Mary having a relationship with a married man, or perhaps Godwin could see the signs of future mental instability in Percy's character and worried about how this would affect his daughter's future life. 'Shelley would go on to harm every one of the Godwin girls whether he meant to or not.' (Gordon, 2015, p. 75)

First travels in Europe and debt

To escape London, Percy and Mary ran away to France, along with her stepsister, Claire. The trip was, in many ways, a failure from the start: Mary was terribly sick on the way and they were soon discovered by Mary's stepmother. Refusing to return to London, they made their way to Switzerland, but soon ran out of funds and were forced to return home. Though brief, the journey proved to be of future benefit, as they discovered 'Castle Frankenstein' and its legend of Konrad Dippel, who tried to bring the dead back to life.

In London, Percy discovered that his financial worries had worsened, as Harriet, his wife, had emptied his bank account. Consequently, Mary, Claire and Percy had to live in relative poverty and as social outcasts. Their woes continued as Harriet give birth to a boy, Percy's son, and Mary also fell pregnant. Claire also spent increasing amounts of time with Percy, taking advantage of his distaste for pregnant women – a situation that upset both women.

In November 1814, after living apart for a time to avoid Percy's arrest for debt, their financial situation improved and Percy, Mary and Claire moved into lodgings together. Interestingly, pages of both Mary and Claire's journals that may have related to this time period have been removed, suggesting that there was still some tension between the three of them, and speculation remains as to the depth and physicality of the relationship between Percy and Claire. Percy then encouraged Mary and his friend, Thomas Hogg, to form a relationship to distract Mary from her jealousy of Claire. Percy wanted to develop his plans for a community based on free love, and Hogg agreed to further this plan. In a bid to please Percy, Mary attempted a relationship with Hogg, but was far too in love with Percy to act on this. She did, however, promise Hogg that she would consider this once her baby was born.

1815: Mary becomes a mother

On 22 February 1815, Mary's first child, Clara, was born eight weeks early, living for just 13 days. She wrote to Hogg: 'My baby is dead... It was perfectly well when I went to bed.' (Bennett, 1995, p. 8) Mary had little support and mourned the loss of her first baby alone. Her grief can be seen in the themes of birth, loss and death in *Frankenstein*. Following the loss of the baby, Percy and Mary retreated to the countryside in April for a few nights, as Percy had become less self-absorbed and more supportive towards Mary.

In June, Mary discovered that she was pregnant for a second time, and she and Percy moved to Bishopsgate, near Eton, and undertook a programme of reading as Mary's pregnancy symptoms improved. In January 1816, Mary gave birth to Willam, affectionately known as Willmouse.

1816: The entrance of Byron

In 1816, Byron became a significant influence in the lives of Mary and Percy, after Claire met him by chance at a theatre in Drury Lane. Claire soon shifted her attention away from Percy and engaged in a variety of ploys to gain his attention. Byron, like Percy, was already married (and also rumoured to be having an affair with his half-sister), but this did not prevent him from encouraging her. She sent dozens of letters to him, portraying herself as a radical woman and, in a bid to entice him further, plotted to bring Byron and Mary together. Once again, missing journal pages prevent us from knowing how Claire brought the two together. Her ploys briefly succeeded, and in the early spring of 1816, Claire became pregnant by Byron. Unfortunately for her and the child, he soon lost interest in her.

Switzerland

In April 1816, Mary, Percy and Claire set off to Switzerland. Percy wished to leave England, as he was frustrated by Godwin's continued refusal to accept Mary and Percy's relationship and by critics' response to his poem 'Alastor'. It was Claire who suggested Switzerland, as she wished to be near Byron, who was heading for Geneva to escape the scandal that he had caused in London. For Mary, who was terrified of losing her son as she had her first baby, the trip seemed potentially beneficial for little Willmouse.

The journey to Switzerland was not exciting. Mary's travel sickness, the disruption in weather patterns and general food shortages made the journey incredibly unpleasant. Like their journey from Switzerland earlier, this scenery eventually found its way into the landscapes in *Frankenstein*.

Once in Geneva, the travellers settled into routines, reading and writing in the Maison Chapuis. Never settled, though, Claire remained anxious in anticipation of Byron's arrival, which eventually came with expected flamboyance, complete with a carriage like Napoleon's and Byron's menagerie. Byron, accompanied by his friend and physician, Dr John Polidori, soon began acquainting themselves with the other guests.

June 1816

As the journey had been hampered by poor weather, so too was their time in Geneva, and the travellers spent much of their time indoors and sheltering from storms. On 15 June, they gathered to read a play by Polidori, which sparked discussions about human nature and creation, Dr Darwin's experiments with electricity and Polidori's notes from a lecture on animals given by William Lawrence, an anatomist. Raised in a household with visitors from various academic fields, Mary was not new to science, and here again we can see the seeds of *Frankenstein* beginning to germinate. The final catalyst needed for *Frankenstein* soon came in the form of Byron setting a challenge to everyone to pen a ghost story.

Mary could not have had a more conducive environment for penning a Gothic classic. Further evenings were spent discussing ghosts and sharing readings of various Romantic and Gothic works, including Coleridge's *Christabel*. At one point, Percy became hysterical and claimed to have seen a horrific vision of a lady with eyes instead of nipples on her breasts, an event that left the party much disturbed.

There are different accounts of Mary's genesis of *Frankenstein*. Percy (1818, preface) and Polidori's accounts differ from Mary's introduction to the 1831 edition. Mary's later account of this event explores the difficulties of the creative process, but Percy's 1816 introduction omits this and is supported by Polidori's diary account. This adds another layer of complexity to our understanding of the creation and writing of *Frankenstein* and the stability of the text. Whatever the true origins, when the men took a trip for a few days, some time between 22 and 30 June, Mary began writing her story, originally opening it with 'It was on a dreary night in November'.

She continued to develop it over the coming days and weeks, layering the narrative with multiple perspectives, exploring her experience of birth and death, and thoughts around the concept of men as creators. She was not alone in writing, and other works generated from the time at Villa Diodati were Polidori's 'The Vampyre', Byron's *Manfred* and Percy's 'Mont Blanc' and *Prometheus Unbound*.

Autumn 1816

In September 1816, Mary and Percy returned to England and moved to Bath to avoid the bills from Bishopsgate. Mary spent the autumn working on her manuscript, deciding to add Robert Walton as an important new character. Her writing process was hampered, however, by personal tragedies.

In early October, Percy received a disturbing letter from Fanny, Mary's half-sister and her mother's first daughter. Percy rushed to Bristol to help Fanny but was unable to, as she had already travelled to Swansea; there, she committed suicide with an overdose of laudanum. Mary grieved heavily for her loss.

Another tragedy occurred in December, as Percy received notice that his wife, Harriet, had also committed suicide. Now free to marry and seeking custody of his two children by Harriet (in whom he had formerly shown little interest), Percy decided that he and Mary should be wed to bring some respectability to their relationship. On 30 December, the two were finally wed. Despite such significant developments, Mary continued to work on *Frankenstein*.

January 1817

In January, Mary discovered that she was pregnant again and wrote anxious letters to Percy, who was away with Leigh Hunt in Hampstead. Percy told Mary to come to London and she then joined him on the 25 January. Once again, Mary was in the company of literary society and also part of a complex household. The Hunt household had many similarities with her family: a husband who was having an affair with his wife's sister and a sister who had mental health issues. Having lost her half-sister to suicide, Mary was also concerned for the health of Claire, who had recently given birth to her child by Byron, Alba, later known as Allegra.

In the spring, Mary and Percy moved to Albion House, Marlow. To support Claire, an elaborate plan was concocted to pass off Alba as one of the Hunt children. In order to do this, the Hunts were invited to stay at Albion House for an extended period of time. It is with this complex backdrop that Mary refined the manuscript of *Frankenstein*.

Mary suffered a long period of exhaustion following the birth of her second daughter. She was unable to produce enough milk to sufficiently feed the baby and she also worried about William's health in the cold and damp Albion House. She longed to return Alba to Byron but by this time, he had disappeared from Italy and gone to Greece or elsewhere. Mary and Percy were also in debt, and their relationship suffered further as he spent time in London with Claire rather than with Mary. His recent publishing of a pamphlet on the death of British liberty caused Mary to fear that he would be hanged as a traitor. She worried too about her own work, fearing that her publishers would raise the issue of Victor's feelings for Elizabeth as, in this edition, they were first cousins.

It took nine months for Mary to complete her final iteration of the 1818 edition of the story. This is not insignificant, as she was writing during pregnancy. Mary recognised this and referred to the novel as her 'progeny' – Gordon (2015) points out that the time of the novel spans from 17 December to 17 September, which links with the pregnancy. By the time her daughter and third child, Clara, was born in September, Mary's novel was complete. In addition to typing a fair copy of the manuscript for publication, Mary also worked on *History of a Six Weeks' Tour* (1817), to which Percy contributed two travel letters and his poem 'Mont Blanc'. This was published in November.

1818

In January, *Frankenstein* was published anonymously in a print run of 500 copies (the convention at the time) by Lackington, Hughes, Harding, Mavor and Jones. As Percy had contributed the preface, many readers and critics inaccurately attributed the novel to him. Despite not being enthusiastically received by critics, the novel's reputation began to build by word of mouth.

In the spring, the Shelleys, Claire and Alba left England for the third time, travelling via Calais to Italy. A factor in their decision to move back to Italy was Percy's health, as the hot climate of Italy was suggested as a cure. At this point, Byron was in Venice and Mary hoped to leave Alba with him. While the trip was mingled with intellectual gatherings, writing and sightseeing, for Mary, their time in Italy was blighted by further tragedy. In September 1818, Clara became ill and died of a fever, and in June 1819, William too became ill and died of malaria. Consumed by grief, Mary fell into a deep depression, feeling cursed by death. Mary also found herself pregnant once again, and eventually began work on her new novel *Mathilda*, which would not be published until 1959.

Mary's final child, Percy Florence, was born on 12 November 1819. Like her other children, he would not survive infancy and, after one final pregnancy resulting in a miscarriage that nearly killed her, Mary would never fall pregnant again.

The 1820s

Throughout the 1820s, Mary continued to write, and she and Percy continued to travel despite their increasingly strained relationship. At one point, Percy had become interested in sailing and bought a boat with a friend. This would prove a fatal mistake. On 8 July, Percy and Edward set sail from Livorno to Lerici. The weather was stormy and the boat was spotted in difficulty. Ten days later, Percy's body would be washed up on the shore. After his friends took relics from the body (including Leigh Hunt taking Percy's heart), the body was burned in a funeral pyre on the beach. Leigh later refused to give Mary the preserved heart, but was eventually persuaded to hand it over. The heart was discovered, 30 years later, preserved inside the pages of 'Adonais', inside Mary's travelling desk.

In August 1823, Mary returned to London after an absence of five years, where she began to plan her novel *The Last Man*, published in 1826. It was at this point that *Frankenstein* had become a play, with five different versions being performed. The play attracted protesters against its monstrous subjects, holding placards, but this served to promote it further.

Due to copyright laws at the time, Mary made no money from this appropriation of the play, so she knew that she had to continue to write to survive, as she only had a tiny allowance from Percy's father. Mary edited a book of Shelley's poems, wrote for the *Westminster Review* and began *The Fortunes of Perkin Warbeck* in 1828 (published in 1830), then *Lodore* (published in 1835), followed by *Falkner*, her last novel, in 1837. Her last non-fiction work was *Rambles in Germany and Italy* in 1844. She also spent 16 years writing short stories for ladies' annuals. In addition, she revised *Frankenstein* for a new edition. This edition is the one set for study for GCSE, as it is the edition most commonly found in English schools.

1831 edition

Mary revised *Frankenstein* so that Bentley, the publisher, would own the copyright and therefore a new edition could be published and sold. This time, 3,000 of the 3,500 copies were sold in the same year. This edition carries the preface written by Mary and is her attempt to revise her life story, implying to readers that she was a married woman in 1816. Spark (2013) comments that Mary had originally written when 'not acquainted with her own mind', but that in 1831 she had reached 'a higher degree of consciousness' (p. 127), preferring the 1831 edition. Mellor (1990) comments that the 1831 edition reflects how Mary's philosophical views 'changed radically', linked to her 'pessimism' caused by the deaths of her children and husband, betrayals by close friends and her financial difficulties. These Mary saw as part of an 'indifferent universe' (p. 100). There are powerful arguments for both texts and no doubt you will have your preferred edition.

This is a list of the main changes to help you with the 1831 edition:

- Elizabeth Lavenza becomes an unconnected orphan and not a cousin, and takes a more passive role.
- The role of Frankenstein's family in encouraging their son's interest in science is changed to that of a stranger.
- The influence of Professor Waldeman on Victor while at Ingolstadt University is more powerful and more evil in intent.
- Fate takes the place of individual choice/free will, and nature is presented as a significant force.
- Male ambition is portrayed as harmful.
- Female characters are innocent but unable to save themselves.
- The glacier at Chamounix is seen by Victor as 'working of an immutable law' rather than just a wonderful spectacle.
- The parallels between Victor and Walton are made stronger, with Walton sharing Victor's craving to achieve the impossible.

- One significant aspect is unchanged in both editions: Victor dies unrepentant, hoping that someone else may have the success that he had not.

- A new preface is written by Mary, focusing on the conception of the story and romanticising the origins at the Villa Diodati.

What is the significance of Frankenstein in our literary and cultural landscape?

'"Frankenstein" is a product of criticism, not a work of literature', states Fred Botting (1995, p. 1). Yet *Frankenstein* is dominant in our literary, cultural and critical landscape. Even from first publication in 1818, the novel received criticism that it was lacking in morality and piety, and it is this and the debates around the novel's themes that have contributed to its fame.

What place does the novel have in our literary heritage? For teachers, it is often a text included in Key Stage 3 as part of a study of the Gothic, but also a set text for some exam boards, which may have been what brought you to this book.

Mary Shelley's imagination and skill, along with the novel's own heritage, linked with Percy Shelley, Byron and William Godwin, has now assured its place in the literary canon and also its significant influence in film and media. The novel was first published in 1818 (with a revised version following in 1831) and then a play by Richard Brinsley Peake was performed in 1823, called *Presumption; or, the fate of Frankenstein*, watched by Mary Shelley herself: '… lo and behold! I found myself famous.' Botting (1995, p. 3) suggests that this play 'signalled Victor's transformation into a modern myth'. Certainly, the nineteenth century saw many mutations of the novel, and the first confusions between the Creature and its creator emerged, leading to the common misconception that the Creature is called 'Frankenstein'. The novel has mutated into its own 'hideous progeny', with Frankenstein the Creature as the star, as seen here in an article for The Student Voice Network:

'When asked to describe Frankenstein, most people will give you an image of a bright green blockheaded, mindless monster with stitches across the forehead and bolts in the neck that walks with the speed of molasses; allowing his victims time to run away, and killing those who don't run fast enough by ripping out their hearts.'

This is likely to be the predominant image that our learners have of the Creature and one that teachers need to counter.

The novel has had considerable influence in the theatre world. Richard Brinsley Peake's production is described – by Beverley Hart writing for Offord (2018) – as one of the first stage adaptations. Another significant production by Henry M. Milner, titled *Frankenstein – Or, The Man and the Monster*, was performed in July 1826. These productions mutated the story, introducing elements that have become common associations: the Creature as a monster who carries our fears and suspicions about what is different, and the hyperbolic depiction of Victor Frankenstein's laboratory and the moment of the Creature's creation. It is these misrepresentations that lead to misconceptions for learners. Hart outlines the progeny of the novel, including Frank N. Furter in Richard O'Brien's *The Rocky Horror Show*.

Early film versions built further on these theatrical interpretations, again showing the creation of the Creature in full cinematic glory, and J. Seale Dawley's film (1910, Edison Studios) can be found on YouTube. While the Edison Film Company wanted to eliminate 'all actual repulsive situations', the Creature's creation is highly dramatic and forms a significant portion of the film's 12 minutes, reaching far beyond Shelley's description of the event – definitely one to watch and discuss with pupils.

Perhaps the most famous incarnation of *Frankenstein* is that directed by James Whale, with the Creature played by Boris Karloff. His visualisation of the Creature is far removed from Shelley's descriptions but established the most iconic image of Victor Frankenstein's creation: tall, monstrous, green-faced and bolt-necked, with a cube-like head.

Having experienced success with this film, and keen to capitalise on it, *Bride of Frankenstein* (1935) was released, followed by a whole franchise. Over time, other studios produced comedy versions, horror ensemble versions and parodies: clear evidence of the centrality of the text to Western theatre and film tradition. Even Mel Brooks produced a version, called *Young Frankenstein* – a parody of the Universal horror films.

Paul O'Flinn (1995, p. 22) states that there 'is no such thing as "Frankenstein", there are only "Frankensteins"'. It is a text that invites rewriting and reproducing, being itself rewritten by Mary Shelley.

What does this mean for teachers?

O'Flinn (1995) posits that texts can alter in three major ways:

1. through the operations of criticism
2. through a shift from one medium to another
3. as a result of history unfolding.

Cultural understanding of *Frankenstein* has been shaped by all three of these. *Frankenstein* is often a point of reference when discussing scientific developments, for example. As such, we must consider where our learners find themselves when they encounter the text. How do we support them to peel away the cultural laminations to grapple with the layers of meaning in the text?

1. Operations of criticism

We need to place the reading and close analysis of the text first, but support our understanding as teachers with the use of literary criticism. Fishelov (2016) states that it was the feminist approaches of the 1970s and 1980s that placed *Frankenstein* as a text of literary significance. Indeed, it was described by D.W. Harding (1957, p. 45) as 'one of those second-rate works, written under the influence of more distinguished minds'. Fishelov comments that 'the novel did not generate a cumulative body of positive criticism or a significant token of appreciation from the contemporary literary elite' (2016, p. 5); instead, Mary Shelley was overshadowed by the literary reputation of her husband. The rise in feminist criticism, such as Moers' *Literary Women* (1978) and Gilbert and Gubar's *The Madwoman in the Attic* (1979), did much to place *Mary* Shelley centre stage, and it is from this standpoint that the current book explores this influential work.

2. Through a shift from one medium to another

Frankenstein and its tropes have permeated the film and TV industries, as well as advertising and journalism; has any other novel been so influential? In addition, the novel has been adapted and adopted by the world of comic books and graphic novels since 1939 (Murray, 2016).

This guide focuses on the literary merits of the text and on centring Mary Shelley as a key literary figure in the landscape of the nineteenth-century novel.

3. As a result of history unfolding

O'Flinn (1995, p. 22) suggests that '*Frankenstein*'s meaning alters as time passes' – for example, changes over time in politics, and industrial, technological and scientific development, as well as war and peacetime. Advances in science, particularly genetics, are often linked with *Frankenstein*, e.g. Frankenstein foods. While the first edition of the novel was written during the 1810s, its impact and presence are still evident today and it has depth and relevance for all learners.

SECTION 1
WALTON'S LETTERS

At a glance

> **Summary quotation:** 'you cannot contest the inestimable benefit which I shall confer on all mankind to the last generation' (Letter 1)

> **Big Question:** How does Shelley use Walton's narrative voice at the beginning of Frankenstein? Why must Walton and Victor meet on the deadly ice floe?

> **Significant plot events:**

Letter 1:

- Walton writes to his sister, Margaret Saville, explaining his progress so far with his Arctic expedition.

- He gives his current and next geographical location: St Petersburgh and then Archangel.

Letter 2:

- In Archangel, Walton writes again to his sister, telling her about his crew.

- He tells her that he is certain of success, and writes of the wondrous Arctic landscape.

Letter 3:

- The length of this letter shows that there seems to be little worth writing to his sister about.

- His crew are as yet unfazed by any of the cold weather or icebergs that they encounter.

- He reassures his sister that he will not 'rashly encounter danger', while also boasting of the anticipated triumph of his expedition.

Letter 4:

- Walton and his crew are surrounded by ice and thick fog.

- Once the fog clears, Walton and his crew catch sight of a gigantic man-like creature being pulled on a sledge.

- In the morning, there is another unexpected encounter with a stranger on a sledge, on the brink of death.

- Walton takes charge of the stranger's care and both men begin talking to each other.

- The stranger insists on telling Walton the story that explains why he is in such a wretched state on the ice floes.

> **Character focus:** Robert Walton, his sister Mrs Margaret Saville, Victor Frankenstein (the stranger), the Creature

> **Key themes:**

  - Knowledge and discovery 🔍

  - Ambition and legacy ⚙

  - Isolation and loneliness 🔒

  - Society and social class ✂

  - Narrator and narration **N**

> **Handle with care:**

  - the portrayal of an emaciated and vulnerable Victor who is close to death

Why?

'Why' is an important question, not only within the world of the text but when also considering authorial intent and meaning.

- In Letters 1 and 2, Walton was certain that his expedition would be a magnificent success. Why is he less certain in Letters 3 and 4?

- Why does Shelley provide the reader with the merest glimpse of the Creature in Letter 4?

- Why does Victor Frankenstein enter the narrative in Letter 4 and not Letter 1?

- Why begin the narrative in the setting of the Arctic?

- Why is it important that readers are introduced to two ambitious men of science, rather than just one?

S-T-R-E-T-C-H questions

- Why does Shelley use a frame narrative?
- Why does Shelley choose to use letters for Walton's narrative?

What?

What happens? ☁

Walton's Letter 1: Early December

Letter 1 is set in St Petersburgh. From here, Walton (Shelley's first narrator) writes to his sister, Margaret Saville. The letters provide us with biographical information about his ambitions, the purpose of his travels and his previous (and failed) attempts at becoming a poet. Here, he describes a rather romantic hypothetical account of what his journey to the North Pole will be like. He proudly narrates his time aboard whaling ships, working among merchant seamen. He informs Margaret of his travel plans to Archangel, giving the reader a clear sense of time and place in his narrative. He ends the letter confidently informing her that he will be successful in his expedition.

Walton's Letter 2: Late March

In Letter 2, Walton is in Archangel, where he continues to tell his sister of the progress of his expedition, informing her that he has begun to collect 'my sailors' for his expedition further north. Early in the second paragraph, he reveals the extent of his loneliness: 'I have no friend' – or rather, no one of equal social status that he can name as a friend. Walton, a gentleman, is unable to truly befriend his crew, who are of a much lower social class. However, he does show the ability to respect and admire one of his crew, the ship's master, who shares the romantic story of his crew-man's youthful love for a Russian woman. As Walton narrates in his letter, when the master learned of who his fiancé really loved, he broke off the engagement so that she could marry for love rather than money.

Later, Walton attempts to articulate the range of emotions that he feels upon the now-inevitable moment of departure across the northern ice floe. He is both excited and terrified, so signs off his letter in a much more doubtful tone than the first.

Walton's Letter 3: Early July

Letter 3 is a short but enthusiastic letter to his sister, informing her that he is safe and 'well advanced on his voyage'. He (or rather Shelley) makes a point of stating that nothing interesting enough has occurred for him to inform her of, bar the odd leak and 'stiff gale'. This is both a literal and figurative calm before the storm of Victor's entrance in the next letter.

Walton ends this short letter with a barrage of rhetorical questions that emphasise his determination to succeed, while also showing his naivety, as he asks, 'What can stop the determined heart and resolved will of man?', while surrounded by a typically Gothic sublime landscape and sailing headlong into weather and temperature conditions over which he has no control.

Walton's Letter 4: Late July

Walton and his ship are surrounded by ice and a dense fog. The fog does not clear until 2.00pm, allowing Walton and his crew to see the vastness of the ice floe in which they are trapped. Out of the mist, the crew report a peculiar sight of a 'being... in the shape of a man' who is 'gigantic in stature' yet as ethereal as 'an apparition', thus providing a moment in the text that veers towards the supernatural and the Gothic genre. Soon, the ice and sea give a little, releasing their grip on the ship.

The next morning, the crew are excited by the appearance of another man on a sledge, drifting towards their ship on a large piece of ice. Exhausted and emaciated, this man is brought aboard the ship and cared for by Walton and his men. The stranger's 'gentle manners' are fascinating to the crew and endearing to Walton, who quickly forms an attachment to him. Soon, Walton begins to love the stranger 'as a brother', meaning that at this moment, Walton's self-imposed loneliness is at an end.

Social and historical context 🏵

Literary context: Shelley's chimera of literary sub-genres

Raised among such a wide range of intellectuals, and incredibly well-read, Shelley had a plethora of genres and conventions with which to play when writing her novel. While it is easy to assume that Shelley borrowed from only two genres (science fiction and horror), her novel is actually a chimera of genres and forms.

These include bildungsroman: a narrative about the events and experiences of the main protagonists as they grow up and become adults. Each narrator – Walton, Victor and the Creature – narrates their life, from their early childhood up to their present adulthood.

The epistolary form of narration can also be found, involving or consisting of letter writing. Walton's letters adhere to the conventions of an early novel in literature: Samuel Richardson's *Pamela; or Virtue Rewarded* (1740). This form, as used by Shelley, evolves the convention (a conceit) of the 'found manuscript', thus:

- framing the events as 'true'

- framing the published text to not really belong to a well-known author.

Letters, and different narrators within narratives, are embedded throughout the text, either explicitly – so that the content is included in the narrative – or implicitly, where a letter is mentioned or implied but not included in the narrative. *Examples of how this applies to the text can be found in the online teachers' resources.* 🖱

Historical context: An Age of Exploration

The seventeenth and eighteenth centuries were the Age of Exploration. Having discovered new worlds since the fifteenth century, several European nations were now keen to capitalise on their maritime success by both establishing new trade routes and also gaining new scientific knowledge. Even landed gentlemen would take great risks for the adventure and potential fame involved in daring and risky expeditions.

Many attempts were made to explore the North West Passage, a sea lane between the Atlantic and Pacific Oceans. If successful, this would open up a new trade route between Asia and Europe, although the seas were hostile and vessels such as Walton's were often stuck in ice. From even a cursory reading of Walton's letters, we are aware of the significance of a successful expedition through the Northern ice floes that would go beyond that of the explorers themselves.

It is likely that Shelley, along with her Romantic contemporaries, was aware of explorers such as William Baffin (c. 1584–1622), a well-renowned Arctic explorer of his day, who, like Walton, gained his sea-faring legs through whaling. Baffin is most well known for the discovery of Baffin Bay – named after him – which is situated between Canada and Greenland.

Literary context: Variations on a theme – Shelley's Byronic hero(es)

Walton, Victor Frankenstein and the Creature each share characteristics of the Byronic hero, but with slight variations in their character.

Oxford Reference defines a Byronic hero as follows:

'Characteristic of or resembling Byron or his poetry; that is, contemptuous of and rebelling against conventional morality, or defying fate, or possessing the characteristics of Byron's romantic heroes, or imitating his dress and appearance.'

Marquette University's 'Glossary of the Gothic' describes Byronic heroes as arrogant, intelligent, rebellious, self-destructive, mysterious, magnetic and attractive (to the heroines, particularly in Gothic literature).

See the *teaching resources* for this chapter about the social and historical context, useful for A level teachers and anyone teaching this to an able GCSE group, covering the following social, historical, literary and geographical contexts:

- the Age of Exploration
- the geographical locations in the letters
- further detail about the concept of the Byronic hero.

Vocabulary in context

Word	Quotation	Definition
Letter 1		
ardent	'I am too ardent in execution and too impatient of difficulties.'	having intense emotion or enthusiasm (Recurs in all letters and Chapters 2, 3, 4, 9, 12, 13, 14, 17, 18, 21, 23, 24)
forebodings	'You will rejoice to hear that no disaster has accompanied the commencement of an enterprise which you have regarded with such evil forebodings.'	in anticipation of something happening, especially approaching or overhanging evil
inspirited	'Inspirited by this wind of promise, my daydreams become more fervent and vivid.'	to put spirit, life or energy into; to quicken, enliven, animate; to cheer, encourage; to incite, stir
fervent		of persons, their passions, dispositions or actions; ardent, intensely earnest, often used in relation to love or hatred (from 17th century onwards)
diffusing	'There, Margaret, the sun is for ever visible, its broad disk just skirting the horizon and diffusing a perpetual splendour.'	to send forth (an immaterial, or abstract thing) in many or all directions; to spread among a large number of people; to disseminate
splendour		magnificence; great show of riches or costly things; pomp, parade (*transitive verb:* to move with splendour)
Letter 2		
dauntless	'those whom I have already engaged... are certainly possessed of dauntless courage.'	not to be daunted; fearless, intrepid, bold, undaunted
assailed	'If I am assailed by disappointment, no one will endeavour to sustain me in dejection.'	to attack with physical violence, assault
endeavour		to try, to make an effort for a specified object (objective); to attempt
inclinations	'my early inclinations'	a person's natural tendencies or preferences

Letter 3		
enterprise	'my courageous, yet sometimes despairing, enterprise'	a project or undertaking, especially one that is difficult
satiate	'satiate my curiosity'	to fully satisfy a desire or appetite
zeal	'how much happier I am than during my earlier zeal'	great energy or enthusiasm in pursuit of a cause
Letter 4		
impertinent	'Certainly; it would indeed be very impertinent and inhuman in me to trouble you with any inquisitiveness of mine.'	not showing proper respect; rude
fastidious	'you are therefore somewhat fastidious'	very attentive to and concerned about accuracy and detail
benevolence	'his whole countenance is lighted up, as it were, with a beam of benevolence and sweetness that I never saw equalled'	the quality of being well-meaning; kindness (Recurs in Chapters 3, 11, 15, 16, 17, 21)
unintelligible	'but there is something so strange and unintelligible in his manner that I could not help remarking it to you'	difficult to interpret or understand; mysterious

PIT STOP ▼

Retrieval point ☁

Many of the words that Shelley uses early in this chapter are words that she uses again and again throughout her novel. For example, the word 'benevolent' is used by several characters to describe themselves or others. Ensuring that learners are clear on the definitions and meanings of these words will enable them to talk about the text in greater depth and to articulate their knowledge of characters.

When exploring the letters, learners should return to the taught vocabulary in a later lesson, assessing whether they can link the vocabulary to:

- Walton's character
- the setting of the start of the novel
- the emerging themes of ambition and legacy, knowledge and discovery, and isolation and loneliness.

Plot and character development

Many of the questions included in this section of each chapter can be used for comprehension of that chapter or can be used or adapted as retrieval questions in further lessons. Some are more 'factual', where others may be more open to interpretation.

1. Who is Robert Walton and what are his letters about? (N)

Robert Walton is a gentleman explorer who is writing to his sister, Margaret Saville. He is an explorer on an expedition to the Arctic north, writing to his sister to tell her about his progress. He also writes about his hobbies: when young, he read a lot of explorers' books and journals. When he was older, and before this voyage, Robert Walton tried to become a Romantic poet, and he also spent time aboard a whaling ship prior to this expedition.

2. Why is Walton travelling?

Walton has spent several years as an explorer, building up his knowledge and skills to undertake ambitious expeditions to explore uncharted passages and areas of the world. He believes that he 'deserves' to achieve his ambition as he has worked very hard for it.

3. Where is Walton? Are the places real?

Letter 1: St Petersburgh

St Petersburg (Petersburgh in *Frankenstein*) is a city to the west of Russia, next to the Gulf of Finland. This western edge of Russia shares borders with Finland, Estonia, Belarus, Ukraine and Georgia. St Petersburg was the capital of the Russian Empire from 1712 until the October Coup of 1918.

Letter 2 onwards: Archangel

This Russian city much further north than St Petersburg was established by the English in the late sixteenth century as a major trade port. This part of Russia largely borders Finland.

4. Why does nothing much seem to happen in Letter 3?

The seemingly dull Letter 3 does more than it appears on the surface: jeopardy and peril are increased by Walton and his men being stuck in the ice. Simultaneously, the calmness of the ice floe is emphasised by Walton – the calm before the 'storm' of Victor Frankenstein arriving into the narrative in Letter 4. Therefore, the reader is lulled into a false sense of security, making what follows much more shocking and surprising.

5. Who do Walton and his crew see before they find Victor?

Walton writes:

> 'We perceived a low carriage... pass on towards the north... a being which had the shape of a man, but apparently of gigantic stature, sat in the sledge, and guided the dogs.' (Letter 4)

This is the first appearance of the Creature in the novel, and it is interesting that we meet him first and not Victor. This glimpse very clearly represents him as something 'other', with 'the shape of a man' (and so *not* a man). This prepares us for what is to follow in Chapters 3 to 5, as Victor prepares, makes and brings to life the Creature seen here.

6. What is Walton's reaction to Victor's arrival?

The key quotation for Letter 2, and a theme of this section of the novel – 'isolation and loneliness' – is Walton's answer: 'I bitterly feel the want of a friend.' Even though Victor is in a wretched state, hovering on the brink of death, Walton believes that he has found a kindred spirit, a fellow 'gentleman'. As a gentleman, Victor is worthy of his time, attention and intellect.

7. Why does Shelley withhold Victor Frankenstein's name from the reader until the end of Letter 4?

Mary withholds Victor's name until the very end of Chapter 4, creating a strong sense of anticipation and a strong desire to know who this character is. It is possible that the reader has already anticipated that this wretched figure on the ice is the one who titles the novel, in which case the reader is satisfied at having been correct.

8. How does Victor's arrival develop Walton's character and the plot? ☁

Walton and his crew are stuck in the ice, 'As idle as a painted ship/Upon a painted Ocean' (Coleridge, 1778). At this point, it seems that neither plot nor character has anywhere to go, and in Todorov's narrative terms (1971, P.39), this is a neat illustration of the equilibrium stage (the 'normal', as established at the early stages of the narrative) of his five-part narrative structure. Victor's arrival marks the 'disruption' stage of Todorov's model. Victor disrupts the static dullness of Walton's ship and crew, with his narrative providing the catalyst for Walton to grow and develop into a man who will save the life of his crew, rather than sacrifice them at the altar of perpetual glory and martyrdom.

S-T-R-E-T-C-H

Absence and negative space

Here, absence of something – the negative space – also constructs meaning. Walton never asks about his sister or about her children's wellbeing. This lack of concern for his only living relatives carries meaning. The 'negative space' of this absence indicates narcissism, a characteristic that Walton shares with Victor, although their levels of narcissism differ. Challenge learners to consider what is noticeable by its absence. Additional examples are the absence of:

- a name for the Creature

- any terms of endearment for the Creature from Victor

- a possessive determiner when Victor narrates the creation of the Creature and his later encounters with him

- paternal and maternal figures in the Creature's life

- hope for the Creature in the latter parts of the novel.

How?

Language

Impressions of loneliness

Key quotation:

'I have no friend, Margaret: when I am glowing with the enthusiasm of success, there will be none to participate my joy; if I am assailed by disappointment, no one will endeavour to sustain me in dejection.' (Letter 2)

Loneliness, a key theme in the novel, is established as early as Walton's letters, when he describes his longing for the companionship of an equal. In this quotation, Shelley repeats 'no' and 'none' to emphasise Walton's feelings of lack and emptiness. Her choice of determiner and pronouns, respectively, echo the desolation of Walton's physical environment, which is a void. To Walton, his lack of a companion on his ship represents different kinds of voids: the social and the emotional. However, we must not forget that this position of isolation is completely self-imposed *and* imposed on his crew.

Secondly, we should pay attention to Shelley's use of the conditional in the clause beginning with 'if'. Conditional sentences (or clauses) suggest a possibility, a set of conditions or a choice to be made. In this clause, Walton contemplates, briefly, the idea that he may not succeed in his expedition, contradicting earlier bravado and boasts about his likely success in this letter.

Common allusions and the pursuit of knowledge

Using literary allusion, Walton admits that his pursuit of knowledge and adventure has led to his sense of isolation. He writes:

'But I shall kill no albatross; therefore do not be alarmed for my safety, or if I should come back to you as worn and woeful as the "Ancient Mariner".' (Letter 2)

Here, Walton makes an explicit reference to Coleridge's *The Rime of the Ancient Mariner* (1778), quite deliberate on Shelley's part, having heard the poem as a small child. However, it is likely that the reference to this text and the 'albatross' may need to be taught explicitly. Walton is alluding to the maritime lore that the albatross, if flying next to a ship in open waters, is a symbol of good luck, but to shoot an albatross will bring misfortune. In Coleridge's text, the Ancient Mariner accidentally shoots an albatross, causing him and his crew to suffer a terrible sea voyage.

By explicitly referring to the albatross, Shelley forewarns the reader that all three narratives – Walton's, Victor's and the Creature's – will expose the dangers of the pursuit of knowledge, especially from a position of ignorance or ego.

Finally, the muted and sombre tone of the effect of isolation and loneliness upon Walton is conveyed by the soft alliteration and long, loping vowel sounds of 'worn and woeful'. For learners, alliteration is often a language technique that is easy to spot but hard to write about well. To help them to write well about use of alliteration, get learners to pay close attention to the choice of consonant sound (hard, soft, low or high pitch, harsh, smooth and so on) and its placement in the text. Focus their attention on the sound using prompts like:

- Why here?
- Why now?
- What do we need to take notice of *because of the use of alliteration*?

Character focus

Walton ✦

Key quotations:

- 'You cannot contest the inestimable benefit which I shall confer on all of mankind' (Letter 1)
- 'I prefer glory to every enticement that wealth placed in my path' (Letter 1)
- 'For my own part, I begin to love him as a brother' (Letter 4)
- 'He must have been a noble creature in his better days' (Letter 4)

As Shelley's first narrator, Walton's character is used to establish a number of key themes and character traits running throughout the text. One of the most obvious characteristics that Walton explicitly shows us here is his desire for god-like immortality, under the guise of his expedition being for the benefit of 'all mankind'. His wealthy family means that Walton has had his pick of careers, dabbling in poetry before becoming a sailor who, despite years of travel, has an idealistic view of the seas. At times, he appears naive and somewhat prejudiced, even being surprised when one of the crew displays noble sentiments despite being from an uneducated and impoverished background.

Victor

Notable quotations:

- 'His limbs were nearly frozen, and his body dreadful emaciated by fatigue and suffering' (Letter 4)
- 'I have lost every thing and cannot begin life anew' (Letter 4)
- 'He must have been a noble creature in his better days' (Letter 4)

Victor is introduced to the story in part of Walton's journal, which continues after Letter 4. He is desperately fatigued and ill from his travels and, to Walton, appears as a figure of wild contrasts. He is troubled and 'wild-eyed' (Letter 4) at times, but is also noted as being 'noble'; he is clearly admired by Walton. Walton also notes that, upon hearing about the Creature, Victor becomes more animated and even suggests that Walton has provided him with a reason for living – a clear indication that he has an interesting tale to share.

Creature

Notable quotation:

- 'The daemon, as [Victor] called him' (Letter 4)

Walton provides almost no details about the Creature in these letters. Instead, what Shelley offers through Walton's writings is Victor's response to the Creature. It is clear that he has some kind of desperate tryst with Victor and that Victor perceives him to be a 'daemon'.

Structure 🏗️

Learners should explore the following examples from the opening and ending of this section and be invited to consider:

- Why has Shelley chosen to begin with this focus on Walton's optimism and end with a metaphor that illustrates Victor's wretched state on board Walton's ship?

Letter 1

Opening: 'You will rejoice to hear that no disaster has accompanied the commencement of an enterprise which you have regarded with such evil forebodings'

Ending: 'Heaven shower down blessings on you, and save me, that I may again and again testify my gratitude for all your love and kindness'

Letter 2

Opening: 'How slowly the time passes here, encompassed by frost and snow!'

Ending: 'Remember me with affection should you never hear from me again'

Letter 3

Opening: 'I write a few lines in haste to say that I am safe – and well advanced on my journey'

Ending: 'Heaven bless my beloved sister!'

Walton's first three letters 🏗️

Shelley uses these particular structural choices to set up the first version of her Byronic protagonists that will narrate this story of horror and wonder. She establishes the following:

- Walton and Victor's shared Promethean and Byronic-hero characteristics
- a very specific audience for Victor's narration: Walton
- an engineered meeting, location and situation that enable Victor to narrate his disastrous tale
- a suggestion as to why Walton is the primary audience for Victor's story: Walton could also be responsible for many unnecessary deaths unless he can be saved from himself
- the conventions of the frame and embedded narratives as favoured by Gothic authors.

Letter 4 🖼

Opening: 'So strange an incident has happened that I cannot forbear recording it'

Ending: 'Strange and harrowing must his story be, frightful the storm which embraced the gallant vessel on its course and wrecked it – thus!'

Letter 4 marks a clear shift away from Walton's thoughts about his own expedition and his sister towards now focusing on Victor and the storm (figurative and literal) that his appearance has ushered in. Notably, this is the first letter that doesn't contain a reference to Margaret in the opening or closing line. Instead, Shelley provides us with a deliberate hint of what is to come.

Although the Creature has entered the story, he remains very much in the background of the narrative. It is not until Victor recounts the Creature's story to Walton that he takes centre stage on his spree of revenge.

Extracts

Extract 1 (Letter 3): How does Shelley use language to develop Walton's character in this extract from Letter 3? 🔍 💡

'But success shall crown my endeavours. Wherefore not? Thus far I have gone, tracing a secure way over the pathless seas: the very stars themselves being witnesses and testimonies of my triumph. Why not still proceed over the untamed yet obedient element? What can stop the determined heart and resolved will of man?'

Use the following prompts to help learners analyse the above extract in detail:

• Shelley's choice of the modal verb 'shall' suggesting a level of certainty of his expedition

• the choice and use of 'crown' as a symbol for the success of his 'endeavours'

• why the oxymoronic phrase 'untamed yet obedient' environment indicates that Walton is naive

• Shelley's use of the rhetorical question 'What can stop the determined heart and will of man?' This rhetorical question will be worth returning to when learners have read up to Chapter 4 of Victor's narrative: the making of the Creature.

An analysis of two paragraphs is provided in the teacher's resources that accompany this chapter.

Extract 2 (Letter 4): How does Shelley use language to introduce her key characters in this extract from Letter 4?

'About two o'clock the mist cleared away, and we beheld, stretched out in every direction, vast and irregular plains of ice, which seemed to have no end. Some of my comrades groaned, and my own mind began to grow watchful with anxious thoughts, when a strange sight suddenly attracted our attention, and diverted our solicitude from our own situation. We perceived a low carriage, fixed on a sledge and drawn by dogs, pass on towards the north, at the distance of half a mile: a being which had the shape of a man, but apparently of gigantic stature, sat in the sledge, and guided the dogs. We watched the rapid progress of the traveller with our telescopes, until he was lost among the distant inequalities of the ice.'

In this extract, Shelley uses a range of language techniques in order to develop the plot; for example, when 'the mist cleared away', she is once again alluding to Coleridge's *The Rime of the Ancient Mariner* (1798), while also making use of the symbolism of the mist itself. Mist tends to obscure light and muffle sound, making the environment uncanny. When the mist clears, it is much like a theatre curtain being raised, allowing new characters to enter 'the stage'. Shelley then once again reminds us of the lethality of Walton's (and his crew's) position by drawing attention to the 'vast and irregular plains of ice', an environment so hostile that any assistance that they might need would be impossible, and the fact that they are unlikely to see another living soul. Once this is established, Shelley interrupts the view of the vast icy plains with 'a strange sight', which is a welcome distraction from the nothingness of what they can all currently see. The sibilance draws attention to the strange and unexpected nature of what Walton can see in the distance.

Threaded through this extract is a sense of ambiguity and uncertainty, achieved via the use of verbs of perception – 'perceived' and 'seemed' – suggesting that what is visible cannot be viewed as 'true'. Shelley builds on this sense of uncertainty when adding some limited detail to the figure in the sledge (which we will later learn is the Creature), who is described as 'a being' who had 'the shape of a man'; both phrases position this sight as something other than human. If it is presented as the 'shape of a man', it is not a man. As well as the being's unexpected presence on the ice, he is othered through the description of his 'gigantic' size. (According to Said (1978), the concept of 'othering' is the process of creating an artificial divide between two groups, often by portraying one group as fundamentally different to the other.) This careful choice of adjective, the ambiguity of the description and the uncertainty conveyed through the choice of verbs of perception present this being as something of which to be fearful. Most importantly, though, the being's interruption and intrusion into Walton's static predicament is what instigates the horrific events of the narrative of *Frankenstein* to begin.

SECTION 2
THE MAKING OF FRANKENSTEIN THE MAN (CHAPTERS 1–3)

At a glance

› **Summary quotation:** 'Chance – or rather the evil influence... which asserted omnipotent sway over me from the moment I turned my reluctant steps from my father's door' (Ch3)

› **Big Question:** What are the key influences in Victor's early life?

› **Significant plot events:**

Chapter 1:

- Victor's parents meet and begin a family.

- Victor receives a 'pretty present' – Elizabeth – who becomes his 'more than sister' and joins the Frankenstein family.

Chapter 2:

- Victor introduces his friend Clerval, a young man from school who becomes a good friend of Victor and Elizabeth.

- Victor discovers 'natural philosophy' and begins an obsessive journey of discovery.

- Victor's father dismisses his choice of scientific literature.

Chapter 3:

- Victor's mother, Caroline, dies.

- Victor begins his time at Ingolstadt University.

- Victor's determination to explore science is solidified.

› **Character focus:** Victor, Alphonse, Elizabeth, Clerval

› **Key themes:**

- Family and companionship 🍼

- Knowledge and discovery 🔍

- Society and social class ✖

- Death and grief ✝
- Obsession 💭
- Destiny and fate 🧬
- Ambition and legacy 🏆

> **Handle with care:**

- the portrayal of women and possessions (Ch1)
- maternal death (Ch3)

Why?

- Why does Shelley have Victor tell us so much about Victor's family?
- Why is it important for us to know about Victor's early life?
- Why are Victor's descriptions of family and science so separate?
- Why does Victor fall in love with science?

S-T-R-E-T-C-H questions

- Why does Shelley change Elizabeth's origin story so much in her 1831 edit?
- Why does Shelley portray women in the way in which she does?
- Why is the relationship between Victor and his father so important to our understanding of Victor's character?

What?

What happens? ☁

Chapter 1

This chapter brings a shift of narrator from Walton to Victor Frankenstein, who introduces his childhood as part of a distinguished family in Geneva. His father, Alphonse, is a respected public figure, who rescued his mother, Caroline Beaufort, from poverty. Victor tells of his childhood of privilege, in which he is adored by both parents. We also learn that when Victor is five, his mother discovers a young girl living in poverty, named Elizabeth. Caroline and Alphonse adopt Elizabeth, who is destined to become Victor's future wife.

Chapter 2

Shelley introduces us to the obsession that drives Victor to create his Creature: 'natural philosophy', or science. He tells of his younger brothers and his talented friend, Clerval, in a chapter that again emphasises his happy feelings about his childhood and friends. Later, he explains his introduction to science: a chance discovery of a book that his father immediately dismisses but with which he becomes rapt. He shares his early scientific learning, particularly seeing a tree destroyed by lightning, which sparks his curiosity and drives him to explore science more deeply.

Chapter 3

Victor begins his life as a young adult away from his family. His plans to begin university are delayed by the loss of his mother, whose death brings grief to all the family. Throughout this time, Elizabeth keeps the family's spirits up, but eventually Victor leaves for Ingolstadt. While there, he meets two lecturers. One abruptly dismisses his current scientific study and the other inspires him by redirecting his studies. Victor determines on setting a new course for himself in unlocking the secrets of nature in a way that no scientist has ever done before.

Social and historical context ✻

It is important for learners to fully understand, appreciate and be able to realistically envisage Shelley's late eighteenth-century setting, language and characters. They may require pre-teaching activities on the following features of social, cultural and historical context so that they can write about them confidently.

Historical context: Settings

Shelley sets Chapters 1 to 3 in two main locations: Geneva and Ingolstadt. Both are significant.

Shelley chooses Geneva as Victor's hometown and it is also the birthplace of the story itself. In 1816, Shelley and her travelling companions stayed in Geneva and exchanged Gothic tales (there's more on this in Chapter 5 of this book). However, the choice of Geneva can also be seen as carrying its own meaning. For many centuries, it has been a forward-thinking centre of theology, literature and philosophy. The city is also the centre of Calvinism (a religious movement founded by John Calvin in the sixth century), with which young Mary Godwin would have been familiar through her father, who himself was the son of a Calvinist minister. Another important 'child' of Geneva is Jean-Jacques Rousseau, who was born in Geneva in 1712 and is said to have been a key influence in the French Revolution. During her stay in Geneva, Shelley spent much time reading his works, and there are several elements and ideas in the novel inspired by his writing.

Ingolstadt – Victor's university town – is also riddled with political and historical connotations. Like Geneva, Ingolstadt is known for its radical and revolutionary thinking – a fitting place for young Victor to study. As the founding place of the Illuminati, the city is associated with unconventional and controversial thinking.

Historical context: Expectations of the early-nineteenth-century man ✷

Victor and his father offer two very different versions of what it is to be a 'man', and to fully explore what Shelley does through these contrasts, it is necessary to understand the role of men and concepts of masculinity at the time at which she was writing. Victor, in many ways, echoes Percy Shelley's erratic and wild pursuits of knowledge and novelty, whereas Alphonse perhaps echoes William Godwin's diligent exploration of politics and consideration of social justice. At a time when there was much conflict about what made a 'man', Mary Shelley explores these contrasts.

Following an eighteenth-century focus on masculine politeness, the turn of the nineteenth century brought a greater focus on etiquette and 'proper' conduct for men and women. Matthew McCormack (2005, p. 33) writes that in the Georgian period, 'politics and masculinity were inseparable in this period: manliness was important in political situations, but politics was also central to the business of being a man'. Mary Shelley's father, William Godwin, aligns with this in many ways, as does Victor's father, Alphonse.

In contrast, Victor arguably aligns more with the ideals of Georgian masculinity that John Tosh (2005, p. 333) explores, stating that 'there was an increasing concern with occupation (or "calling") and a corresponding elaboration of work ethic'. This brought with it a requirement for men to be occupied with work, away from the domestic sphere. Shelley portrays this separation clearly in Victor, as he strains to be separate from the domestic sphere and assert himself as a real 'man'.

It is clear that Shelley explores different versions of masculinity within Victor and Alphonse, and that there are distinct elements of Percy Shelley and William Godwin within those characters. As a result, Shelley enables herself to explore and critique a range of elements of masculine ideals within her novel, to encourage her readers to reflect on those ideals and their potential impact on others in society.

Scientific context: Victor's self-made curriculum 🔍

Of all the chapters of the novel, it is perhaps this one that best demonstrates Shelley's own knowledge of science. In the scientists that Shelley references in Victor's self-created curriculum, she includes, as described by Nick Lane on Radio 4's *The Infinite Monkey Cage*, 'basically the history of science up until 1816' (BBC Sounds, 2016).

At the time when Shelley was writing, scientific exploration and discovery were exploding, as England continued on its journey towards becoming the centre of a global empire and reaped the financial and intellectual rewards that came with this. Young Shelley was fortunate to spend time with many influential scientists of the time, including Humphry Davy,

William Nicholson and Erasmus Darwin (grandfather of Charles Darwin). As part of an intellectual scene, Shelley was familiar with many works by scientists of varying degrees of credibility. As such, her choices for Victor's key influences are likely to be deliberate.

Key scientists that Shelley features are:

- **Cornellius Agrippa (1486–1535):** A noted 'black magician' of the Renaissance, whose works promised to connect the material and spiritual world through classical mathematical patterns. For a time, Agrippa was much celebrated, but later in life was declared a heretic and was forced to flee public life (something of which Shelley was either unaware or chose to make Victor unaware).

- **Paracelsus (1493–1541):** A doctor, chemist and reformer who travelled Europe gathering medical and scientific knowledge. While many of his ideas are now perceived as 'quack medicine', he replaced some of the pillars of ancient medicine with more modern thinking, particularly around the causes of disease. Paracelsus is said to have created laudanum by combining alcohol with morphine.

- **Albertus Magnus (1200–1280):** A religious man and teacher in the thirteenth century. Having studied newly translated works by ancient figures such as Aristotle and Arabian philosophers, Magnus is credited with having legitimised the role of science and scientific experiments within Christianity.

PIT STOP ▼

S-T-R-E-T-C-H

It may be worthwhile connecting with your science department to explore which scientists your learners are familiar with and when they lived. It is not the case that these scientists are earlier or later than the scientists still featured on our schools' curricula; rather, they are absent from it for their now-debunked ideas. Ask your learners:

- What does this tell us about the history of people's beliefs around science?

- Why might Shelley have chosen these scientists?

- What is it that these scientists allow Shelley to explore that other scientists may not have?

Biographical context: Percy Shelley as inspiration for Victor

It is well known that Percy Shelley had an enormous influence on the young Mary Godwin and her writing. Less known, however, are the parallels that Mary Shelley creates between Percy Shelley and her protagonist, Victor. These parallels include:

- the name 'Victor', which was a playful pseudonym used by Percy as a child

- the name 'Elizabeth', from Percy Shelley's favourite sister

- Victor having similar interests to Percy and the inclusion of some of Percy's favourite scientists

- similarities between Victor's descriptions of himself and Percy's descriptions of himself.

Percy was deeply interested in the occult, as his friend Thomas Hogg describes. He:

'even planned how he might get admission to the vault, or charnel house...
and might sit there all night, harrowed by fear, yet trembling with expectation,
to see one of the spiritualised owners of the bones piled around him'
(Hogg, 1858, pp. 33–4).

In a more extreme exploration of the relationship between Percy Shelley and Victor, Scott Douglas de Hart's book, *Shelley Unbound: Discovering Frankenstein's True Creator* (2013), argues that Percy is the novel's true author.

Putting aside this theory, the idea that Percy Shelley was used by Mary Shelley as inspiration for Victor, requires readers to consider Mary Shelley's relationship with Percy, who, at the time of the novel's conception, was married to another woman; who, at the time of publishing, was her husband; and who, at the time of her 1831 edition, had widowed her. Weissman (1976) argues that the relationship between the real Percy and Shelley's Victor 'suggests a distinct, though perhaps unconscious, unhappiness with the revolutionary politics of her husband and his political predecessors'. Whatever the purpose – conscious or unconscious – of the use of Percy Shelley as inspiration, and whatever it may reveal about Mary Shelley's thoughts about Percy, the connection between the two men is undeniable.

Literary context: Changes between edition

Chapters 1 to 3 vary significantly between the original edition in 1818 and the 1831 edition used by most GCSE exam boards. Some key differences are explored below.

In 1818, Elizabeth is a blood relative: the child of Alphonse's late sister, who is adopted by Alphonse without hesitation when her father wishes to remarry. By rescuing Elizabeth, Alphonse becomes the rescuer of both the key women in Victor's life and enables his son to fulfil a saviour's role, as he is marked to marry Elizabeth, thus setting his son up for a future as a figure of responsibility and chivalry (Shelley, 1818).

In 1818, Alphonse is portrayed as knowing much more about science and even explains the lightning-struck tree to Victor. In 1831, however, Shelley removes Alphonse's positive influence and he becomes a more distant figure to Victor. This change in parenting role both alters the perspective that readers are given of Alphonse and also has an impact on our perspectives of science, as it becomes the domain of removed, non-familial men, rather than being connected with Victor's own loving, intelligent father.

Vocabulary in context

Word	Quotation	Definition
Chapter 1		
distinguished	'One of the most distinguished families'	a respected or admired person or their work
Chapter 2		
sublime	'the sublime shapes of the mountains'	of great or excellent beauty; extreme or unparalleled
virtue	'the virtues of heroes, and the actions of men were his theme'	having strong or high moral standards; good actions undertaken (these will often benefit others)
genius	'Natural philosophy is the genius that has regulated my fate'	a very intelligent person; a person regarded as having influence over good or evil
galvanism	'the explanation of a theory which he had formed on the subject of electricity and galvanism'	a branch of science named after Galvani, an Italian scientist who experimented on animals with electricity
Chapter 3		
malignity	'Her watchful attentions triumphed over the malignity of the distemper'	the quality of intending to cause harm
sacrilege	'It appeared to me sacrilege so soon to leave'	the act of treating something holy without respect
pioneer	'I will pioneer a new way'	to develop or be the first to use or do something; a person who is one of the first to do something

Retrieval point: Establishing vocabulary ☁

Much of this vocabulary is used frequently by Shelley in other chapters, exploring how these words can be applied to different characters to explore their different facets. Ensuring early on in teaching that learners are familiar with them will be beneficial later in the text.

Example:

- As the Creature is portrayed as benevolent here, who does he take after: Victor or Alphonse?

- In what ways can both Victor and the Creature be described as 'indefatigable'?

- Victor comes from a long line of distinguished public figures. In what ways could he now be described as 'distinguished'?

Retrieval point: Chapter 3 ☁

This chapter marks a juncture between Victor's family life and his growing interests in science. As the previous chapter focused largely on his initial interactions with science rather than his family, before reading this chapter with learners, it would be beneficial to recap with them the key characters of the Frankenstein family and their traits.

- Who are Victor's parents? How could we describe them?

- What are Victor's feelings towards his mother?

- How did Victor's mother present Elizabeth to him?

- How many members of the Frankenstein family are there?

- What was Victor's father's response to Victor's scientific readings?

Plot and character development

1. Who are Victor's family and friends? What do they do?

- **Alphonse:** Alphonse is a respected public figure who 'rescued' Victor's mother from poverty.

- **Caroline Beaufort:** Much younger than Alphonse, Caroline is the daughter of a merchant, who cared for him when he fell into ruin.

- **Elizabeth:** A poor orphan who was adopted into the family when Victor was five, Elizabeth is adored by everyone.

- **Clerval:** A friend that Victor makes at school, Clerval is romantically minded and theatrical. He, unlike Victor, follows in his father's footsteps and begins working in the family trade.

2. How does the Frankenstein family develop in Chapters 1 to 3?

This section provides readers with the key information on the Frankensteins that they will require for the novel. Having been adventurous explorers with young Victor and Elizabeth, the family settle down following the birth of a second son, Ernest, and they return to the ancestral home city of Geneva. It is here that another new character is introduced to Victor's social circle: Henry Clerval, with whom Victor attends school. Except for Victor's Creature and minor characters, this nearly completes the character list for the novel.

The family changes slightly through these chapters, as Victor grows older and Caroline dies. Most notably, Victor grows away from the family and finds his own interests, while Elizabeth remains with the family.

3. How does Victor's relationship with his father change in Chapters 1 to 3? 🐝

In the first chapter of Victor's narrative, his relationship with his father, Alphonse, seems largely positive. Alphonse is portrayed as a loving and dedicated father (at least on the surface), of whom Victor speaks very positively. However, in Chapter 2, the differences between Victor and his father emerge swiftly and strongly.

Alphonse is a respected public man. In contrast, Victor 'confesse[s]' that neither languages, nor governance, nor politics 'possessed attraction for [him]' (Ch1). Victor also contrasts with Alphonse on matters of science, and Alphonse even dismisses the works of Agrippa, which Victor adores. After Alphonse's dismissal of Agrippa's writings, Victor is quick to blame his father for not explaining the reasons for his rejection, suggesting that this may have changed Victor's story. Arguably, the fracture between father and son is one that foreshadows the divide between Victor and his Creature, who, in time, Victor will also reject and blame.

4. Why is Geneva important to the Frankenstein family? 🕸

Shelley makes it clear that the Frankenstein family has a clear connection with Geneva. As one of 'the most distinguished' (Ch1) families in the city, many of whom have been public figures, we could say that Geneva has been shaped by generations of Frankensteins contributing to its public business. In turn, Victor is shaped by the events that take place in Geneva (including several of the murders committed by Victor's Creature). It is interesting not only that Victor will fail to follow the role of public service to Geneva that he is due to inherit as eldest son, but also that the most cutting consequences of his failures will be realised there instead.

5. How does Victor discover science? 🔍

In Chapter 2, Shelley has Victor tell us that during a rainy day in a nearby town, he 'chance[s]' to come across a volume of works by Cornelius Agrippa and finds 'a new light' in his life. This love of science builds, as he acquires and reads further works by similar men and delights in witnessing a tree being destroyed by a lightning bolt. It is the combination of the intense promises of medieval writers and the destructive power of nature that captures Victor and has him determine that science – rather than public service – will be the way in which he makes his mark on the world.

This develops further in Chapter 3, as Victor moves to university and meets his professors. While his first professor is, like his father, abruptly dismissive of his reading choices, his second takes time to explain the relationship between their work and current thinking, particularly in chemistry. This attentive explanation seizes Victor's interest and thus his future in science is set.

6. What is Elizabeth's influence on Victor and Clerval?

Victor and Clerval are very different men. However, they are equally influenced by Elizabeth's presence. Victor admits that he 'might have become sullen in my study' and 'rough', without her being the 'living spirit of love', and that he believes that Clerval 'might not have been so perfectly humane, so thoughtful in his generosity' without her (Ch2). We might interpret, then, that she has an almost feminising influence on the young men, particularly Clerval, in whom she evokes 'kindness and tenderness amidst his passion for adventurous exploit' (Ch2). It is this feminising, calming influence that Shelley limits, as she confines Elizabeth to a domestic life in contrast to her young male friends.

7. How does Shelley portray Victor as he comes of age?

Shelley provides much more information on Victor's temperament in Chapter 2. We learn that he has a 'violent' temper and 'vehement' passions for uncovering 'the hidden laws of nature', which bring a 'gladness akin to rapture' (Ch2). He is clearly a young man who is passionate to an obsessive level, with strong determination. However, Shelley also suggests that he is naive, or perhaps ignorant. The divine and devilish promises of the 'scientists' with whose works he is rapt in his youth are never questioned by him but wilfully believed. Even when his father rejects his choice of book, this makes Victor more determined to forge his own path and determine his own future.

How?

Language

Personal pronouns and possession 🔍

Key quotations:

- 'I, with childish seriousness, interpreted her words literally and looked upon Elizabeth as mine – mine to protect, love, and cherish' (Ch1)
- 'my more than sister, since till death she was to be mine only' (Ch1)

Critic Schoene-Harwood (2000) comments that Elizabeth's 'rescue from an undignified life in squalid destitution comes at the high price of total commodification' (Schoene-Harwood, 2000, p. 6), and we can see this clearly through Shelley's use of pronouns in the final paragraph of Chapter 1.

Victor says that Elizabeth was introduced as a 'pretty present for my Victor', suggesting that even Caroline sees Elizabeth as a commodity. When we look at the pronouns within this paragraph, Elizabeth is referred to as 'it' and Shelley's use of possessive personal pronouns has Victor use the words 'my' and 'mine' no less than ten times. Elizabeth is described as 'my more than sister, since till death she was to be mine only'.

PIT STOP ▼

S-T-R-E-T-C-H

The introduction of Elizabeth and Caroline in this chapter is ripe for exploring critical lenses, particularly the feminist lens. You might ask learners:

- How has Shelley portrayed female characters so far?
- What is their relationship with the male characters?
- What role do these female characters play?

Victor's language around science

Key quotations:

- 'I took their word for all that they averred, and I became their disciple' (Ch2)
- ' I read and studied the wild fancies of these writers with delight' (Ch2)
- 'always... been imbued with a fervent longing to penetrate the secrets of nature' (Ch3)

As this is the first chapter in which we see Victor's love of science begin to emerge, it is important that learners grasp how much pleasure and thrill he experiences as a young man.

Shelley's language reveals how positively Victor views science, but also how his relationship with science is obsessive and hungry. In reference to his wild, unconventional 'scientific' reading, Shelley uses overly positive language related to pleasure – 'delight', 'wild fancies', 'treasures' (Ch1) to emphasise how special Victor considers these works to be and to highlight how enthralled he is with them. She has Victor describe himself as a 'disciple' of the scientists that he has discovered, to suggest how devoted he is to their ideas and teachings. In contrast, he describes his feelings of being 'discontented' and 'unsatisfied' (Ch1) with more conventional scientists (such as those with which we might be familiar, such as Newton).

However, there is an invasive and aggressive undertone to the language that Shelley uses for Victor's description of his early scientific pursuits. Victor states that he had 'always... been imbued with a fervent longing to penetrate the secrets of nature', using the language of sex and invasion to capture his determined intentions. Later, he describes admiringly how his chosen muses had 'penetrated deeper' into the 'citadel of nature', at once using language of military conquests but also language of sex again (Ch3). The violence of his temper in relation to this is further illustrated when his imagination is captured after seeing a tree struck by lightning in a storm, and he is in awe of how it is 'entirely reduced to thin ribbons of wood' and 'utterly destroyed' (Ch1).

It is important here that learners understand Victor's obsessive and violent pursuit of scientific knowledge, which stands aside from his family. This could be achieved by either providing key extracts or even simply using a selection of single-word quotations as a catalyst for discussion. The use of the word 'disciple', for example, carries religious connotations that learners may be able to discuss.

PIT STOP ▼

When exploring the language that Shelley uses to portray Victor's feelings about science, it is useful to contrast this with the language that she uses to portray Victor's feelings about his family. It may be useful here to undertake some retrieval practice around the language and descriptions of the Frankenstein family, so that this can be compared to the language around science. ☁

The language of grief ✝

Key quotations:

- 'that most irreparable evil, the void that presents itself to the soul' (Ch3)

- 'the reality of the evil, then the actual bitterness of grief commences' (Ch3)

Shelley has Victor describe his grief in two stages: the first of overwhelming sentiment and the latter of pragmatic resignation (or perhaps numbness?). The first phase contains words that strongly suggest that he deeply feels the loss of his mother: 'void', 'despair', 'evil', 'forever', 'extinguished' (Ch3). However, 'when the lapse of time proves the reality of the evil', Victor admits that the 'bitterness of grief commences' and that he 'still had duties' (Ch3). This contrast offers us a range of interpretations to discuss and debate with learners: is Victor a pragmatic man who is striving to continue with life despite his loss, or is he repressing his feelings? With older learners, we might also consider how much of Shelley's own perspective on life with grief she echoes in Victor. It is interesting, too, that bar a single punctuation mark, Shelley makes no edits to this paragraph between 1818 and 1831.

Character focus

Victor

Key quotations:

- 'I was their plaything and their idol, and something better – their child, the innocent and helpless Creature bestowed on them by heaven' (Ch1)

- 'I feel exquisite pleasure in dwelling on the recollections of childhood, before misfortune had tainted my mind' (Ch2)

- 'The raising of ghosts or devils was a promise liberally accorded by my favourite authors, the fulfilment of which I most eagerly sought' (Ch2)

- 'The time at length arrives when grief is rather an indulgence than a necessity' (Ch3)

- 'I will pioneer a new way, explore unknown powers, and unfold to the world the deepest mysteries of creation' (Ch3)

Victor's character grows and changes significantly in this section. In Chapter 1, Shelley creates the impression that he is indulged and loved, even spoilt (there is perhaps an element of idealisation, which makes us question how reliable his feelings about his childhood are and how much he looks through rose-tinted glasses at his life before he found science). In Chapter 2, Victor's life shifts away from his parents, as he grows into a young man with his own desires and drive, who is temperamental and sometimes violent. In Chapter 3, Victor is contrastingly pragmatic and sentimental (perhaps this sparks distrust in his narrative voice). Notably, Victor also becomes aspirational and determined to make his mark on the world.

Alphonse

Key quotations:

- 'He was respected by all who knew him for his integrity and indefatigable attention to public business' (Ch1)

- 'There was a sense of justice in my father's upright mind which rendered it necessary that he should approve highly to love strongly' (Ch1)

- 'When I mingled with other families I distinctly discerned how peculiarly fortunate my lot was, and gratitude assisted the development of filial love' (Ch2)

- 'My father looked carelessly at the title page of my book and said, "Ah! Cornelius Agrippa! My dear Victor, do not waste your time upon this; it is sad trash."' (Ch2)

Alphonse is clearly a public figure who is loved and respected by his son, but he is also portrayed as absent at times and – to modern readers – perhaps questionable in his actions when he marries the vulnerable daughter of one of his closest friends. In Chapter 1, Victor largely portrays his father in a positive light and seems to admire him, but in Chapter 2, this changes as Victor deeply feels Alphonse's rejection of his new love of science. Alphonse seems pragmatic (or unfeeling?) when he insists on Victor's move to university shortly after Caroline's death.

Caroline

Key quotations:

- 'Caroline Beaufort possessed a mind of an uncommon mould, and her courage rose to support her in her adversity' (Ch1)
- 'On her deathbed, the fortitude and benignity of this best of women did not desert her' (Ch3)

Caroline is portrayed as a strong and determined woman, who suffered difficult circumstances yet is generous and noble. She provides a lifelong friend and future wife for her son and, when Elizabeth is ill with scarlet fever, sacrifices herself in order to nurse her. In death, she cements her wish for Elizabeth and Victor to be married, and explicitly passes her role of mother to the young Frankenstein boys to Elizabeth. These final acts have been interpreted in many ways by literary critics and academics: some perceive her to be a noble martyr while others consider her to be irresponsible and a limiting, anti-feminist force on the future of her adopted daughter.

Elizabeth

Key quotations:

- 'The beautiful and adored companion of all my occupations and my pleasures' (Ch1)
- 'She busied herself with following the aerial creations of the poets; and in the majestic and wondrous scenes which surrounded our Swiss home' (Ch2)
- 'The saintly soul of Elizabeth shone like a shrine-dedicated lamp in our peaceful home' (Ch2)
- 'Never was she so enchanting as at this time, when she recalled the sunshine of her smiles and spent them upon us' (Ch3)

At first, Elizabeth is portrayed largely as a possession of Victor. She is presented as being able to bring joy to others and admired by many. Elizabeth has a 'calmer and more concentrated disposition' (Ch2) than Victor and enjoys being in nature and exploring the dramatic scenery of Geneva. In the first paragraph of Chapter 2, Victor certainly appears to have quite an admiration of Elizabeth for this. He also describes her influence over him and Clerval.

Here, Shelley is perhaps hinting at the individuality of women and their feminine power. Victor, however, does not see this and often talks about Elizabeth as an object, particularly in reference to domestic objects, reinforcing her place in the family home. In Chapter 3, this becomes more prominent as she, despite being a similar age to Victor, is bound further to the home as she takes on Caroline's role as mother – a stark contrast to Victor's upcoming freedom as he attends university.

S-T-R-E-T-C-H

Considering the novel as a whole, we can see that it is this tie to Geneva and to Victor that is ultimately Elizabeth's undoing. It is because of her importance as a relation – or possession – of Victor's that his Creature kills her in an act of revenge. It is this portrayal of her ill-fated domestic attributes that is ripe for exploration through a feminist lens. While admired by Victor's male gaze for these, the very fact that they result in her death can be interpreted as a sharp commentary on the consequences of restricting women to a domestic sphere.

Clerval

Key quotations:

- 'He was a boy of singular talent and fancy' (Ch2)
- 'And Clerval – could aught ill entrench on the noble spirit of Clerval?' (Ch2)
- 'But when I spoke, I read in his kindling eye and in his animated glance a restrained but firm resolve not to be chained' (Ch3)

There are parallels between Clerval and Elizabeth: both are taken with poets, adventures and romantic notions. However, as a man, Clerval is granted the opportunity to be ambitious and 'noble' for these. He is a clear contrast to Victor, but Shelley has Victor describe Clerval with deep love and adoration. In Chapter 3, Clerval and Elizabeth share similar grief at the prospect of losing their friend to university, and Victor is dismissive of Clerval's father's 'narrow-minded' views, which mean that Clerval does not attend university with him. Victor does, however, note a determined glint in Clerval's eye, which suggests that he won't be tied to following the footsteps of his father.

Structure 🖧

This section begins with a very logical point (perhaps echoing Victor's logical and scientific character): the origins of Victor himself, and his story up to the point of the creation of his Creature.

Chapter 1

Opening: 'I am by birth a Genevese, and my family is one of the most distinguished of that republic'

Ending: 'No word, no expression could body forth the kind of relation in which she stood to me – my more than sister, since till death she was to be mine only'

As Chapter 1 marks the transition from Walton's narrative to that of Victor, learners should be invited to consider the following:

- What has Shelley already told us about Victor Frankenstein before his narrative begins?

- How does Victor's idealistic recounting of his childhood contrast this?

Although this chapter is the first narrated by Victor, we have already heard his voice in Walton's writing. We also know that, even though it is Victor's narrative, it is Walton who captures and relays it: Walton remarks to his sister in his notes that 'I have resolved, every night... to record, as nearly as possible, in his own words, what he has related.' Moreover, Walton's words that he will, in the future, read it with 'interest and sympathy' arguably allude to further bias in this: not only do we have Victor's story told through none other than his perspective, but we also read it through the records of a 'sympathetic' fan.

When discussing this with learners, teachers might use the following questions as prompts:

- Why does Shelley open Victor's section with Victor's entire life? What is the impact of readers hearing about Victor's family and childhood, rather than simply his life in science?

- What impact does the sharing of the origin stories of Caroline and Elizabeth have on readers' understanding of women in the Frankenstein family?

PIT STOP ▼

S-T-R-E-T-C-H

In starting Victor's narrative, we begin a new timeframe – one that takes place many years before Walton's. Importantly, this places the reader in the position of knowing the outcome of the story – or, at least, part of it. We know that, regardless of how cheerfully Victor paints the picture of his early life, his life takes tragic turns and he ends up desperate. To challenge learners' understanding of authorial intent, it is worth asking them:

- How does our knowledge of Victor's current situation impact our view of his childhood?

- Does our knowledge of his current situation influence how reliable we consider him to be as a narrator?

Chapter 2

Opening: 'We were brought up together; there was not quite a year difference in our ages'

Ending: 'Destiny was too potent, and her immutable laws had decreed my utter and terrible destruction'

Chapter 2 very much marks the shift between Victor's domestic life and his existence as he discovers science and begins a more academic life. Shelley uses her structure to reflect these distinctly separate worlds. The first half of Chapter

2 is centred on Victor and the relationship between him and his family. However, once Victor discovers the work of Agrippa, Shelley notably shifts the focus of the chapter so that Victor is far more centred on himself and his own desires, none of which involve anyone beyond himself. The image of lone Victor exploring science reflects the isolation that he will later feel as a result of his pursuit of science (as reflected in the final line of the chapter). This is a pattern that Shelley maintains throughout the novel, which is, in part, enabled by the confinement of Shelley's female characters to domestic spheres.

Foreshadowing 🧬

Where we have heard Victor's voice already, it is from the emaciated and broken man that Victor has become. Before beginning his narrative retelling to Walton, he states that he has suffered 'great and unparalleled misfortunes' and that he has 'lost everything, and cannot begin life anew'. Before even reading the 'main' narrative of the text, we might reflect and consider what information Shelley has already given us. We enter the main narrative knowing that Victor is miserable, and sees himself as suffering great tragedies as a fallen, failed man. Shelley plays on this across her early chapters, as Victor often reflects back on moments that defined or determined his 'destiny', foreshadowing the events to come while also frequently reminding readers of the dangerous consequences of the behaviours and views shared in his narrative.

PIT STOP ☁ ▼

Shelley ends both Chapter 1 and Chapter 2 with a reminder of Victor's later downfall. The end of these chapters is a good point to highlight this to learners as a deliberate choice that Shelley makes to prevent her readers from falling too much into engaging with Victor's past.

As retrieval practice, you may ask learners:

- Where before has Shelley included a reminder of Victor's downfall?
- What might be the reason for this?
- What is the impact on the reader of this?

Chapter 3 ✝

Opening: 'When I had attained the age of seventeen my parents resolved that I should become a student at the university of Ingolstadt'

Ending: 'Thus ended a day memorable to me; it decided my future destiny'

In Chapter 3, the shift between family and scientific study is further emphasised, and the chapter even opens with a declaration of the decision for Victor to leave his childhood home. Victor's split from the domestic sphere is echoed through the tone of the chapter, which begins in grief and sorrow and later shifts to curious independence. This shift is quite suddenly marked in the third paragraph of the chapter, when Shelley deftly moves Victor's narrative from news of his mother's death, to his all-consuming and bewildering grief, and then suddenly to an almost coldly practical perspective, in which grief is indulgent and the family 'must continue [their] course'. Shelley's use of the conjunctions 'but', 'yet' and 'and' allow her to shift between perspectives without interrupting her narrative flow. Perhaps this in itself reflects Victor's coldly pragmatic and unfeeling character.

PIT STOP ▼

S-T-R-E-T-C-H

It is worth highlighting to learners that throughout Victor's story, women and science sit very separately. What begins as a split focus in a single chapter grows into vast geographical distances and long gaps between instances of Victor's interaction with females. With A level learners, the context explored earlier in this chapter around the Georgian sense of masculinity should prove a rich topic of discussion, with questions such as:

- What are the advantages to Victor of being so far from home?

- What is Shelley telling us about the lives of women in the early chapters?

- What does Shelley set her readers up to expect of the different lives and freedoms of Victor and Elizabeth in the early chapters?

Extracts

Extract 1 (Ch1): How does Shelley use language to present Victor's feelings about Elizabeth?

'And when, on the morrow, she presented Elizabeth to me as her promised gift, I, with childish seriousness, interpreted her words literally and looked upon Elizabeth as mine – mine to protect, love, and cherish. All praises bestowed on her I received as made to a possession of my own. We called each other familiarly by the name of cousin. No word, no expression could body forth the kind of relation in which she stood to me – my more than sister, since till death she was to be mine only.'

Given that we now see the language that Victor uses as troubling, you may wish to handle this extract carefully with learners. You might debate the following interpretations:

Shelley presents Victor's feelings for Elizabeth as:

- heavily loving and full of admiration and adoration?

- brotherly?

- possessive?
- self-gratifying?

Shelley presents Victor's feelings towards Elizabeth as possessive. She has Victor repeatedly use the words 'mine' and 'my' to highlight how much Victor believes himself to be her owner, or at least to suggest that he considers himself to have a special relationship with her. This impression is further emphasised when Shelley writes that Victor saw any praise given to Elizabeth as 'a possession of my own', revealing that he even saw other people's admiration of her as belonging to him.

PIT STOP ▼

S-T-R-E-T-C-H

This is a prime extract to use when introducing learners to the feminist lens. When exploring this, you might ask learners to discuss or debate how we might read and interpret Victor's language around Elizabeth versus how one of Shelley's contemporaries may have interpreted it. Moreover, you might refer to this later when discussing what Shelley might want us to think of men who talk about women in this way: does she intend for this to build sympathy for Victor when Elizabeth is killed, or is his adoration of her the seed that leads to her demise?

Extract 2 (Ch2): How does Shelley use language to foreshadow Victor's destructive passion for science?

'I feel exquisite pleasure in dwelling on the recollections of childhood, before misfortune had tainted my mind and changed its bright visions of extensive usefulness into gloomy and narrow reflections upon self.'

In this extract, Shelley presents Victor's childhood as something that brings him pleasure and comfort. Victor says that he feels 'exquisite pleasure in dwelling' in thoughts of his childhood, suggesting that he finds happiness in these thoughts. The word 'exquisite' highlights the strength of happiness and pleasure that these thoughts bring him, and the verb 'dwelling' reveals that he enjoys reliving them, with a hint that he would like to do so more often. The words that he uses to describe the 'bright visions' of his childhood contrast with the 'gloomy and narrow' feelings he has about his later life. The word 'gloomy' suggests that these later experiences were much less happy, and the word 'narrow' highlights a feeling of being trapped or tightly bound to those gloomy days.

Extract 3 (Ch2): How does Shelley portray Elizabeth and her influence on Victor?

─────────── 66 ───────────

'Her sympathy was ours; her smile, her soft voice, the sweet glance of her celestial eyes, were ever there to bless and animate us. She was the living spirit of love to soften and attract; I might have become sullen in my study, rough through the ardour of my nature, but that she was there to subdue me to a semblance of her own gentleness.'

─────────── 99 ───────────

In this extract, Shelley portrays Elizabeth as a beautiful and almost heavenly character. The words 'the sweet glance of her celestial eyes, were ever there to bless and animate us' creates the impression that Elizabeth exists to inspire and bring joy to others. The adjective 'celestial' highlights how angelic and heavenly her appearance is, alluding to her being almost divine rather than human. This is reinforced when Shelley portrays Elizabeth as able to 'subdue' Victor and 'soften' the 'rough ardour of [his] nature'. The verb 'subdue' suggests that she has a calming and soothing influence on Victor, offering comfort and joy to him.

PIT STOP ▼

S-T-R-E-T-C-H

As with the language that Shelley has Victor use to describe Elizabeth's introduction to him, in this section Victor continues to objectify Elizabeth and see her as a facilitator of his life, rather than the owner of her own life and character. The phrasing of the first sentence of the extract suggests that her sole purpose is to 'bless and animate' Victor and Clerval, as she is 'ever there', implying that she has no other function. Shelley also has Victor focus on shallow elements of her character: her smile, voice and eyes. The thoughts behind her 'celestial eyes' and the words spoken in her 'soft voice' are aspects that Victor neglects to share with Walton, reducing Elizabeth to a beautiful servant.

Extract 4 (Ch3): How does Shelley present Victor's determination?

"

'As he went on I felt as if my soul were grappling with a palpable enemy; one by one the various keys were touched which formed the mechanism of my being; chord after chord was sounded, and soon my mind was filled with one thought, one conception, one purpose. So much has been done, exclaimed the soul of Frankenstein – more, far more, will I achieve; treading in the steps already marked, I will pioneer a new way, explore unknown powers, and unfold to the world the deepest mysteries of creation.'

"

Victor's determination to forge a legacy is one inherited from his father. However, rejecting politics and public service, it is science through which he determines to make his mark on the world. The metaphor of Victor 'grappling with a palpable enemy' is indicative of the aggressiveness of his determination and the violent disregard that Victor holds for those who doubt him, his beliefs and his abilities. This intense feeling is juxtaposed with the connotations of the word 'mechanism' that Victor uses to describe the core of his 'being'. Considering himself in this way, Shelley foreshadows the unfeeling, unthinking and almost inhuman drive to create life that we see in his extraordinary actions in the following chapter. There is a strong sense of superlative and extreme action throughout the quotation – a determination to follow existing science but push far beyond this in a quest to embrace 'unknown powers' and share the knowledge of these with the world. Two things could be noted here, the first being the determination to explore 'powers' and the second to claim these as his own and intertwine them with his legacy.

SECTION 3
VICTOR'S LABOURS
(CHAPTER 4)

At a glance

> **Summary quotation:** 'Learn from me... how dangerous is the acquirement of knowledge' (Ch4)

> **Big Question:** Why does Victor persist in his ambition to create a new life? Is everything scientifically possible ethically justifiable?

> **Significant plot events:**

  - Victor arrives at Ingolstadt University, meeting Professors Krempe and Waldman. He prefers Waldman over Krempe, partly because he finds Krempe ugly and partly because Waldman flatters his ego.

  - Victor's admiration and friendship with Professor Waldman develops.

  - Victor becomes fascinated with life and death, and begins to consider the possibility of reanimation.

  - Victor has an (unrevealed) epiphany about the secret of the creation of life, and begins collecting the body parts of dead humans and animals, obsessively assembling them into a creature.

  - Victor's obsessive work is detrimental to his health and his relationships with others.

> **Character focus:** Victor Frankenstein, Professor Krempe, Professor Waldman

> **Key themes:**

  - Knowledge and discovery 🔍
  - Isolation and loneliness 🧎
  - Ambition and legacy 🏗️
  - Obsession 💭
  - Power and responsibility 💡

> **Handle with care:**

  - gruesome misuse of corpses

Why?

The 'whys?' for this chapter could seem a little banal; however, Shelley carefully sets up and prepares us for Victor's brutal rejection of the Creature in Chapter 5.

- Why is Victor's continued dislike for Krempe significant in this chapter?
- Why, after his scientific epiphany, does Victor never query the ethics of his experiment?
- Why are the details of this scientific epiphany never revealed?
- Why is he motivated to carry out such gruesome tasks in the name of 'science'?
- Why is he driven to obsession while making the Creature?
- Why does he isolate himself so completely from friends and family?

What?

What happens? 📄 🔍 ☀

After the untimely death of his mother in Chapter 3, Victor is settled at Ingolstadt University and becomes fully absorbed in the study of natural philosophy (the study of nature and the physical universe – we might call this 'natural sciences'). Despite Victor's dislike of M. Krempe's physical appearance, he concedes that Krempe has 'sound sense', although he prefers the more aesthetically pleasing M. Waldman, whom he regards (perhaps mistakenly) as a 'true friend'.

Working day and night until early morning, Victor believes that he has mastered what he needs to know of natural philosophy and turns his attention to 'the structure of the human frame'. He takes a very pragmatic approach to the dead bodies of people, meaning that he views a human corpse as an object to use as he sees fit.

After intensive study of human physiology, Victor has an epiphany (a sudden moment of great revelation or realisation) about the knowledge and power of creating human life. From here, Victor gathers 'materials' (human and animal body parts) so that he can assemble and bring to life a human being of his own creation. His obsession to do so has completely isolated him from his family and friends, while physically he has become a ghost of himself. Emaciated, delirious with a fever but still resolutely determined, Victor decides to proceed with his experiment.

Social and historical context ⚙

Historical context: Grave robbing – the 'Resurrectionists'

Before the Murder Act of 1751, human cadavers were not dissected for the purpose of exploring human anatomy; instead, scientists used pigs and apes. In 1751, the Murder Act prevented the bodies of convicted and condemned murderers from being buried, and so they were strung up to rot in public or used for medical science.

The nineteenth century saw great progress in engineering, technology and the sciences, alongside an increasing number of medical schools being opened. This gave rise to great demand for cadavers, which the supply could not meet. Savvy – and poor – Georgian entrepreneurs saw a gap in the market and began exhuming recently deceased bodies and selling them.

Although morally repugnant, at this time dead bodies were not viewed as being owned by anyone, so this was not illegal. Despite many security efforts being installed in graveyards – gates, stone tombs and mausoleums – this did not stem the tide of grave robbers (Resurrectionists), and supply could not keep up with demand.

Shelley's audience would not be unfamiliar with the concept of grave robbing and the Resurrectionists. Nor would they be unfamiliar with dissections, as these were often viewed by the public in medical school theatres, which welcomed the public in. Knowing this is helpful for learners so that they understand the pragmatic regard that corpses were given at the time.

Literary context: The Gothic

The Castle of Otranto by Horace Walpole (1764) is regarded as the first text that truly acquired the label 'Gothic', containing a blueprint of characteristics that have been moulded, developed, critiqued, parodied and conjoined to numerous other genres ever since. These traits included:

- **setting:** an isolated medieval castle that is dark and disorientating

- **supernatural:** hauntings, prophecies, ghosts and spectres, metamorphosing monsters

- **dark atmosphere:** dark in terms of the gloominess of the castle, but also dark in terms of tone and subject matter

- **women in distress:** what we would now call a 'scream queen' – a woman under physical and sexual threat

- **tyrannical males:** fathers and husbands controlling and killing women by shocking means

- **twisted (morally shocking) events:** such as the father ending up killing his own daughter in *Otranto*

- **hidden identities:** often revealed in a big twist, e.g. one character is revealed to be the true prince of Otranto

- **exploring the human psyche:** that is, the darker taboo recesses of the human psyche – sexual desire, sexual deviance, death, murder, jealousy and so on.

While Shelley only utilises some of these traits in Frankenstein, her novel is now viewed as a key Gothic text.

Hubris – what is it and why does it matter to this text?

The Cambridge Dictionary defines hubris neatly as 'a way of talking or behaving that is too proud', which is certainly the most common modern usage of the word. In Ancient Greece, it was the act of an intentional use of violence that was to punish or humiliate. Aristotle, who explored the term in his treatise *Rhetoric* (quoted in Britannica, 2024), defined it differently:

'Hubris consists in doing and saying things that cause shame to the victim... simply for the pleasure of it. Retaliation is not hubris, but revenge... Young men and the rich are hubristic because they think they are better than other people.'

The last sentence in this short extract from Aristotle's *Rhetoric* shows how the modern usage of behaving and being 'too proud' came to be common.

Hubris is an interesting avenue to explore with all types of learners of this text. Ask them to consider whether Victor's hubris in particular is deserving of the punishment meted out to him by his creation.

Vocabulary in context

Word	Quotation	Definition
natural philosophy	'From this day natural philosophy, and particularly chemistry, in the most comprehensive sense of the term, became nearly my sole occupation'	the study of all natural phenomena in the physical world (in the nineteenth century)
physiognomy	'I found even in M. Krempe a great deal of sound sense and real information, combined, it is true, with a repulsive physiognomy and manners'	the physical appearance of the face
infallibly	'A mind of moderate capacity which closely pursues one study must infallibly arrive at great proficiency in that study'	in a way that is never wrong or never fails
minutiae	'I paused, examining and analysing all the minutiae of causation'	small or unimportant details

Vocabulary builder

The combination of key vocabulary and key quotation revision is both fruitful and efficient. Learners could consider the question and quotation below:

1. To whom does Victor Frankenstein refer to in this quotation? *(Answer: Prof. Waldman)*

   'His gentleness was never tinged by dogmatism, and his instructions were given with an air of frankness and good nature that banished every idea of pedantry.'

2. Usually, the words 'dogmatic' (dogmatism) and 'pedant' (pedantry) are used pejoratively (to show contempt or disapproval). This is not the case here. How and why have these terms become a compliment to Waldman instead?

This will enable recall of the 'facts of the text', as well as allowing learners to better develop their understanding of writers making choices – that words, *and specific combinations of words*, are not arrived at by chance or accident.

Academic writing and emerging themes of the text

To encourage deeper thinking about the text, and the form of the Gothic that Shelley presents us with here, it is worthwhile asking learners to consider and cross-reference how some key concepts are presented in Walton's letters and Victor's narration thus far:

- **Isolation and loneliness:** Walton and Victor impose this isolation and loneliness on themselves. To what extent should the reader feel sympathy for their loneliness?

- **Obsession and obsessiveness:** Both Walton and Victor share the characteristic of obsession, but is it the same for both characters? If there is a difference, where and when is that observable and why?

- **Cost and consequence(s):** There is a cost and a consequence to being completely obsessed by something. What might be the cost to Victor and is the 'cost' commensurate to (equal to, appropriate to) the 'crime'? What is to be learned because of the consequences of obsession for Victor and, to a slightly lesser degree, Walton?

Plot and character development

1. Why is Victor's continued dislike for Krempe significant in this chapter and the next?

Victor's distaste for Krempe is much more explicit in the 1818 version of this text, but is still made some use of in this edition. Victor has an obvious and visible disgust for ugliness, which is exemplified in his description of Krempe, who he states has a 'a repulsive physiognomy and manners', and his favouring Waldman on account of his more pleasing face. Here, Shelley effectively signposts the dramatic rejection of his creation in Chapter 5 by making Victor's disgust at what is ugly fairly clear. Narrative signposting prepares the reader for other bigger moments in the text, where the desired response may well be shock but it should not be a surprise.

2. Why, after his scientific epiphany, does Victor never query the ethics of his experiment? 🔘

Victor narrows his studies down to natural philosophy and chemistry – the only tools that he believes he needs to get his experiment completed. What is absent from his studies? Morality and ethics. Victor has little interest in what is ethical or moral; rather, he is determined to complete his experiment without consideration of whether he should or not.

3. Why are the details of this scientific epiphany never revealed?

There are several sound reasons, in terms of character and narrative, as to why Victor never reveals the truth of his discovery.

• It shows *some* element of Victor having learned from his mistakes.

• The overall purpose of this narrative, which is told to the narratee Walton, is to prevent Walton from making similarly terrible mistakes. Walton's potential terrible mistake is to sacrifice his own life and those of his crew for the sake of recognition, glory and immortality, by being immortalised in the history books. Victor's narrative is to show him that chasing immortality can only end in disaster – not just for Walton but for everyone whom he holds dear.

4. Why is Victor motivated to carry out such gruesome tasks in the name of 'science'? 🔘

Victor is able to disassociate himself from his actions as he gathers his 'material' for his experiment. Having said that, learners (and teachers) must never discuss characters in terms of being 'real people' – they are a construction of the author – but the concept of disassociation (commonly associated with the condition of psychopathy) has its uses, in that it allows learners to understand the pragmatic approach that Victor takes to raiding graves and cutting up corpses. Victor uses science to justify actions that would be ethically and morally unacceptable under any circumstance. He believes, just as Walton does as he sets off across the ice, that his work will benefit all mankind, and that is reason enough to pursue his 'unhallowed arts' (Ch6).

5. Why is he driven to obsession while making the monster?

It is here that Shelley fully exploits her version of the Byronic protagonist – a character that is emotionally overwrought, wallows in suffering and does so in self-imposed isolation. Obsessive behaviour is part and parcel of the DNA of a Gothic protagonist: Dracula obsesses over Mina Harker, Jekyll obsesses over his creation of Hyde and Victor is driven to the point of near death to make sure that his experiment succeeds – which indeed it does. Alongside the characteristic of obsession, Shelley takes pains to illustrate the cost of this: to Victor's health and, latterly in the narrative, to all those whom he loves and cares for.

6. Why does he isolate himself so completely from friends and family?

It is in this chapter that Shelley builds up the momentum for the big event in the early part of her novel: the birth of a 'monster'. However, we should not forget that this chapter, along with Chapters 1 to 3 of Victor's narration, also creates a monster, although this particular character's monstrosity is internal, while it is the Creature's (predictable) ugliness that marks him as a failure, a monster and a 'daemon' in the eyes of his creator.

How?

Language

How and why does Shelley use language of conception, gestation and birth in this chapter? 🔍

Shelley was a young woman, who was acutely aware that her existence cost her own mother her life. Within a few weeks of her birth, Shelley's mother, Mary Wollstonecraft, died of a postpartum infection. Shelley's relationship with her mother was predominantly via Wollstonecraft's written work, alongside conversations with her father, William Godwin. For further reading about Shelley and her mother, Charlotte Gordon's (2015) *Romantic Outlaws: The Extraordinary Lives of Mary Wollstonecraft & Mary Shelley* is a very well-researched source and a great read.

'After so much time spent in painful labour, to arrive at once at the summit of my desires, was the most gratifying consummation of my toils.' (Ch4)

Given the context of Shelley's own life, it becomes less of a shock as to why her novel explores pregnancy and labour in the way that it does, although here she places the burden of pregnancy (gestation) upon the male.

The phrases below demonstrate how the quotation on page 60 considers the processes of conception and birth in reverse:

- **consummation:** the act of sexual intercourse (which validates a marriage)
- **summit of my desires:** the climax
- **painful labour:** the result of the two actions above – a new life that enters the world.

So not only are Victor's actions ungodly and sinful, but they are also an equally terrible crime against nature. The inversion of the natural processes of creating a new life, as we have here, presents the act of creating the Creature as unholy and unnatural.

Light: Symbolises knowledge that man should not possess (Promethean interpretation) ℚ

Key quotation:

- 'until from the midst of this darkness a sudden light broke in upon me – a light so brilliant and wondrous' (Ch4)

It is in Chapter 4 that Victor has his scientific epiphany: he finds the answer to the question 'How does one create life?', although this secret remains as such right until the last words of the novel.

Interestingly, it is here that one of the key themes of the text – knowledge and discovery – receives some of its best and most startling imagery. A perfectly sound and reasonable interpretation of light and dark imagery would be a biblical one: God is light and dark relates to evil or sin. An alternative interpretation, which is more in keeping with the novel's subtitle 'the modern Prometheus', is that 'light' symbolises powerful and godly knowledge (the fire that Prometheus stole from the gods to give to man), while 'dark' and 'darkness' symbolise a lack of knowledge or ignorance.

The final phrase, 'a light so brilliant and wondrous', illustrates how completely dazzled Victor is by this discovery, to the extent that he is blinded by it in all respects. What does this light obscure from Victor's sight? The ethics and morals of completing an experiment that places Victor in the position of a god.

Character focus

Victor ♟

Key quotations (Ch4):

- 'a churchyard was to me merely the receptacle of bodies deprived of life, which, from being the seat of beauty and strength, had become food for the worm.'
- 'at the end of two years, I made some discoveries in the improvement of some chemical instruments, which procured me great esteem and admiration at the university.'

- 'None but those who have experienced them can conceive of the enticements of science.'

- 'Two years passed in this manner, during which I paid no visit to Geneva, but was engaged, heart and soul, in the pursuit of some discoveries, which I hoped to make.'

In this chapter, Victor reaches full maturation as an educated young man in charge of his own pursuits. Victor's obsessive and determined young self becomes dogmatic and practical. His raiding of churchyards and tunnel vision when conducting his experiments reveal his disregard for moral consequences and for his beloved family.

He is overly ambitious in his pursuits too, deeply desiring public recognition of his excellence (a likely parallel drawn by Shelley between Victor and the mythical Prometheus). Ironically, it is this desire for legacy and excellence that leads him to isolation while conducting experiments and building his Creature.

PIT STOP ▼

S-T-R-E-T-C-H

This chapter is key to Shelley's positioning of the reader, where she lays a foundation for the reader's relationship with Victor. Questions to which to return frequently when exploring this throughout the novel are:

- Who is the reader with?

- Who is the reader against?

- How do you know?

PIT STOP ▼

Victor's Creature is a chimera, a combination of human *and* animals. Victor wanted to construct a 'super-human', which he could only achieve by adding animal parts to the human.

This is what also makes the Creature an abomination (a thing that causes disgust or loathing). Ask learners to consider why the Creature might be viewed as an abomination against:

- God and the church

- nature.

You can find teacher notes giving more detail about the concept of a chimera and its origins from Greek mythology in the online resources. 🖱

Structure 🗂

Learners should explore the following examples from the opening and ending of this section and be invited to consider:

- Why has Shelley chosen to begin and end with this focus on the cause and effect of Victor's obsessive pursuit of forbidden knowledge?

- What consequences for Victor can the reader anticipate that Victor cannot? Why is this?

Opening: 'From this day natural philosophy, and particularly chemistry... became nearly my sole occupation'

Ending: 'Sometimes I grew alarmed at the wreck I perceived that I had become;... I promised myself both of these [exercise and amusement] when my creation should be complete'

Ask learners to consider this opening and ending in light of the concept of reader privilege. Reader privilege concerns who has access to what kind of information (as well as insight and foresight) and when.

Ask learners to consider:

- Does the reader have more knowledge on which to base judgements than the characters in the text?

- If so, what conclusions can the reader draw because of this position of privilege?

Victor's obsessiveness acts as a pair of blinkers on a working farm animal (such as a Shire horse), completely narrowing his field of vision and field of reference, so that all rational perspective has been removed.

Reader privilege is a continually useful concept for this text, but especially when learners have read Walton's opening narrative, Victor's narrative and the Creature's, thus forcing us to compare one against the other.

Extracts

Extract 1 (Ch4): How does Shelley use language to present the discovery and temptation of taboo knowledge in this extract? 🔍

'I paused, examining and analysing all the minutiae of causation, as exemplified in the change from life to death, and death to life, until from the midst of this darkness a sudden light broke in upon me – a light so brilliant and wondrous, yet so simple, that while I became dizzy with the immensity of the prospect which it illustrated, I was surprised, that among so many men of genius who had directed their enquiries towards the same science, that I alone should be reserved to discover so astonishing a secret.'

In this extract, Shelley presents the discovery and temptation of taboo knowledge as something that is so overpowering that Victor is unable to resist its lure. Shelley exploits the rhetorical form of chiasmus – 'life to death, and death to life' – to foreground the nature of the taboo knowledge that Victor chases. The circular nature of this structure mimics that of the natural world, while 'life' and 'death' in religious teachings are the preserve of God only. Shelley illustrates the overwhelming power of Victor's discovery by using light imagery, which references Prometheus's theft of fire (knowledge) from the gods. Victor views this knowledge as 'brilliant and wondrous', not able or wanting to see its dangerous potential. Victor's willingness to view this knowledge as 'wondrous' demonstrates a frightening lack of foresight, which is exemplified later in this extract when Victor believes himself to be the 'sole discoverer' of this extraordinary knowledge, not stopping to wonder whether his predecessors may have also discovered it but chosen not to use it. Finally, Shelley has presented us with an inverted version of Eve tempted by the apple or Pandora unable to resist the temptation of Pythos (the jar), showing us that man can be the cause of the downfall of man, and in a far more repugnant fashion than that of either Eve or Pandora.

Extract 2 (Ch4): How does Shelley use language to demonstrate Victor's obsessive, destructive character in this extract from Chapter 4? 🔊

'Who shall conceive the horrors of my secret toil, as I dabbled among the unhallowed damps of the grave, or tortured the living animal to animate the lifeless clay? My limbs now tremble, and my eyes swim with the remembrance; but then a resistless, and almost frantic, impulse, urged me forward; I seemed to have lost all soul or sensation but for this one pursuit.'

The following are some example responses when planning key language features for scaffolding:

1. Shelley maintains her use of the semantic field of conception, pregnancy and birth with 'conceive'.

2. Shelley uses the possessive determiner 'my' to show ownership of Victor's 'secret toil'. The secrecy of his work contradicts his desire for adulation and recognition for his great discovery. The secrecy also demonstrates a sense of cowardice or shame with his experiment, indicating that he knows that it is morally and ethically wrong but persists anyway.

3. Victor then seems to perceive his motivation for completing his experiment as something supernatural – 'resistless', 'frantic', 'impulse' – all of which imply that *something* is in control of his actions and it isn't him. This is one of many times that Victor abdicates any and all responsibility for his actions.

4. Victor's compulsion to complete the experiment costs him both his 'soul' and 'sensation' at the expense of all else.

Here is another instance of Victor's lack of foresight, as he can only consider the harm that his experiment has done to him and not the harm that its existence could mean for his family and for humanity as a whole.

PIT STOP ▼

S-T-R-E-T-C-H

One of the most simple but effective techniques for language analysis is to look for patterns and, with a specific word or words, look for frequency of usage.

An example of how to direct learners to look for patterns and frequency of usage is to consider how many times Shelley refers to or alludes to labour and pregnancy in this passage, chapter or section, or to look for usage of the words 'labour', 'conceive', 'conception' and 'birth'.

- Which is the most frequently used?
- Where is it most frequently used?
- Why is it most frequently used at that specific place in the text?
- What does this frequent use of 'X' achieve?

You could also direct learners' attention to what is infrequent or absent altogether (using the idea of negative space referred to in the section on Walton's letters, page 27) and how that also creates meaning.

SECTION 4
BIRTH OF THE CREATURE
(CHAPTER 5)

At a glance

> **Summary quotation:** 'How can I describe my emotions at this catastrophe, or how delineate the wretch whom with such infinite pains and care I had endeavoured to form?' (Ch5)

> **Big Question:** Why does Victor view his experiment as a complete failure?

> **Significant plot events:**

- Victor's experiment is brought to life, but rather than celebrate, Victor suddenly sees the Creature's ugliness and considers him a terrible failure.

- The Creature reaches out to his creator, which Victor interprets as a threat, and so runs away out of his apartment into a nearby church courtyard.

- Clerval suddenly arrives in Ingolstadt, which delights Victor, who is relieved to see that his Creature has fled.

- The relief of the empty apartment provokes maniacal laughter in Victor. Soon afterwards, Victor faints with a fever.

- Clerval nurses him back to health, and the chapter ends with news of a letter received from Elizabeth.

> **Character focus:** Victor Frankenstein, Clerval, the Creature

> **Key themes:**

- Family and companionship 🌐
- Knowledge and discovery 🔍
- Ambition and legacy 🎲
- Rejection and its consequences ⊗
- Power and responsibility 🔆

> **Handle with care:**

- The main sensitive issue in this chapter is that of Victor's abandonment and neglect of his creation (his child)

Why?

- Why can Victor's behaviour be regarded as 'Promethean'?

- Why might the reader's relationship with Victor change here?

- Why does Victor misinterpret the Creature's gesture of reaching towards him?

- Why is it Clerval who nurses Victor back to health, and not Elizabeth?

S-T-R-E-T-C-H questions

- At the point of the Creature's birth, with whom is the reader positioned and why?

- At the point of the Creature's rejection, does the reader's positioning change? Why?

This allows us to consider Chapter 5's Big Question: Why does Victor view his experiment as a complete failure?

PIT STOP ▼

Retrieval point ☁

With learners, remind them of Victor's childhood and specifically the moments where he learned that the aesthetically pleasing (what is beautiful) is valuable, and so, by default, the aesthetically displeasing (the ugly) is valueless. It is important that the learners can grasp the inevitability of Victor's rejection of his creation. Once the moment of rejection has been read, it is worth posing the following question:

Are we surprised by Victor's rejection of the Creature? Explain your thinking. (Or, if not, why not?)

What?

What happens? ☁

The most significant events of the chapter, which have a bearing on what follows, are:

1. the birth of the Creature

2. Victor's rejection of his creation

3. Victor's fever and Clerval (not Elizabeth) nursing him back to health

4. Elizabeth's letter – as it is Elizabeth who communicates the Frankenstein family's bad news to Victor.

With an impending sense of Gothic doom, set up by the gruesome explanation of how the Creature is made in Chapter 4, Victor narrates the birth of his creation. However, the narration is biased against the Creature even before the Creature (or, if we want to be more Freudian about it, Victor's child) takes his first breath. Why is this? In Chapters 1 to 3, focusing on Victor's childhood and adolescence, Victor is taught by his parents that beauty is valuable. Therefore, if beauty is valuable, ugliness is valueless, worthless and disposable. The focus of the opening section of this chapter is almost entirely on the aesthetics of the Creature. Indeed, Victor believed himself to have stitched together – from a range of dead human and animal parts – something that was as beautiful as Michaelangelo's David; he bemoans that he 'had selected his features as beautiful'.

After the melodramatic moment of the Creature's birth (he does effectively emerge from an artificial womb), Shelley amplifies the drama with the moment of Victor's rejection of the Creature.

After this, Victor cowers in a nearby courtyard, fretting about the discovery of his failure until the morning, at which point Clerval arrives just in time for Victor's hysteria to peak. Clerval, assuming the same role for Victor as Walton does at the start of the novel, takes care of Victor while he is in a feverish stupor.

Meanwhile, the Creature is at large in Ingolstadt.

Social and historical context ⚙

Literary context: Prometheus – the overreacher

Who is Prometheus and why is he relevant to Chapter 5? There are three main parts to the Promethean (name meaning 'foresight') myth:

1. Prometheus, feeling pity for man's struggling state on the earth, steals fire from Zeus and gives it to man.

2. As part of Zeus's punishment for Prometheus's hubris, and to punish mankind, Pandora is created to tempt his brother Epimetheus (name meaning 'hindsight') into marriage, which works. Their marriage gift is a jar (Pythos) for Pandora, which *she must not open*. Succumbing to curiosity and temptation, just as Zeus intended, she opens the jar. The jar spews out many evils, which fly out into the world, although one thing is left in the jar: hope.

3. A further punishment for Prometheus's hubris is much more direct. Zeus has Prometheus chained to a rock in the Caucasus mountain range, and sends an eagle to peck out his immortal liver every single day.

Note here that fire can be interpreted literally as the state of combustion that produces heat (so Prometheus brings warmth to a struggling human race) or, more metaphorically, as the 'essence of life'. Before Prometheus's interventions, man (the race) was milling around on the earth like ants: existing, but not living. Prometheus enables man to live beyond merely existing, thus elevating humans above mere animals.

In this chapter, it is the act of 'overreaching' that turns this story on its generic heels: adventurer's journal (of assumed exploration glory) to bildungsroman (within Walton's bildungsroman) to a terrifying science fiction horror story.

There are further teacher notes about the Prometheus myth and how it can be applied to this text in the online resources.

Vocabulary in context

Word	Quotation	Definition
dreary	'It was on a dreary night of November, that I beheld the accomplishment of my toils'	boring, making you feel unhappy
accomplishment		something that is successful or achieved with a lot of effort
dismally	'It was already one in the morning; the rain pattered dismally against the panes'	in a way that makes you feel sad and without hope
convulsive	'it breathed hard, and a convulsive motion agitated its limbs'	movements of muscles in your body that you cannot control
dun	'that seemed almost of the same colour as the dun white sockets in which they were set'	of a greyish brown colour

PIT STOP

Retrieval point

Here are some prompts, using some of the words from the vocabulary table in a different form, to enable analysis and discussion of Shelley's vocabulary choices:

1. Why does Victor view his creation as a 'catastrophe'?

2. What did Victor 'accomplish' on that 'dreary night of November'?

3. What might be disturbing about the convulsive movement of the Creature?

4. What connections can you make between the Creature's convulsive movements here, the inspiration for Victor's experiment (lightning hitting a tree) and the energy source that brings the Creature to life?

PIT STOP ▼

Academic writing: 'But, because, so' sentences

Directing learners to use specific conjunctions with the same sentence stem enables them to learn that specific conjunctions serve specific purposes.

Examples:

- Victor's experiment is a success, because the Creature is living, breathing and moving.

- Victor's experiment is a success, but he believes it to be a complete failure.

- Victor's experiment is a success, so that when he rejects it, the reader can see the flaws in Victor's character.

For a second example and a more detailed rationale, explanation and source for this approach to teaching grammar, see the resources that accompany this chapter of the book.

Plot and character development

1. What is the most significant moment of this chapter?

Chapter 5's 'birth of a creature' is the pivotal moment in the text, because it is where Victor overreaches in the most Promethean of ways. The 'Context' section of this chapter provides a summary of the Prometheus myth; *some detailed examples of how Shelley uses it are in the online resources.* 🖱

In terms of this moment in the text, it is difficult to disentangle Victor, the character, from this significant plot moment. The birth of the Creature is a catalytic moment for all the death and destruction that follows it. Additionally, this moment – to state the obvious – is when the other significant character of the text emerges in the narrative: blinking, vulnerable and innocent.

2. What is even more significant than the birth of the Creature? 🔧

The birth of the Creature is not the only significant moment in this chapter nor, perhaps, the most significant. Instead, it is Victor's rejection of his creation that informs everything that follows this moment – and this chapter:

'one hand was stretched out, seemingly to detain me, but I escaped, and rushed down stairs'

By perceiving the Creature's actions as aggressive, Victor condemns the Creature to a life of misery and suffering. At this moment, Victor becomes a distant and uncaring 'god', unworthy of the responsibility of creating life. Here, Shelley builds upon and utilises the gruesomeness of Victor's grave robbery in Chapter 4, in order to change the reader's relationship with – and to – Victor. Where, in Chapters 1–3, he may have had some redeemable qualities that the reader could like or admire, here he seems to have none, thus altering the reader's relationship with him to one of distance, criticism and judgement.

3. What is the significance of the Creature's successful creation? 🧩 ☀

The significance of the Creature's successful creation is far reaching, in that every other event that occurs in the novel is as a result of the Creature's birth and rejection.

When one considers the 'big ideas' of this text, Victor's creation of life by artificial means foregrounds a huge range of concepts and questions, such as what happens when:

1. man takes on the role of God and succeeds?

2. the mortal 'god' is unable to take responsibility for the new life that he created?

3. a man rejects his child, and so rejects his role as father?

4. a child's education (the Creature's) is left to chance?

5. a child (the Creature) never experiences love or compassion?

6. a mortal 'god' tries to improve upon God and nature's work by creating a human who is in fact 'super-human'?

7. the woman's role of bearer of children and carer of newborn life is taken away, and taken over, by a man?

PIT STOP ▼

These questions demonstrate why this novel is called a novel of ideas. Periodically track the key ideas of the text, perhaps in a table.

4. How does Victor feel about this Creature before he brings it to life? 🔍

Chapter 4 presents us with a driven, determined and obsessed character, forging ahead with proving that he has discovered the secret to life. Just before he brings his creation to life, he is in a state of heightened emotion, 'With an anxiety that almost amounted to agony'. While in Chapter 4 Victor appeared boastful and assured, in Chapter 5 he seems frightened of what he is about to do. He is not frightened of the experiment itself as such, but fearful of failure.

S-T-R-E-T-C-H

To explore the significance of the birth and rejection of the Creature by Victor, provide learners with a statement around which they can form an opinion. For example:

'Victor's rejection of his creation is completely predictable.' To what extent do you agree with this statement?

This type of task focuses on the skill of evaluation, using a GCSE English language question focus, and should force a decision from pupils. In terms of preparing learners for A level study, discourage 'sitting on the fence'; push learners to make a decision. This allows you to make use of retrieval practice for moments and events in Chapters 1 to 4 that prepare the reader for this moment. ⛅

5. What does Victor think about his Creature after it comes to life? ⊗

Although his experiment is clearly a success – he has successfully given life to a patchwork quilt of body parts – Victor perceives his creation to be a complete failure due to his ugliness.

> **"**

'I had selected his features as beautiful. Beautiful! – Great God! His yellow skin scarcely covered the work of muscles and arteries beneath'

> **"**

After fixating on the failure of his experiment, Victor indulges in some regret – 'the beauty of the dream vanished' – closely followed by cowardice: 'Unable to endure the aspect of the being I had created, I rushed out of the room.'

> **"**

'the beauty of the dream vanished, and breathless horror and disgust filled my heart... I rushed out of the room, and continued a long time traversing my bedchamber, unable to compose my mind to sleep.'

> **"**

Why is he horrified? Why is he disgusted? The Creature's aesthetics are not what he intended. He regrets the 'failure' of his experiment; consequently, he feels deep shame. Victor's shame and horror at his perceived failure is what drives him to conceal the truth of the Creature's existence from his family and friends. His secrecy will be fatal for all of them.

6. What is Victor's response to these feelings?

In keeping with the characteristics of the Byronic protagonist, as discussed in Chapter 5, Victor's response to his creation coming to life is emotionally overwrought and focuses on his suffering (at the hands of his own actions).

7. What is the significance of Clerval's entrance?

Clerval is Victor's closest friend, and upon his arrival Victor states that 'Nothing could equal my delight on seeing Clerval'. Victor's joy at seeing Clerval provides a welcome distraction from the aftermath of his experiment coming to life, enabling Victor to push the 'failure' of the experiment to the back of his mind without much effort.

8. What is Clerval and Victor's relationship like?

In Chapter 3, Clerval and Victor's relationship as friends is very fraternal; so close are they that Clerval too wishes to study at Ingolstadt with Victor:

'Clerval spent the last evening with us. He had endeavoured to persuade his father to permit him to accompany me, and to become my fellow student; but in vain.' (Ch3)

This desire to go to university with Victor gives the impression that Clerval is in thrall to Victor's brimming intelligence and the friendship is somewhat unbalanced. This becomes clearer as the characters exchange dialogue:

• 'I have lately been so deeply engaged in one occupation' (Ch5)

• 'I hope...that I am at length free' (Ch5)

There is deliberate ambiguity in the choice of the phrase 'one occupation'. This lack of specificity to Clerval shows that Victor is clearly being deliberately obtuse. The ambiguity continues, with Victor's 'hope' that he is 'free', while withholding from Clerval what he wants to be 'free' from.

If Victor is keeping the truth (of his experiment coming to life) from Clerval, why do so? For whose benefit is this secrecy? (It won't be the Creature's and it won't be Clerval's.) Victor's lying by omission implies that he does not care or love Clerval quite as much as he states to the reader in his narration.

Finally, through such ambiguous comments, Shelley fully exploits reader privilege (the reader is party to more information about events and characters than the other characters in the text) so that *only* the reader is fully aware that Victor is not being honest with Clerval.

PIT STOP ▼

S-T-R-E-T-C-H

With this in mind, ask learners to consider the degree of honesty in Victor's comments to Clerval at the end of the chapter. Does the reader believe what Victor says to Clerval? Why? Why not?

How?

Language 🔍

How does Shelley use language to present Victor's disgust and disappointment in his creation?

Victor Frankenstein others his creation from his first breaths ⊗ 🔔

Key quotation:

- 'How can I describe my emotions at this catastrophe...?' (Ch5)

The first clause of Chapter 5 shows that Victor's response to his creation coming to life is governed by emotion and not reason. Shelley's framing of this response as an interrogative sentence, alongside Victor's inability to 'describe' his range of emotions, shows that he has rejected science and reason, thus exposing his very human flaws, the most notable being that he is (and always was) a man very unsuitable to play God.

The othering of the Creature is immediate when Victor refers to him using the impersonal pronoun 'this', which frames his creation as an object only. Combined with the noun 'catastrophe', this sets up the Creature as less than human in Victor's eyes, so unworthy of any compassion or, worse yet, any paternal responsibility being considered by Victor.

As he comes to life, the Creature is othered through Victor's choice of adjectives

Key quotations:

- 'the dull yellow eye'
- 'His *yellow* skin scarcely covered the work of muscles and arteries beneath'

Victor does notice *some* aesthetically pleasing features:

- His hair is a 'lustrous black'.
- His teeth have a '*pearly* whiteness'

However, for Victor, these aesthetically acceptable achievements only serve to *foreground the ugliness* of the Creature's other features.

- They 'formed a... horrid contrast with his watery eyes'.
- They made the '*dun white* sockets' all the more noticeable.
- Victor focuses on his '*shrivelled* complexion' and '*straight black* lips'.

Note that the Creature is Victor's creation, thus giving him some conscious choice in the Creature's appearance.

The Creature is othered through the absence of possessive determiners and personal pronouns

The predominant pronoun that Victor uses in relation to his creation is the impersonal 'it', which is preceded by the noun 'thing' in the very first paragraph of this chapter. This reiterates to the reader that the Creature is an object, and therefore there is no need to give a specific name to him. The Creature remains nameless for the entirety of this novel.

- 'I might infuse a spark of being into the lifeless thing that lay at my feet'
- 'it breathed hard, and a convulsive motion agitated its limbs'

To fully appreciate the careful signposting of Victor's rejection of the creation that he *perceives* as an ugly failure, refer back to his descriptions of Elizabeth's beauty in Chapter 1 and his differing reactions to Waldman and Krempe in Chapter 4.

The Creature is othered through Victor's use of derogatory epithets

An epithet is an adjective or phrase expressing a defining quality of the person or thing mentioned. Here are some typical derogatory epithets from this chapter:

- 'its hideous guest'
- 'the dreaded spectre'
- 'the monster'

The combination of the derogatory epithets, with the definite article 'the', more commonly used to refer to an object than a living being, others the Creature as less than human – more something spewed from Hell.

However, the first derogatory epithet that Victor uses to name the Creature is 'wretch', which in this chapter occurs five times. The chapter was copied and pasted into Word and the 'find' tool was used to look for specific words. Upon searching for the noun 'wretch', the search also found:

- 'I passed the night wretchedly' (adverbial form)
- 'I afterwards learned that... how wretched my sickness would make Elizabeth, he spared them this grief' (adjectival form)

Although it is the Creature who is 'a wretch', only Victor can suffer 'wretchedly' or describe his state of illness as 'wretched'. From Victor's narrative point of view, it is only Victor who has the capacity to suffer.

Developing language analysis: Depth/breadth 🔍

Below is one of the most well-known quotations from this chapter and, indeed, the whole text. Contained within it are some contradictions, highlighted in bold:

> 66

> *'It was on a dreary night of November, that I beheld the accomplishment of my toils.'*

> 99

It is worth focusing on specifics of language choices and *placement* to give learners a more precise grasp of the choices that writers make and why they might make them.

Ask learners to consider why:

- Shelley chooses to use the adjective 'dreary' to describe the 'night of November' that Victor uses to bring his experiment to life, which has obvious connotations of doom or foreboding.

- Shelley chooses to use the noun 'accomplishment', which, according to most dictionaries, means the *successful completion* of a task.

- Shelley chooses to use the adjective and noun above in the same sentence, which seem to have contradictory uses and meanings. What might this tell us about Victor as a character and how he feels at this specific moment?

Character focus

Victor

Key quotations:

- 'one hand was stretched out, seemingly to detain me, but I escaped, and rushed down stairs. I took refuge in the courtyard... where I remained during the rest of the night'

- 'I struggled furiously, and fell down in a fit'

- 'I was lifeless, and did not recover my senses for a long, long time'

In this chapter, Shelley provides two thresholds for Victor. In creating life, he becomes almost God-like, as he achieves something beyond any man before him. However, in running desperately from his Creature from the moment at which it begins its life, he becomes a coward.

His perception of the Creature's stretched-out hand as an act of aggression highlights his inner fragility, and that perhaps he is not as boldly confident as he had previously believed. This is further emphasised by his physical weakness and prolonged illness in response to the shock of the outcomes of his long-planned-for experiments.

Clerval

Key quotation:

- 'nothing but the unbounded and unremitting attentions of my friend could have restored me to life'

In this chapter, Clerval's role is to rescue and nurse Victor. In many ways, Clerval is Victor's foil – a rather gentle, loyal character, whose pursuits are the arts rather than science, and who conveys far more compassion than Victor. Interestingly, while Victor interprets the Creature's reaching out as aggression, Clerval responds to Victor's reaching out with care.

The Creature

Key quotation:

- 'one hand was stretched out, seemingly to detain me'

This is the first chapter in which the Creature is a living, breathing being. However, the only insight that Shelley provides on him is through Victor's perspective. Through Victor's eyes, the Creature is aggressive, terrifying and threatening.

Structure

Opening: 'It was on a dreary night of November, that I beheld the accomplishment of my toils'

Ending: 'Is that all, my dear Henry? How could you suppose that my first thought would not fly towards those dear, dear friends whom I love, and who are so deserving of my love'

Of particular note to how the chapter ends above, once Victor is nursed back to health, is how he does not give the Creature a second or even third thought... until news of William's death is delivered.

Shelley bookends this chapter with a focus on different ideas of family. One is unconventional and artificial – creator and created – while the other is what society accepts to be a family.

The setting of a 'dreary night of November' prepares the reader for the horror of the Creature's birth, leading to the even greater moral horror of his rejection by Victor.

Most tellingly, in the quotation taken from the end of the chapter, Victor is a fickle god who decides who is 'deserving' of his love. The choice of this verb in particular is loaded with implications – that the Creature is not deserving (and never will be) of Victor's love. We should not forget that while he was making the Creature, Victor did not return to Geneva for six years, and nor did he communicate with the family who was deserving of his love over that time. Victor will continue to contradict his words with his actions as the novel progresses.

Narrator and narration

When texts have multiple narrators, it is a good opportunity to introduce learners to the concept that narrators need not be reliable and that we cannot always trust what they tell us. The narrator's unreliability may also be as a result of their own biases and prejudices. Therefore, encourage learners to have some healthy scepticism of all of this text's narrators.

Useful terms to apply when teaching texts with embedded narration and narrators include:

- **narrator:** the entity that tells the story to the reader and/or implied reader
- **narratee:** the entity that receives the narrative
- **implied reader:** the entity who is the intended recipient of the text (Walton's sister is the implied reader of Frankenstein)
- **implied author:** the authorial entity or character that a reader infers from the text, based upon how the text is written and constructed (Walton is the implied author of *Frankenstein*, because it is he who diligently writes down the story that Victor narrates to him).

Extracts

Extract 1 (Ch5): How does Shelley use language to present Victor's state of mind in this extract?

──────── 66 ────────

'I thought I saw Elizabeth, in the bloom of health, walking in the streets of Ingolstadt. Delighted and surprised, I embraced her; but as I imprinted the first kiss on her lips, they became livid with the hue of death; her features appeared to change, and I thought that I held the corpse of my dead mother in my arms; a shroud enveloped her form, and I saw the grave-worms crawling in the folds of the flannel.'

──────── 99 ────────

The following prompt questions should enable purposeful analysis of the extract.

In this extract, Shelley uses disturbing and transgressive imagery to show the reader the extent of Victor's troubled mind.

- What can we infer about Victor from the symbolism of disturbed sleep?
- How does Shelley exploit the Gothic tropes of nightmares and metamorphosis when he narrates how Elizabeth transforms into his (dead) mother?
- In Chapter 4, Victor views corpses as food for the grave-worm; how is this different when he refers to the image of his dead – and rotting – mother?
- The image of Elizabeth metamorphosing into a corpse creates a sense of narrative foreboding – why?

Further points to consider for this extract are below:

- How might this moment be relevant to events later in the text?
- To what extent would Shelley's contemporaneous audience find this imagery disturbing?
- What significance might dreams and nightmares hold in the text as a whole?

A short analysis of this extract can be found in the accompanying online resources. 🖱

Extract 2 (Ch5): How does Shelley use language to describe Frankenstein's rejection of his creation in this extract? ⊗

'I started from my sleep with horror; a cold dew covered my forehead, my teeth chattered, and every limb became convulsed: when, by the dim and yellow light of the moon, as it forced its way through the window shutters, I beheld the wretch – the miserable creature whom I had created. He held up the curtain of the bed; and his eyes, if eyes they may be called, were fixed on me. His jaws opened, and he muttered some inarticulate sounds, while a grin wrinkled his cheeks. He might have spoken, but I did not hear; one hand was stretched out, seemingly to detain me, but I escaped, and rushed down stairs. I took refuge in the courtyard belonging to the house which I inhabited...'

Shelley uses a range of different language techniques to build upon the horror of the Creature's first few moments of life. This extract begins with a focus on Victor's physical and emotional response to the results of his experiment: he 'started' from his sleep 'with horror'. His startled awakening shows us that Victor is fearful of the life that he created, *and fearful that others will find out about his terrible 'catastrophe' of an experiment.* Shelley then draws attention to the physicality of his fear with some precisely chosen dynamic verbs: 'chattered' and 'convulsed', both of which are automated, physical responses to fear, showing that Victor is not in control of his body – nor his mind.

Later in the same sentence, focus shifts away from Victor and towards the Creature in its first few moments of life. However, the verb choices of 'forced', 'fixed', 'muttered', 'wrinkled' and 'stretched' all present the Creature, from *Victor's point of view,* as a deeply threatening 'other'. This is not to say that Victor's interpretation of the Creature's actions is correct here, because it is not. During the Creature's narration in Chapter 11, the same event is told from the Creature's perspective, where it will be shown that the Creature's outstretched hand was that of a newborn seeking comfort from his parent. At the moment of his birth, the Creature is innocent and helpless, although Victor can only judge him (and does so wrongly) on the basis of his appearance, and Victor's own perception that his experiment is that of a complete failure.

Victor's horror at his own failure, combined with the horror of the Creature's appearance, gives us one of literature's greatest and most memorable moments of cowardice. He narrates to Walton his response to the Creature's supposedly aggressive actions: 'I escaped, and rushed down stairs.' Shelley's dynamic verb choices of 'escaped' and 'rushed' show that Victor's only concern is for himself, and not for the life he has just created, nor the family and friends that he has so willingly left behind. The moment at which the Creature came to life, Victor relinquished any and all responsibility to him. Therefore, whatever sympathy Victor believes that he may be entitled to, at this point the reader will not be able to provide it.

At a glance

> **Summary quotation:** 'I beheld those I loved spend vain sorrow upon the graves of William and Justine, the first hapless victims to my unhallowed arts' (Ch8)

> **Big Question:** How does Shelley present the first consequences of Victor's actions?

> **Significant plot events:**

Chapter 6:

- Elizabeth writes to Victor concerned with how ill he has been.

- Justine is introduced to the reader in the letter.

- William is also mentioned in the letter.

- Victor introduces Clerval to the university professors.

- Victor and Clerval undertake a two-week tour around Ingolstadt.

Chapter 7:

- Victor learns of William's murder while reading a letter from his father.

- By the end of the letter, he learns that Justine is accused of the murder.

- Victor is certain that the Creature is the murderer and that Justine is innocent.

Chapter 8:

- Justine's trial begins; she is calm and dignified.

- The prosecution advocate (lawyer) presents all the circumstantial evidence against Justine, which she cannot explain. (Justine has no 'advocate for her defence'.)

- Victor does not speak up in Justine's defence, even though he knows that she is innocent.

- Elizabeth speaks to the court, aiming to argue for Justine's innocence. This backfires, and the court is even more convinced of Justine's guilt.

- A priest who visits Justine in her prison cell convinces her to confess to her guilt in order to absolve her soul.

- Victor spends some time on the lake and in nature, while in the distance lightning plays on the tops of the mountains.

> **Character focus:** Justine, Victor, Alphonse, Elizabeth, the Creature (via Victor's thoughts)

> **Key themes:**

- Family and companionship 🏵
- Knowledge and discovery 🔍
- Death and grief ✝
- Crime and justice 🗡
- Prejudice 👥
- Society and social class ✂
- Rejection and its consequences ⊗
- Revenge ⚙
- Betrayal and guilt ↫

> **Handle with care:**

- infanticide: the murder of a child
- the blaming – and conviction – of an innocent woman
- imprisonment of an innocent person

Why?

These 'why' questions cover Chapters 6, 7 and 8, keeping the focus upon Shelley's exploration and critique of justice and social class at the time at which she was writing.

- Why is Justine framed for the murder of William?
- Why is Justine introduced via Elizabeth's letter?
- Why are the public (within the world of the novel) so quick to believe her guilt?
- Why do both Justine *and* Elizabeth's words fail to make a difference to Justine's fate?
- Why is Justine's death instrumental to the overall narrative?
- Why does Justine's death change our (the reader's) relationship with Victor Frankenstein?

What?

What happens? ☁

Chapter 6

In Chapter 6, an ill Victor Frankenstein receives a letter from Elizabeth. Elizabeth informs him that Justine, who worked for the family before, has returned to the household. Justine is a welcome addition to the Frankenstein household, and they hold her in high regard.

However, Frankenstein is unable to bear mention of his former studies as he introduces Clerval to the professors. Frankenstein's journey home to Geneva is delayed until the spring. This is further delayed by a two-week tour of the environs of Ingolstadt; narratively, this is all constructed by Shelley to delay Frankenstein until after the murder of William. This delay is narratively positioned to link with the theme of justice and in order for the reader to consider the impact of the death of William.

Chapter 7

Chapter 7 begins with Victor receiving a letter from his father, Alphonse. The purpose of Alphonse's letter is not just to inform Victor of his younger brother William's death, but also to narrate the circumstances of the death. Alphonse also narrates the impact of William's death on the family that Victor left behind while he indulged in making his Creature.

We learn from the letter who set out on the walk to Plainpalais: Alphonse, Elizabeth 'my niece' and Victor's two younger brothers, William and Ernest, with William being the youngest of the whole party. However, not all return home, and William remains missing until his body is discovered by Alphonse, with 'the print of the murderer's finger... on his neck'. This piece of information alone is enough to affirm for the reader that Justine, who is the accused a little later in this chapter, is innocent, allowing us to infer correctly that the probable perpetrator is the Creature.

Chapter 8

This chapter recounts the unjust murder trial of Justine Moritz, which is another consequence of Victor's actions in Chapter 5. The Creature has condemned her through the placing of a locket belonging to William on her person. Frankenstein conceals the truth that the Creature is the murderer, because he does not want to admit to his responsibility for its creation. The chapter ends with the significant line 'the first hapless victims to my unhallowed arts'. The deaths of William and Justine are the result of Frankenstein's narcissism and hubris, which are the weaknesses in his character that prevent him from being honest. Later on, these flaws will lead to the deaths of Elizabeth, Alphonse and Clerval.

PIT STOP ▼

S-T-R-E-T-C-H ⊗ ✏

Ask learners to explore the following statement:

In Frankenstein, innocent victims have suffered, and will continue to suffer, at the hands of Victor's arrogant and selfish actions.

To what extent do learners agree with this statement? They should consider:

- the relevance of the Promethean myth and the concept of hubris
- Victor's character development thus far
- Victor's rejection of his creation in Chapter 4
- ideas about justice and consequences.

Social and historical context ⚙

Biographical context ✿

Shelley's philosophical viewpoint changed after the death of her own children; these events convinced Mary Shelley that human events are decided not by personal choice or free will, evident in the revisions to the 1831 edition. This links to the birth/death narrative theme of the novel. Moers (1978) comments that Shelley is one of the few, if only, nineteenth-century novelists to have written while being a mother, so the murder of William as a narrative device and an act of revenge is important. Death comes to haunt Victor as punishment for his hubristic challenge to the natural order of the world, where women carry and birth children, whereas Victor can only usurp this female ability through laboured scientific experiment.

'Mary Shelley's infant son (b. 24 January 1816) was named William after her father. Her arranging to have his namesake in the novel murdered has prompted some wonder. Certainly, there was no lack of maternal affection: William Shelley's death in Rome on 7 June 1819 was a devastating blow to Mary Shelley, issuing in something approaching a nervous breakdown.' (Moers, 1978)

William's death is indirectly Victor's responsibility, as a result of creating and abandoning the Creature. Brennan's (1988) essay 'The landscape of grief' explores Mary's unresolved grief for the loss of her mother, linking this with her portrayal of Victor's grief for the loss of his mother. Chapters 7 and 8 explore the impact of William's death on the Frankenstein family, Justine and Clerval.

Historical context: The presentation of the eighteenth-century justice system ✎

The most useful thing to make explicit to learners is what is absent in the justice system as it is presented in the novel. The common legal principles below are what we take for granted in our current legal system.

There is no principle of 'innocent until proven guilty'

Although this principle dates back to Roman law, this is very much absent in Justine's trial in the text. It is the cornerstone of justice systems around the world, and was enshrined in the Human Rights Act of 1998 (UK law) and the United Nations Declaration of Human Rights (1948). Justine, and people like her – her gender and social class – had no such access to the human rights that we now have. If you were male and wealthy, you had much better access to justice than anyone in the working classes... or female.

There is no concept of 'beyond reasonable doubt'

In current UK law (and that of many other Western nations), the concept of 'beyond reasonable doubt' means that 'the evidence must be so strong that there is no other logical explanation for the defendant's guilt' (Watts, n.d.). In Justine's case, it is only plausible circumstantial evidence that is enough to convict her.

Is it better that a guilty man go free or that an innocent man is imprisoned?

Fortunately, an eighteenth-century English jurist, William Blackstone (1765), decided for us, and he stated that 'it is better that ten guilty persons escape than that one innocent suffer'. Justine is afforded no such principle in her trial; rather, it is the idea that a woman can kill a child – one of the worst societal taboos, both then and now – that is on trial in the novel.

The defendant is not entitled to legal representation

In the novel, Justine is left to advocate for herself in the court, while the prosecution has legal representation. Here, Shelley makes rather explicit the degree to which the scales of justice are imbalanced – and very heavily imbalanced against the accused when you do not have financial means for legal defence in court. The court is also quick to bow to public pressure and mob rule, with a swift conviction being the aim, rather than convicting the right person. This demonstrates the weaknesses in the justice system, as Shelley saw it, when it is so easily swayed by public opinion.

Vocabulary in context

Word	Quotation	Definition
Chapter 6		
convalescence	'It was a divine spring; and the season contributed greatly to my convalescence'	the process of becoming well again after an illness or injury
dilatoriness	'The winter, however, was spent cheerfully; and although the spring was uncommonly late, when it came its beauty compensated for its dilatoriness'	the quality of being slow and causing delay
perambulations	'We passed a fortnight in these perambulations: my health and spirits had long been restored, and they gained additional strength from the salubrious air I breathed, the natural incidents of our progress, and the conversation of my friend'	the activity of walking around a place, especially for pleasure and in a leisurely way
salubrious		describing something that is pleasant, clean and healthy to live in
encomiums	'his [Krempe's] harsh blunt encomiums gave me even more pain than the benevolent approbation of M. Waldman'	pieces of writing or speeches that praise someone or something highly
exculpate	'such a declaration would have been considered as the ravings of a madman and would not have exculpated her who suffered through me'	to remove someone from blame
ignominy	'Could the dæmon who had (I did not for a minute doubt) murdered my brother also in his hellish sport have betrayed the innocent to death and ignominy?'	public embarrassment or shame
obdurate	'He threatened excommunication and hell fire in my last moments if I continued obdurate'	extremely determined to act in a particular way and not to change, despite what anyone else says

Chapter 7		
wretchedness	'What would be your surprise, my son, when you expected a happy and glad welcome, to behold, on the contrary, tears and wretchedness?'	the state of being unpleasant or of low quality; the feeling of being very ill, or unhappy
Plainpalais	'Last Thursday (May 7th), I, my niece, and your two brothers, went to walk in Plainpalais.'	a neighbourhood in Geneva, Switzerland
conjectured	'This account rather alarmed us, and we continued to search for him until night fell, when Elizabeth conjectured that he might have returned to the house.'	a guess about something based on how it seems, rather than proof
console	'Come, dearest Victor, you alone can console Elizabeth.'	to make someone who is sad or disappointed feel better, usually by giving them comfort or sympathy
prognosticated	'Is this to prognosticate peace, or to mock at my unhappiness.'	to give a judgement about what is likely to happen in the future, especially in connection with a particular situation
Chapter 8		
obliterated	'now all was to be obliterated in an	an action that destroys something completely
ignominious	ignominious grave; and I the cause!'	describes an action or experience as embarrassing because it was unsuccessful
solemnity	'her countenance, always engaging, was rendered, by the solemnity of her feelings, exquisitely beautiful'	the state or quality of being solemn (very serious)
indignation	'a murmur of horror and indignation filled the court'	the feeling of shock and anger when you feel that something is unfair
protestations	'But I do not pretend that my protestations should acquit me'	a strong declaration that something is true or not true
bewildered	'That she had been bewildered when questioned by the market-woman was not surprising, since she had passed a sleepless night'	confused and not understanding something or being able to decide what to do
timorous	'but fear, and hatred of the crime of which they supposed her guilty, rendered them timorous'	frightened and nervous of other people and situations (relates to the verb 'timid')

Vocabulary

Below are examples of questions that will aid understanding of Shelley's usage of some of her vocabulary.

Chapter 6:

- What does Victor's dilatoriness as he travels home to Geneva tell us about his character at this moment in the text?

- Will the Frankenstein family be able to exculpate Justine from her fate?

Chapter 7:

- At this point in the text, who is the most diabolical character?

- Who wants to inflict retribution on whom in this chapter?

Chapter 8:

- Why does Victor believe that 'all was to be obliterated'?

- What does Justine's 'solemnity' in the face of a biased court tell us about her character?

- Why were witnesses 'timorous' when speaking in support of Justine's character in court?

Etymology 👥 ✂ ✏

In this section of the novel, it is a good opportunity to explore the abstract noun 'justice', its origins, changes of meaning and use over time, and different forms of justice in the text.

The table below is chronological, with the oldest root first.

Origin	Meaning
Latin *iustus*	upright, just
Latin *iustitia*	righteousness, equality
Old French (eleventh century)	justice, legal rights, jurisdiction

Through Justine's unjust trial, Shelley wishes to explore and expose a justice system that is unbalanced, favours the wealthy and is unable to be fair and just to the poorest in society.

Key question: At this point in the novel, which characters seem to have access to justice and which characters do not? Why is this?

Plot and character development

1. How do Clerval and Victor respond to William's death? ✝

Clerval is informed of the murder of William and, as is consistent with his character, is quick to sympathise and console Victor. Just as in keeping with Victor's character, Victor takes possession of the tragedy of William's murder and calls it 'my misfortune' (Ch7). The combination of the possessive determiner 'my' with the abstract noun 'misfortune' serves to remind us of Victor's narcissistic nature. Additionally, by calling a deliberate act of murder 'misfortune', Victor attributes this tragedy to bad luck, rather than truly accepting responsibility for it.

2. How are Victor's feelings influenced by his environment?

Having left Ingolstadt, Victor procrastinates and spends two days in Lausanne, taking time to bathe in the sublime of the 'snowy mountains' (Ch7). These 'calm and heavenly' environments restore his strength and he heads back to Geneva. On the surface, this appears to be a lovely moment; however, his procrastination here only reminds us of the selfishness of his character.

While getting close to his Genovese home, the landscape and nature continue to put on a pleasing display of the Romantic sublime, where the sky is 'serene' and even the lightning puts on a display of 'the most beautiful figures' (Ch7). This soon shifts into the Gothic sublime, and the sky becomes a 'vast sheet of fire', alluding to the fury of Zeus reigning down from Olympus. Here, it is worth reminding learners of the subtitle of this novel – 'Or the Modern Prometheus' – and the severity of Zeus's punishment of Prometheus. Lesser gods and man *should* be fearful of Zeus, as should Victor.

3. How does Shelley use weather when reintroducing the Creature to the narrative?

During a particularly violent lightning flash, Victor catches a glimpse of his creation – 'the object' with 'its shape plainly to me; its gigantic stature' (Ch7). The noun choice of 'object', along with the impersonal pronoun 'it', is used to bring to the fore the dehumanising language that Victor uses to describe the Creature. From here on in, a dramatic lightning flash will signify the arrival of the Creature into a scene of the novel.

4. How do the Frankenstein family respond to Victor's return? 🐘

After his procrastination in the glories of the Swiss landscape, Victor eventually arrives home, to be greeted warmly (despite his six-year absence, with little or no communication) by his 'Beloved and venerable' father, Alphonse (Ch7). His brother, Ernest, also welcomes him home warmly. Both Alphonse and Ernest hold the belief that Victor's presence will heal the emotional wounds of William's death. Ernest informs Victor of the devastating effect that William's death has had upon Elizabeth, who is troubled by 'vain and tormenting self-accusations' (Ch7). Here, Elizabeth accepting the blame and responsibility for William's death is an illustration of issues faced by women for centuries: to take the blame and to feel guilt, whether one is truly responsible for it or not.

5. How does Shelley exploit the reader's knowledge of Victor's experiment in Chapter 7? 🖊 ✍ 🔍

Once Victor learns more about the events of William's death, the aftermath of this tragedy quickly unfolds. Ernest informs Victor that 'the murderer has been discovered', leading Victor to jump to conclusions: 'Good God! how can that be? who could attempt to pursue him?' Given the reader's position of privilege here (we know more than Ernest about what Victor had been doing for the past six years), it's a reasonable conclusion to reach, although reference to 'him' in Victor's comment above confuses Ernest, who then informs Victor that it is Justine who is the accused.

Upon learning this, Victor is emphatic in his belief of Justine's innocence, stating, 'I know the murderer... poor Justine is innocent.' Shelley has now given Victor a moral dilemma with which to wrestle:

1. Save Justine by confessing the creation of his Creature, and thus legally and morally hold the Creature to account for the murder of William.

2. Keep quiet to maintain appearances and his reputation, which is justified because no one would believe that he created a living being from dead body parts – he would just sound mad.

Unsurprisingly, Victor takes the latter option, letting the events of the trial unfold before him, while doing nothing to help Justine and prevent her conviction and eventual death.

It is in these moments – how Victor responds to the actions of his creation – that the reader's relationship with Victor shifts away from a character that is (partly) likeable to start towards one that we actively dislike if not loathe.

How?

Language

Victor's perceived contentment 👥

Shelley establishes a pattern of contentment, using such phrases as 'our placid home' and 'our contented hearts' (Ch6), which, on subsequent readings, we know will be contradicted by the death of William. Later, when we read the Creature's narrative, the reader will reflect back on Victor's ability to feel contentment when compared to the Creature that he abandoned and left to fend for himself. Shelley deliberately provides contrasting and contradicting perspectives on the same events via her two main intradiegetic (within the story) narrators.

Shelley alludes to William's cherubic innocence

Key quotation:

• 'I must say also a few words to you... of little darling William...; he is very tall of his age, with sweet laughing blue eyes, dark eyelashes, and curling hair. When he smiles, two little dimples appear on each cheek, which are rosy with health.' (Elizabeth's letter, Ch6)

The use of the word 'cherubic' in the subtitle is not accidental, and nor is Shelley's depiction of William accidentally cherubic. Cherubic angels derive from Abrahamic religions, and are often illustrated as small, winged children. In Christian faith, the Cherubim attend to God and his throne, so are higher orders of angels. Shelley's focus on William's cherubic features of 'blue eyes', 'dark eyelashes' and 'dimples' that are 'rosy with health' foreground William's sense of unearthly innocence and childlike beauty. This only serves to make his imminent and brutal murder all the more terrible and tragic.

Couples, doubles and antithesis 🌸

Shelley also puts forward the theme of the couple in her choice of the phrase 'one or two little wives' (Ch6). The Creature desires a mate, Victor desires Elizabeth and we have the idealised parental figures in Victor's mother and father. Yet William will never be part of a couple because the Creature murders him, and we have the ever-present pair of life and death. This is then followed by a list of engagements, which emphasises the significance of marriage, with the implication of procreation following. Shelley builds the mood of contentment and happiness to the end of the chapter. The use of the pastoral is significant, as this is used to both create and mirror the characters' emotions.

Victor's suffering: Hyperbole, modality and an aspect of desire

Key quotation:

• 'A thousand times rather would I have confessed myself guilty of the crime ascribed to Justine... such a declaration would have been considered as the ravings of a madman' (Ch8)

As a character and narrator, Victor is not one to shy away from emotive and melodramatic language, for it is Victor who suffers most in the narrative... according to Victor. This quotation begins with a hyperbolic claim – 'a thousand times' – which also seems to undermine the content of this assertion. Given his treatment of his creation (running away) and the fact that he has lied by omission about the Creature's existence to Clerval, we already have reason to be sceptical of the honesty of Victor's narration of events. Because Victor is narrating this sequence of events, it is Victor's emotional distress that is foregrounded in the text – here by the hyperbole of 'A thousand times...'.

When Victor asserts 'rather would I' and 'would have', Shelley is using what is known in stylistics as modality and modal shading in narration. Examining the modality of Victor's narration is particularly useful when considering the flaws of his character (of which there are many) and the reader's relationship with him, which shifts as the text progresses.

Victor chooses to do nothing to save Justine, so why discuss this via the lens of modality?

'*rather would I* have confessed'

The combined effect of the adverb 'rather' with the modal verb 'would' presents what ought to be a (moral) obligation: to tell the truth, which could free Justine from this miscarriage of justice and certain death. It is presented as a 'want' or a 'desire' – something that he was desperate to do but ultimately could not.

In the second example of hyperbole in the above quotation, Victor excuses himself of the responsibility and obligation towards truth and honesty, and towards freeing Justine. He dismisses the option of being honest, because it 'would be considered as the ravings of a madman'. Shelley's use of boulomaic modality (expressions that highlight aspects of desire) is one of many methods that she deploys which undermines the authority and integrity of our 'gentleman' narrator, Victor Frankenstein. Consequently, we can see that Shelley is in full control of our (the reader's) relationship with Victor, which includes our growing frustration with, and horror at, his character's actions.

See the accompanying resources for an explanation of the different terms and forms of modality. This will be especially useful for teachers of A level English courses and high-prior-attaining GCSE groups. 🖱

Metaphor and zoomorphism, monsters and monstrosity

Key quotation:

- 'The fangs of remorse tore my bosom* and would not forgo** their hold' (Ch8)

In this instance, *zoomorphism* is the tool that Shelley uses to continue the hyperbole of Victor's suffering. Be careful with the choice of the noun 'fangs' that is used in this zoomorphic hyperbole. It would be easy to make the incorrect assumption that Shelley is alluding to vampires or Bram Stoker's *Dracula*. *Dracula* was published in 1897, well after this latter edition of Frankenstein. A more sensible interpretation is reference to a fanged venomous animal: a snake (or a serpent, if we want to draw on biblical allusions from Genesis). This choice of noun to construct the zoomorphism is also a nice example of a hyponymy, a way of viewing the relationship between more general and specific words – here, the noun 'fangs' represents the whole animal: a snake. In rhetoric, this is also known as synecdoche – where a part of something can stand for the whole (and vice versa).

*the upper chest area on a human; **to not be able to do something enjoyable

Clearly, 'fangs' does not in and of itself construct the zoomorphism used here. It is the verb choices that do the bulk of the labour in constructing any metaphor that can be regarded as 'morphic': zoomorphism, personification, anthropomorphism or chremamorphism. It is not just that there are verbs that animate a noun; it's the very precise *choice* of verb that constructs such a strong and purposeful image.

Shelley *chose* to use 'tore', 'forgo' and 'hold'. What do these specific verbs convey about what type of animal is referred to in the zoomorphism? Sometimes it is not as simple as being able to identify the precise genus of animal referred to; sometimes, it is much broader: predator or prey?

Here, it is guilt for Justine's unnecessary death that 'tore' at Victor's chest, with this verb choice conveying a rather rabid, fierce predator ready to consume him. This imagery emphasises the relentless and painful nature of his regret, while also being used to justify his inaction to himself. The Gothic sublime – nature that is at once vast, beautiful and terrifying – interacting with this kind of vast, powerful nature is potentially fatal. Nature's power far outweighs that of man's:

- 'The storm appeared to **approach** rapidly' (Ch7)
- 'It **advanced**;... its violence quickly **increased**' (Ch7)
- 'the thunder **burst** with a terrific **crash** over my head' (Ch7)
- 'vivid **flashes** of lightning **dazzled** my eyes' (Ch7)
- '**illuminating** the lake, making it **appear** like a vast sheet of fire' (Ch7)
- 'The most violent storm **hung** exactly north of the town' (Ch7)

The words in **bold** are the verbs – or, at least, the verbs that do the most work in this section. For example, 'approach', 'advance', 'burst' and 'hung' seem to give the storm above his head an element of predation and sentience.

Character focus

Victor

Key quotation:

- 'The tortures of the accused did not equal mine; she was sustained by innocence, but the fangs of remorse tore my bosom and would not forgo their hold' (Ch8) 📖

Fitting the mould of the Byronic protagonist perfectly, Victor claims quite emphatically that his suffering is greater than Justine's. A Byronic – and, by extension, a Gothic – protagonist focuses on and narrates the greatness of their suffering. Although the aim of the narration of Victor's emotional distress is engineered to garner sympathy, it is unlikely to be garnered from the reader. Walton, who is deeply enamoured by Victor's presence, is the only likely source of any sympathy or empathy heading in Victor's direction. Although Justine, who was hanged for a murder that she did not commit, has suffered far more than Victor, Victor is only capable of some form of competitive suffering.

Elizabeth ✝

Key quotations:

- 'Elizabeth was sad and desponding; she no longer took delight in her ordinary occupations; all pleasure seemed to her sacrilege toward the dead; eternal' (Ch7)
- 'She had no doubt of her innocence; and she was so inflexible in her determination not to admit her guilt, she persisted in asserting her innocence' (Ch8)

In the earliest parts of the novel, Elizabeth is presented as beatific, with a character beyond reproach. At the start of Chapter 6, in her letter to Victor, she is presented as chatty, lively and keen to gossip. There are elements in the subtext of the letter that reveal a sense of jealousy of Justine. Once William's death is discovered, Elizabeth is shown to be a hugely sympathetic and empathetic character, who suffers greatly from William's death. However, for all of Elizabeth's admirable qualities presented to the reader in earlier parts of the text, in Chapter 8 her character is shown to be quick to judge and hypocritical. Elizabeth is certain of Justine's innocence until she hears that Justine has confessed, at which point Elizabeth does not hesitate to condemn her. Here, we see a rather more bitter, fickle character than the angelic child with which we are presented in Chapter 1.

Justine 🖋

Key quotations:

- 'Justine was calm; she was dressed in mourning,* and her countenance, always engaging, was rendered, by the solemnity of her feelings, exquisitely beautiful' (Ch8)
- 'Justine, also, was very ill; but her countenance expressed affection even in death, and I burned with indignation and despair' (Ch8)

While Victor's language is melodramatic and verging on the hysterical, Justine suffers the consequences of being at the wrong place at the wrong time with quiet dignity and grace. It should be noted, too, that Justine, like all other female characters who suffer in this text, does so with beauty.

The greater tragedy of Justine's fate in the text is the confession forced by a priest, who is meant to offer spiritual comfort and compassion before she is hanged. Instead, for fear of spiritual torment in the afterlife, she confesses to a crime that she did not do (and could not have done), thus going to her grave as a convicted and confessed perpetrator of infanticide.

*a formal dress of black, which, given her status as a servant, would have been her smartest dress in which to appear in court

Alphonse

Key quotation:

- 'I wish to prepare you for the woeful news, but I know it is impossible; even now your eye skims over the page to seek the words which are to convey to you the horrible tidings' (Ch7)

In this short extract from Alphonse's letter to Victor that begins Chapter 7, Alphonse attempts to soften the blow of the terrible news of William's death. Alphonse is a paternal figure that consistently acts with kindness and compassion. Frankenstein is a novel of recurring motifs, and one of these is the paternal and the absence of the paternal. He provided a model of the paternal for Victor to follow. Victor could have been just this kind of father to his creation, but instead he runs away. Shelley, by describing Alphonse's kind, paternal treatment of his son Victor, asks us to remember how Victor treated his creation when newly born.

Structure 🗂

Chapter 6

Opening: 'Clerval then put the following letter into my hands. It was from my own Elizabeth'

Ending: 'My own spirits were high, and I bounded along with feelings of unbridled joy and hilarity'

In the previous chapter, Victor successfully creates and then abandons a new life. So grateful and relieved that he does not have to face the consequences of his actions, Victor begins to blossom back into the previous 'pre-Creature' version of his character. The opening of the chapter, with the letter from home, and the end, that foregrounds his improved health and good mood, give the impression that all will be well once again for Victor. This upbeat end to the chapter effectively creates a volta, as the atmosphere of optimism changes permanently from the opening of Chapter 7.

Chapter 7

Opening: 'You have probably waited impatiently for a letter to fix the date of your return to us; and I was at first tempted to write only a few lines, merely mentioning the day on which I should expect you'

Ending: 'If she is, as you believe, innocent, rely on the justice of our laws, and the activity with which I shall prevent the slightest shadow of partiality'

- Why has Shelley chosen to begin and end with a dramatic shift in tone compared to Chapter 6?

- What predictions might there be, based on Shelley's change of tone?

Alphonse Frankenstein's words book-end the start and end of this chapter. The element of ambiguity that begins Alphonse Frankenstein's letter – 'I was at first tempted to write only a few lines' – invites speculation from the reader, and we would correctly speculate that something is going to be amiss. Through the shock and horror of William's murder, to the brutal and unjust accusation of Justine for this murder, Alphonse Frankenstein acts with kindness and compassion to all of those whom he regards as children. By using this character to book-end the chapter, Shelley invites the reader to make comparisons with Victor's approach to parenting, which is somewhat lacking.

Chapter 8

Opening: 'My father and the rest of the family being obliged to attend as witnesses'

Ending: 'I beheld those I loved spend vain sorrow upon the graves of William and Justine, the first hapless victims to my unhallowed arts'

- Why has Shelley chosen to begin and end with this focus on the Frankenstein family's obligation to Justine, and to end with a focus on the innocent victims of his Creature?
- What predictions might there be based on Shelley's focus on the death of innocent characters at this point in the novel?

Shelley effectively devotes Chapter 8 to exploring issues of justice and injustice. She foregrounds, via Justine's trial, who in society has access to justice and who does not. By opening with the term 'obliged' in relation to the Frankenstein family's attendance at the trial, we are given a sense of begrudging compliance, rather than willingly supporting a member of the household falsely accused of murder.

Most tellingly of all are Victor's final few words of the chapter, when he described William and Justine as 'the first hapless victims of my unhallowed arts'. While 'first' neatly foreshadows that there will be many more victims, the adjective 'unhallowed' (unholy) finally shows Victor as admitting the immorality and irreligious nature of his experiment.

Extracts

Extract 1 (Ch7): How does Shelley use language to present the impact of Justine's perceived guilt?

'I do not know what you mean,' replied my brother, in accents of wonder, 'but to us the discovery we have made completes our misery. No one would believe it at first; and even now Elizabeth will not be convinced, notwithstanding all the evidence. Indeed, who would credit that Justine Moritz, who was so amiable, and fond of all the family, could suddenly become capable of so frightful, so appalling a crime?'

[Victor] 'Justine Moritz! Poor, poor girl, is she the accused? But it is wrongfully; every one knows that; no one believes it, surely, Ernest?'

This short extract follows Victor almost giving away the secret of his creation when he exclaims, 'who could attempt to pursue him?' when his brother Ernest tells him that William's murderer has been discovered and caught. Victor's slip-up, with the pronoun 'him', will be in agreement with the reader's assumptions as to who William's murderer is. This reminds us that the rest of the characters in this text are (fatally) ignorant of the Creature's existence. Shelley is exploiting the shared knowledge between the reader and the character of Victor Frankenstein.

Ernest's 'wonder' at who the accused is serves to delay the naming of the accused in the narrative. Before naming the accused, Ernest, as emotively as Victor would, states that the news of who the accused is 'completes our misery'. The suffering of the Frankenstein family is fully underway, just as the Creature intended.

When Ernest refers to Justine, he presents completely contradicting versions of that character (whom the reader has only 'met' via Elizabeth's correspondence thus far). She is both 'amiable, and fond of all the family' while also capable of 'so frightful, so appalling' a crime. While telling Victor this, Ernest seems incredulous.

Victor is also incredulous, but for entirely different reasons. Here, he is emphatic when asserting that 'everyone' knows her innocence and 'no one' will believe her guilt. He can only be so emphatic because he, of all the characters in the text, knows who the real perpetrator is. What we do not yet know, and will not know until we are reading the Creature's narrative, is the motivation for killing William and framing Justine.

Extract 2 (Ch8): How does Shelley use language to present Victor's suffering?

'We passed a few sad hours, until eleven o'clock, when the trial was to commence. My father and the rest of the family being obliged to attend as witnesses, I accompanied them to the court. During the whole of this wretched mockery of justice I suffered living torture. It was to be decided, whether the result of my curiosity and lawless devices would cause the death of two of my fellow-beings: one a smiling babe, full of innocence and joy; the other far more dreadfully murdered, with every aggravation of infamy that could make the murder memorable in horror.'

Use the following prompts to aid detailed analysis of the above extract:

- Why does the opening clause frame the consequences of Victor's actions as a collective suffering of the Frankenstein family?

- Where and when is there a shift of focus from Justine's to Victor's suffering?

- Why does Victor admit to the uncontrolled 'curiosity' that created the Creature?

- In what ways can the Creature's creation be deemed as 'lawless'?

- Victor avoids using Justine and William's names, using 'one' and 'the other' instead. What might this show to the reader? Why?

PIT STOP ▼

S-T-R-E-T-C-H

How might the Creature's narration of the same events differ from Victor's? What differences could be anticipated?

SECTION 6
CREATOR AND CREATED (CHAPTERS 9–10)

At a glance

> **Summary quotation:** 'a weight of despair and remorse pressed on my heart, which nothing could remove' (Ch9)

> **Big Question:** How does Victor Frankenstein react to William's death?

> **Significant plot events:**

Chapter 9:

- Victor suffers from ill health as an emotional reaction to the death of William.

- The family move from Geneva to their residence at Belrive and grieve for both William and Justine.

- Victor decides to travel to Chamounix.

Chapter 10:

- Victor explores the valley and then climbs to the summit of Montanvert.

- Victor and the Creature meet.

- The Creature begins his narration.

> **Character focus:** Victor Frankenstein, the Creature

> **Key themes:**

- Death and grief ✝

- Betrayal and guilt ♡

- Power and responsibility ☀

- Prejudice ♟

- Society and social class ✖

- Isolation and loneliness ♨

> **Handle with care:**

- reference to suicide

Why?

- Why does Victor choose to travel? What does this reveal about his character?
- Why does Shelley choose this point to introduce the Creature's narrative?
- Why is the landscape significant?

These allow us to consider Chapters 9 and 10's Big Question: How does Victor Frankenstein react to William's death?

What?

What happens?

Chapter 9

Victor's ill health is worsened by Justine's execution, following his abandonment of the Creature and William's death. Alphonse observes his deep despair and encourages him to moderate his emotions to recover. Victor sails on the lake in response, as he is afforded greater freedom at the Belrive house rather than the enclosed city of Geneva. Elizabeth reflects on the injustice of Justine's execution and William's death, creating further distress for Victor and his hidden guilt. Consequently, Victor seeks solace in travel and leaves for Chamounix.

Chapter 10 ☀

The next day, the weather changes and the landscape becomes sinister. The higher that Victor climbs, the more isolated he becomes. Descending to the glacier provides a natural amphitheatre for the arrival of the Creature, where Victor greets him with 'words expressive of furious detestation and contempt', provoking an angry response and a command to Victor: 'Listen to my tale.' The Creature states his terms, saying, 'I will leave them and you at peace; but if you refuse, I will glut the maw of death.' They talk and 'For the first time, also, I felt what the duties of a creator towards his creature were' – a significant point at which to end a chapter, with Victor referring to his responsibility as a creator, which he has long rejected.

Social and historical context ⚙

Social context: Social class and multiple residences ⚛

Shelley was familiar with the residences of the wealthy, such as Villa Diodati, from her European travels. Victor is a privileged and advantaged young man, who has established his social status at the start of his narrative – 'I am by birth a Genevese; and my family is one of the most distinguished of that republic' (Ch1) – and so has residences both in Geneva and outside: 'About this time we retired to our house at Belrive... The shutting of the gates regularly at ten o'clock... had rendered our residence within the walls of Geneva very irksome to me. I was now free' (Ch9). Victor feels imprisoned in Geneva, but the house at Belrive offers greater freedom. Like Percy, Victor 'passed many hours upon the water' (Ch9), delighting in the freedom of sailing and the oneness with nature that it offers.

Social context: Mourning

Mourning was an important part of social etiquette, governing clothing, house decorations (e.g. a wreath on the front door) and the drawing of curtains for a period of time. These customs were all to show respect for the dead. Victor states: 'Our house was the house of mourning' (Ch9). However, Shelley focuses not on the customs of mourning but on the emotions of the characters: Elizabeth's sadness and her focus on the lack of justice for Justine; Alphonse's deterioration of his health; and Victor's emotions, principally guilt.

Literary context: The Romantic sublime

This concept dates back to the Roman philosopher Cassius Longinue, 213–73 CE, resurging in the Romantic movement (the movement of Shelley and her contemporaries). Philosopher Edmund Burke (1729–97), in *A Philosophical Enquiry into the Origin of Our Ideas of the Sublime and Beautiful* (1757), explores the different types of aesthetics and the human response to these. He differentiates between the beautiful and the sublime:

- **beautiful:** something that is well formed and pleasing to look at

- **sublime:** something that inspires awe and wonder in the perceiver.

PIT STOP

Give learners images to categorise into either beautiful or sublime, linked to descriptions in the text to reinforce these concepts. Students can also categorise references in the text.

Literary context: Intertextuality

'Mutability' (1816) by Percy Shelley, lines 9–16, is quoted in Chapter 10. Mutability is a good word to discuss with learners: the ability to change or the fact of being likely to change. Mercer (2015) comments: 'The poem's almost universal application to any "man" who lives on to the "morrow" may be why Mary Shelley chose to place... (ll.9–16) in her first novel.' Victor's life has changed dramatically since bringing the Creature to life. This poem emphasises the significance of change – that change is all we know: 'Nought may endure but mutability.' The reader sees that the poem reinforces Victor's philosophical musings about man's desire to think rather than just exist. His use of 'brute' seems to imply that a more natural existence is better – 'more necessary beings' (Ch10). However, his encounter with a 'brute' of his own making contradicts this. The poem also acts as a precursor to his second encounter with his creation, which will lead to further change.

Vocabulary in context

Word	Quotation	Definition
Chapter 9		
remorse	'The blood flowed freely in my veins, but a weight of despair and remorse pressed on my heart which nothing could remove.'	a feeling of sadness and being sorry for what you have done
serenity	'instead of that serenity of conscience which allowed me to look back upon the past with self-satisfaction, and from thence to gather promise of new hopes, I was seized by remorse and the sense of guilt'	the quality of being peaceful and calm
immoderate	'but is it not a duty to the survivors that we should refrain from augmenting their unhappiness by an appearance of immoderate grief?'	too much or many, or more than is usual or reasonable
augmented	'But it was augmented and rendered sublime by the mighty Alps, whose white and shining pyramids and domes towered above all, as belonging to another earth, the habitations of another race of beings.'	made greater or more intense
Chapter 10		
immutable	'the thunder sound of the avalanche or the cracking, reverberated along the mountains, of the accumulated ice, which, through the silent working of immutable laws, was ever and anon rent and torn, as if it had been but a plaything in their hands.	not changing, or unable to be changed
solemnising	'The sight of the awful and majestic in nature had indeed always the effect of solemnising my mind and causing me to forget the passing cares of life'	observe or perform with dignity or gravity (seriousness)
despondence	'I walked about the isle like a restless spectre, separated from all the world, deserted and most wretched, in a state of despondence and solitude'	a state of low spirits caused by loss of hope or courage
abyss	'I felt as if I were walking on the edge of an abyss, beyond which was the destruction I so fearfully dreaded'	a deep or seemingly bottomless chasm; a profound difference or unfathomable situation

PIT STOP ▼

Return to this vocabulary in a later lesson, assessing whether learners can link each key word to the relevant character(s). For a bonus point, develop each link into an analysis of how the writer's choice presents that character, setting or theme.

Chapter 9:

1. Why does Victor feel 'remorse' in Chapter 9?

2. Should Victor feel 'serenity' after Justine and William's deaths?

3. What is it that causes Victor's suffering to be 'augmented' in Chapter 9?

Chapter 10:

1. What is 'solemnising' Victor's mind in Chapter 10?

2. What is the cause of Victor's 'despondence' in Chapter 10?

3. What might be symbolic about Victor's 'conflagration fading away' at this point in the chapter?

Plot and character development

1. How do the deaths of William and Justine impact upon the Frankenstein family? ✝

The characters' emotions are central to the first part of Chapter 9, showing the significance of innocent William's death, compounded by the execution of Justine; the repetition of the noun 'pain' shows their deep sorrow and grief. Elizabeth is 'sad' and Alphonse's health is 'deeply shaken by the horror of the recent events', as he talks of his love for William: 'No one could love a child more than I loved your brother.' Despite his grief, Alphonse is more focused on Victor's feelings. Victor's self-absorption is a recurring theme and is evident here, 'with a look of despair, and endeavour to hide myself from his view'.

Elizabeth makes an impassioned speech about the lack of justice for both William and Justine – 'but she was innocent. I know, I feel she was innocent' – but with greater focus on Justine. She identifies, without irony, that the murderer is walking free. Victor knows that he is the murderer, having rejected the Creature, and experiences 'the extremest agony'. Now he has to carry the burden of guilt, conscious of the consequences of his 'deeds of mischief'.

2. How does Victor respond to William's death? ✝

Victor, as narrator, focuses on his own emotions – principally despair – which predominate in this chapter, in contrast to his father's advice: 'excessive sorrow prevents improvement or enjoyment' (Ch9). Although Victor wishes to find 'some relief' from his 'intolerable sensations' (Ch9), the reader may perceive him as self-indulgent. He offers little comfort to either his father or Elizabeth. His characteristic reaction, as we have seen before, is to travel in response to difficulty or when recovering from illness. This affords plot progression, and now Victor is unknowingly travelling towards his second meeting with the Creature. This is foreshadowed by Elizabeth's rhetorical question: 'what can disturb our peace?' (Ch9) Shelley then uses a journey once again to effect the meeting between creator and created: 'that I [Victor] suddenly left my home' (Ch9). He goes to Chamounix, where he finds a short-lived 'long-lost sense of pleasure' (Ch9).

3. What happens between Victor and the Creature – the creator and created?

Victor's journey to Chamounix takes him to Mont Blanc and the Mer de Glace, in preparation for the meeting with his nemesis. The power of the sublime landscape 'afforded [him] the greatest consolation' (Ch10). The reader may have expected him to find consolation with his father and Elizabeth, but he abandons both of them to pursue isolation. As the landscape becomes more threatening, the Creature appears: 'I suddenly beheld the figure of a man' and Victor re-experiences his fear – 'I was troubled' – and he is seized by a 'faintness' (Ch10). He then feels rage, anger and hatred. The Creature shows 'bitter anguish' in his face. In contrast, Victor sees 'disdain and malignity', which reveals his own disdain for his creation (Ch10). Their confrontation is used to lead us up to hearing the Creature's narrative, concealed at the heart of the novel.

How?

Language

This analysis ranges from the micro-elements, which are more granular, to the macro-elements, which can be tracked as literary and grammatical patterns.

Lightning as a motif

Key quotation:

- 'watching the pallid lightnings that played above Mont Blanc'

This phrase occurs in the penultimate sentence of Chapter 9. Lightning has already played a significant role in the narrative as Victor's inspiration to create life. Here, the motif will take on new significance for the Creature, and acts as a narrative signpost for his arrival 'on stage' into the narrative.

This image serves as an anaphoric reference to the Creature's creation, as well as an allusion to Zeus and Mount Olympus from Greek mythology. This is a recurring motif throughout the narratives of Victor and the Creature:

- A similar storm inspired Victor to make the Creature and bring him to life, using the electrical power that it generated.

- In Chapter 7, we see Victor's fascination with a powerful, melodramatic storm, and Victor experiences the Creature's first act of vengeance.

- In Chapter 19, Victor will refer to himself as 'a blasted tree' – the same one that instigated his obsession with creating new life.

- At the end of Chapter 9, lightning signifies the arrival of the Creature into the narrative.

- Lightning will continue to signify the Creature's arrival into the narrative as the story progresses, until he enters the present of Walton and the dying Victor.

Landscapes

Shelley's choice of landscape is notable, as it is rooted in her own travels and experiences (see the biography section, page 7). Her journals support vivid recall of place, and there are parallels between her own experiences of different landscapes and those that she gives her characters as they travel.

Following William's death, Victor repeatedly seeks solace in pastoral spaces: these become a means of spiritual healing for him. In Gothic and Romantic literature, the landscape assumes great significance, almost as an active participant in the narrative, influencing or echoing the emotions of key characters. Brennan (1988, p.38) comments that 'Victor could sometimes handle his overwhelming despair, and so relieve his "intolerable sensations"' through three experiences of nature:

1. the experience of the natural sublime that induces the forgetfulness of sorrow

2. the experience of the natural sublime that both induces forgetfulness and contributes a comforting maternal power

3. the experience of the maternal power of nature without the sublime.

In Chapter 9, Victor introduces his trip to the valley of Chamounix:

'Sometimes I could cope with the sullen despair that overwhelmed me: but sometimes the whirlwind passions of my soul drove me to seek, by bodily exercise and by change of place, some relief from my intolerable sensations.'

Here, Victor delights in and is restored by his surroundings and experiences the sublime of the Alps: 'But it was augmented and rendered sublime by the mighty Alps, whose white and shining pyramids and domes towered above all, as belonging to another earth, the habitations of another race of beings' (Ch9). The final phrase is carefully chosen to remind us of the Creature following Victor. Yet Victor is reminded of his youth and is restored by 'maternal nature', which 'bade me weep no more' (Ch9) – the second experience of nature. Despite this comfort, his grief returns, but the 'lullaby' created by the sound of the river lulls him, just as an infant is comforted.

Chapter 10 begins with the beauty of the valley, with its typically Gothic features of 'unstained snowy mountain-top, the glittering pinnacle, the pine woods, and ragged bare ravine; the eagle, soaring amidst the clouds – they all gathered round me, and bade me be at peace'. The valley makes Victor feel 'elevated... from all littleness of feeling' (the third experience of nature) and it has an additional tranquillising effect on Victor. However, overnight, the scene has changed dramatically, foreshadowing the arrival of the Creature, of which Victor is unaware of: '[T]he presence of another would destroy the solitary grandeur of the scene' (Ch10). This is a clear signal to the reader of the coming confrontation.

The sea of ice is the Mer de Glace, visited by Shelley in Switzerland in *History of a Six Weeks' Tour* (1817). This is the backdrop to the confrontation – 'this wonderful and stupendous scene', 'place of awe and majesty', 'The sea, or rather the vast river of ice, wound among its dependent mountains' (Ch10). But Victor is not going to be comforted – 'this faint happiness' (Ch10) – by the sublime, nor does nature show its maternal aspects here. The Creature confronts Victor in this icy desert, symbolising coldness, loneliness and isolation, where 'The desert mountains and dreary glaciers are my refuge' (Ch10). They then 'crossed the ice' and sought shelter in a hut by a fire, an instance of civilisation that the Creature has constructed under 'bleak skies' (Ch10).

Character focus

Victor ✏

Key quotations:

- 'I was seized by remorse and the sense of guilt, which hurried me away to a hell of intense tortures such as no language can describe' (Ch9)

'I shunned the face of man; all sound of joy or complacency was torture to me; solitude was my only consolation – deep, dark, deathlike solitude' (Ch9)

'I, not in deed, but in effect, was the true murderer' (Ch9)

This section shows us Victor's emotional suffering with 'guilt' and 'remorse', where he still dwells heavily on the deaths of Justine and William. His brief moment of confession conveys this further, though its delivery to a listener who cannot act upon this confession, nor absolve him of his guilt, suggests that he is not willing or ready to take full responsibility for this.

In this section, Victor also chooses to isolate himself again, leaning into his suffering and even suggesting that he must be suffering more than anyone else alive, a further indication of his inability to truly recognise his guilt.

Alphonse

Key quotation:

- '"Do you think, Victor," said he, "that I do not suffer also? No one could love a child more than I loved your brother;"' (Ch9)

As is consistent with Alphonse's character throughout the text, we are presented with a kind, benevolent paternal figure, capable of showing empathy to others. He exists (along with the elderly De Lacey) as an alternative representation of fatherhood, enabling us to compare and judge Victor's lack of paternal care for his creation. We notice that Alphonse is aware of the suffering of others, while also suffering terrible grief. Victor cannot do the same.

Elizabeth

Key quotations:

- 'But I was restrained, when I thought of the heroic and suffering Elizabeth, whom I tenderly loved, and whose existence was bound up in mine' (Ch9).

- 'now misery has come home, and men appear to me as monsters thirsting for each other's blood' (Ch9, Elizabeth to Victor)

In this section, Elizabeth is again idealised by Victor as a woman who simultaneously suffers and yet is able to save him. Victor is 'restrained' from a temptation to 'plunge into a silent lake' by Elizabeth, as her beauty and 'heroic suffering' are enough to save him from himself.

Structure 🔠

Chapter 9

Opening: 'Justine died; she rested; and I was alive'

Ending: 'I remained at the window... listening to the rushing of the Arve... The same lulling sounds acted as a lullaby... sleep crept over me;... and blest the giver of oblivion'

- Why has Shelley chosen to begin a focus on Justine's abrupt death and end with a focus on Victor's ability to be soothed by nature (the Romantic sublime)?

- What predictions might there be, based on Shelley's shift of focus from the human to the sublime?

This is similar to the blissful calm that Victor experiences at the end of Chapter 6, prior to discovering that William is murdered and Justine accused. Shelley deploys the same technique here, just before the Creature enters the stage to tell his own narrative from the moment of his birth.

However, what is notable in both the beginning and the ending is Victor's urge or longing for death. At the start of Chapter 9, he is full of envy for Justine being at rest. By contrast, at the end, Victor is full of self-pity for still living. The final word of the chapter is 'oblivion' – that he is 'blest' to be in this state shows that, while he narrates his story to Walton, death is desired.

Chapter 10

Opening: 'I stood beside the sources of the Arveiron, which take their rise in a glacier, that with slow pace is advancing down from the summit of the hills, to barricade the valley'

Ending: 'The air was cold, and the rain again began to descend: we entered the hut, the fiend with an air of exultation, I with a heavy heart, and depressed spirits. But I consented to listen;... he thus began his tale'

- Why has Shelley chosen to begin and end with this focus on the setting of the glacier?
- What similarities are there between this setting and the one of Walton and Victor's present?

Due to the complex layered narrative, Shelley is able to make use of the concepts of doubles and mirroring. The setting of the glacier mirrors Walton and Frankenstein's present, as they sit, stuck in the northern ice floe. Similar to the setting of Walton's frame narrative, the glacier is a purposeful use of the Gothic sublime, and it is also a setting that the Creature will be able to endure far better than Victor, thus it serves as a reminder of his supernatural strength compared to Victor's mental fragility.

Monologue and dialogue as structure

Chapter 9: Monologue ✝

Victor's internal monologue is in response to Alphonse's advice to show some dignity in his grief:

> *'I should have been the first to hide my grief, and console my friends, if remorse had not mingled its bitterness, and terror its alarm with my other sensations'*

The modal verb 'should' expresses the idea of an unfulfilled obligation towards Victor's family, and an obligation to protect them, which he never fulfils. The conditional 'if' here – 'if remorse... its bitterness' – implies a foolish hope for a different outcome. Additionally, Shelley anthropomorphises both 'remorse' and 'terror', appearing to make Victor helpless against the lingering, lurking power of the Creature. From Victor's point of view, the language conveying his helplessness aims to engender sympathy. Walton, similar in nature to Victor, provides that sympathy; the reader is more reluctant.

Students will need frequent reminding of the differences between character and reader responses to Victor and the Creature's narratives. Learners should pay attention to how and why Shelley does this.

Chapter 10: Dialogue

Dialogue between the Creature and Victor shows significant differences between the two. Victor initiates the conversation with an exclamatory question, addressing the Creature as 'Devil', which shows his fear and contempt. He attempts to threaten the Creature with 'fierce vengeance', despite the Creature's superior size and strength. Victor's dialogue is fuelled by anger and a desire for revenge, which the Creature recognises: 'You purpose to kill me.' Victor's dialogue is also characterised by imperatives – 'Begone! I will not hear you' – and negatives, conveying Victor's unwillingness to acknowledge the pleas of his creation. Victor's inhumanity is very evident here, with his desire to annihilate, 'that I may trample you to dust!'.

The Creature's language is characterised by greater eloquence and rhetorical phrasing, showing the fruits of his self-education (Chapters 12 to 15). The Creature repeatedly uses 'you' and 'your' as emphatic forms of direct address; he also emphasises the pain of his suffering, which causes him to be 'miserable'. His first part of the dialogue is threatening, showing his anger at being rejected and recognition of Victor's desire to destroy him.

When the Creature responds to Victor, he changes pronouns from 'you' to 'I' as he 'entreats' Victor to listen to his needs, because 'Everywhere I see bliss, from which I alone am irrevocably excluded'. The Creature recognises his loneliness and how cruelly he has been treated: '[M]isery made me a fiend.' There is a significant pattern of language related to Christianity, with reference to Adam and fallen angels, as well as fiends and devils. *Paradise Lost* is frequently alluded to in the novel and is an underpinning narrative influence. Its importance is shown by its role in the Creature's education, hence the imagery used in his dialogue. The influence of *Paradise Lost* is also evident in the Creature's use of 'thee' and 'thou' pronouns, elevating his dialogue to biblical and an authoritative tone.

PIT STOP ▼

See the teaching resources for further work on the Creature's eloquence/ use of rhetoric. 🖱

Extracts

Extract 1 (Ch9): How does Shelley use language to present Victor Frankenstein in this extract?

'The blood flowed freely in my veins, but a weight of despair and remorse pressed on my heart, which nothing could remove. Sleep fled from my eyes; I wandered like an evil spirit... I was seized by remorse and the sense of guilt, which hurried me away to a hell of intense tortures, such as no language can describe.'

Shelley shows Victor's melodramatic nature, foregrounding Victor's overwrought emotional state through anthropomorphosis of his emotions 'despair' and 'remorse'. This type of metaphor draws attention to Victor's self-inflicted burden of suffering, through the noun 'weight' and the dynamic verb 'pressed'. This is repeated at the end of the extract, where 'remorse' and 'guilt' 'seize' him. The dynamic verb 'seize' presents the emotions as sentient and predatory, thus rendering Victor helpless in their grip.

Victor's melodramatic nature is explored further through the use of hyperbolic imagery. Victor continues to be shown as helpless through the personified motif of sleep that has 'fled' from Victor. Here, as in many other works of literature, disturbed sleep symbolises a mind disturbed and tortured by guilt. Shelley then uses a carefully constructed simile – 'I wandered like an evil spirit' – which, unbeknown to him, will mirror the Creature's early childhood and the impossibility of him ever being accepted by, and into, mankind. We see the absolute power that the emotions of remorse, guilt and despair have over him, rendering him 'other', as a form of living ghost.

Extract 2 (Ch10): How does Shelley use language to present Victor Frankenstein's attitude towards his creation in this extract from Chapter 10?

'"Why do you call to my remembrance," I rejoined, "circumstances, of which I shudder to reflect, that I have been the miserable origin and author? Cursed be the day, abhorred devil, in which you first saw light! Cursed (although I curse myself) be the hands that formed you! You have made me wretched beyond expression. You have left me no power to consider whether I am just."'

Consider the context of the extract with learners: 👥

- This is the end of Chapter 10, a liminal place in the narration, where the Creature and Victor's narrations overlap.

- It follows their first encounter, on the glacier.

- The Creature is shown to be calm and articulate before Victor speaks (*see teaching resources*).

- The Creature then takes over the narrative.

Here, Shelley shows Victor's rage and disgust at his creation using anaphoric reference, to remind the reader of the moment of the Creature's birth and abandonment (Ch5): 'circumstances I shudder to reflect'. The noun choice 'circumstances', showing Victor's squeamishness, is deliberately ambiguous and euphemistic, although both the reader and the Creature understand that he refers to the Creature's birth. Additionally, the verb choice 'shudder' indicates that Victor's emotional state is physically overwhelming. Later in the same interrogative sentence, he labels himself as 'the miserable origin and author' of his creation, while at the same time not fully comprehending – yet – why the Creature has turned to evil.

SECTION 7
THE CREATURE'S NARRATIVE (CHAPTERS 11–14)

At a glance

> **Section summary quotation:** 'What was I? The question again recurred to be answered only with groans' (Ch12)

> **Big Question:** How does the Creature's life begin?

> **Significant plot events:**

Chapter 11:

- The Creature realises that he is alive.

- Unsure of where he is or who he is, he feels scared and flees Victor's rooms, finding himself in the woods.

- In the woods, the Creature meets a man who is terrified of him. He is confused, and finds a similar reaction when he comes across a village.

- After some time, the Creature finds a hovel near a family's cottage and shelters there.

Chapter 12:

- The Creature watches the family in the cottage and develops affection for them.

- After noticing that they are poor, he begins to help them.

Chapter 13:

- The Creature is delighted that the family enjoy his secretive aid.

- A young woman arrives to join the family. As she learns to speak their language, so too does the Creature.

- The Creature learns to read too, and begins to discover more about the world, particularly about rich and poor and about property.

Chapter 14:

- The Creature learns the history of the De Lacey family.

- He also learns the history of Safie, the young woman, and how her father betrayed the De Laceys.

- He learns about the imprisonment, release and changing reputation of the De Lacey father.

> **Character focus:** the Creature, the De Laceys, Safie

> **Key themes:**

- Family and companionship 👥
- Isolation and loneliness 🧎
- Knowledge and discovery 🔍
- Betrayal and guilt 🫱
- Rejection and its consequences ✖
- Society and social class ✂
- Prejudice 👥

> **Handle with care:**

- the separation and imprisonment of family members
- archaic language around race: Arabian, Muhammadan, Turk (definitions for these are provided below

  Arabian: historically, a person who is from Arabia, a large area in the Middle East

  Muhammadan: an obsolete term for a Muslim

  Turk: historically, this term referred to anyone who spoke the Turkic languages (a range of languages spoken across Asia)

Why?

- Why is the Creature's early 'life' important?
- Why is the Creature's repeated rejection significant?
- Why does Shelley show a benevolent side to the Creature?
- Why does Shelley create the De Lacey family as she does?

S-T-R-E-T-C-H questions

- Why does Shelley include the De Lacey family?
- Why does Shelley provide further examples of women in need of protection and rescue?

What?

What happens?

This section marks the change from Victor's narrative to that of the Creature (which is relayed by Victor to Walton, who relays it to his sister). Either deliberately or otherwise, Shelley writes in a voice much the same as the previous narrators, although the experience and perspectives shared are vastly different.

Chapter 11

The Creature begins his narrative by explaining the distress that he experienced when brought to life: confused, overwhelmed and hungry. After waking, he flees into a forest and slowly begins to understand his surroundings. He enters a small hut with a man in it, who runs away, causing confusion for the Creature. Similarly, when he finds a village, the villagers chase him away. Finally, he finds himself a small hovel in which to hide, and considers it a 'palace' in comparison to some of the other places in which he has sheltered. Nearby is a cottage and he watches the family who inhabit it, finding them enchanting and idyllic.

Chapter 12

The Creature watches the family from his hovel and develops a deep affection for them and their love for each other. He sees that they are unhappy, but cannot understand why. Over time, he realises that they are poor and hungry too, so regrets stealing from them and begins to help them by completing simple daily tasks. The family begin referring to the Creature as a 'good spirit', which makes him very happy. He begins to learn to speak by imitating them, but also increasingly notices the contrast between them and him. He notices his reflection in a pool and describes himself as a 'monster', but is still determined to win over the family with his kindness.

Chapter 13

A woman arrives, and Felix – the young man of the cottage – is 'ravished with delight' at her arrival. Despite her speaking another language, it is clear that they are a couple. As the woman learns to speak their language, so too does the Creature – but at a much quicker pace. He also listens to the books that Felix reads to her and learns more about humankind and its history. He learns of wealth, class and property, and begins to understand his current place in the world. He is upset by this, but is even more distressed when he realises that humankind has families and relationships, yet he is alone.

Chapter 14

The Creature learns the history of the family that he admires, who were, until recently, respected and wealthy. He learns that Safie, the young woman whom Felix loves, is the daughter of the man who ruined them. He shares this story of betrayal, heartbreak and separation, but also of how the family are reunited and come to be in their current cottage.

Social and historical context ☼

Historical and literary context: Orientalism ☸

Orientalism is typically described as the style or portrayal of characters or traits that are considered Oriental. Nowadays, 'Oriental' is often considered to be the Far East, although 'Orientalism' extends to include peoples and races from the Middle East and across the Indian subcontinent. As trade and power between the East and West became Europe-dominated in the eighteenth century and, particularly, the nineteenth century, this was reflected in some of the art and literature of the time: an idea termed 'Orientalism' by Edward Said (1978). In his seminal book *Orientalism* (1978), he notes that 'European culture gained strength and identity by setting itself off against the Orient as a sort of surrogate and even underground itself.' (p. 3)

Orientalism features in *Frankenstein* in several ways:

- The Creature is 'othered' in two ways: he is both non-human and is also described as having typically non-European physical traits. Terri Pinyard (2016) writes that the Creature's 'yellow' skin and 'black hair' (Ch5) allow Victor to define the Creature as 'other' through his appearance, 'therefore making him a generalisation of an entire race' (Pinyerd, 2016, p. 55).

- Safie and her family are described as 'Arabian'. Pinyerd argues that her character is 'greatly objectified by both Felix and the monster' (2016, p. 55) and highlights that she is described as a 'treasure which would fully reward [Felix's] toil and hazard' (Ch14). Her position as 'treasure' is reinforced by her position as the subject of dialogue rather than a participant, which reduces her character to one of physical appearance rather than intellectual offering (which the Creature notes in Chapter 13 is not as swift as his), and the repeated mention of her beauty as a 'lovely Arabian' (Ch14).

- When learning about different 'manners, governments and religions', the Creature learns about 'slothful Asiatics' versus the 'stupendous genius and mental activity of the Grecians' (Ch13).

- Safie's father is repeatedly referred to as 'The Turk' (Ch14) rather than being given a name (interestingly, a trait that he shares with the Creature).

- Safie's father 'loathes' (Ch14) the idea that she marry a Christian, despite being married to a Christian himself – an act that suggests ingrained prejudice and hypocrisy within his race.

- Safie's mother is described as being 'seized and made a slave by the Turks' (Ch14).

- Safie's education is described as teaching her to 'aspire to higher powers of intellect and an independence of spirit forbidden to the female followers of Muhammed' (Ch14).

- The De Laceys are apparently betrayed by Safie's father, the 'treacherous Turk' (Ch14); also note the following 'tyrannical mandate' that she return to her home country.

Interestingly, Shelley seeks to distinguish Safie from her father and, perhaps, from her race. As well as being educated in a more Western tradition, Safie is 'enchanted' by the idea of marrying a Christian and holding social rank in Europe (Ch14), and finds the idea of returning to Turkey 'abhorrent', as 'her religion and her feelings were alike averse to it' (Ch14). While it could be argued that this favourable portrayal is another sign of the bias of Shelley's narrators and the Creature's attraction to Safie, it could also be interpreted that Shelley makes use of Orientalism here to reflect her own strivings to make her life with Percy against the disapproval of William Godwin.

Literary context: The second bildungsroman

Chapter 11 brings with it a change of narrators, as Shelley provides us with a first-hand account of the Creature's perspective on his existence and life thus far. This is arguably her third coming-of-age narrative of the novel, following that of Walton and Victor. Schoene-Harwood (2000 p. 7) states that Shelley offers us 'three men [who] are preoccupied with the various processes of their coming of age', and highlights that the story offered by the Creature is just as indulgent and lengthy as Victor's. As the narrative voices of the three vary very little, this may be an intentional attempt by Shelley to establish the similarities between Victor and his Creature, but also to provide contrasts that serve to highlight each character's nature and the origin of each character's sufferings.

PIT STOP ▼

S-T-R-E-T-C-H

For A level learners, this argument prompts a close examination of the language and sentence structures used by each character. More enriching, however, could be the discussion around why Shelley chooses to have similar voices for both characters (Victor and the Creature). This could be prompted by this sequence of questions:

- What are the similarities and differences in the characters' narrative styles?

- Do we believe Shelley to have done this on purpose?

- If so, what is Shelley's aim in this? What is she communicating?

Vocabulary in context

Word	Quotation	Definition
Chapter 11		
seized	'A strange multiplicity of sensations seized me'	to take something quickly and keep or hold it
liberty	'I now found that I could wander at liberty'	the freedom to live as you wish or go where you want
enchanted	'I was enchanted by the appearance of the hut'	affected by magic or seeming to be affected by magic
Chapter 12		
affection	'Interchanging each day looks of affection'	the feeling of liking for a person or place
sufficiently	'I improved... but not sufficiently to follow up any kind of conversation'	enough for a purpose
Chapter 13		
endeavouring	'She was endeavouring to learn their language'	to try to do something
rank	'Of rank, of descent, and noble blood'	a particular position, higher or lower than others
noble		belonging to a high social rank in society, especially by birth
Chapter 14		
obnoxious	'He became obnoxious to the government'	very unpleasant or rude
treacherous	'The treacherous Turk'	deceiving someone who trusts you, or having no loyalty

Plot and character development

1. What are the Creature's first experiences of the world?

As the Creature awakes in the world, his first experiences are instinctive and focused on his senses. Initially, he is passive in the world, but he soon realises that he can move and begins to walk. After this, he notices temperature and covers himself in clothes, before venturing into the world, where one of his first sights is the moon. The changes between day and night captivate him for several days, before he then progresses to explore the world more, through interaction and experimentation with nature and people.

PIT STOP ⏏

The Creature's first interactions with the world in this section hold parallels with Victor's but also contrasts. This provides a ripe opportunity for retrieval of Victor's early chapters and his description of his childhood.

Comparisons might include:

- the people involved in the lives of each character and how they are introduced

- the guidance with which each character is provided and who provides this

- the character traits that each character conveys in their first chapters.

PIT STOP ▼

As this is the first time that learners experience the Creature's narrative, in contrast to Victor's depiction of him, this is a ripe time at which to discuss narrative perspectives and the bias of narrators.

Victor has consistently portrayed the Creature as 'monstrous' (Ch5) from the moment of his coming alive. To Victor, the Creature represents a failure of himself to create beauty, and also a threat (at least to begin with, this is limited to a threat to Victor's scientific legacy).

Students should be asked:

- Having known him only through the perspective of Victor, does he seem as malicious and demonic as Victor has portrayed him?

- How do we feel about the newborn 'monster' for whom Shelley now provides a voice? Is it enough to provoke our sympathy?

- If the Creature's narrative is so contrasting to Victor's, can we trust Victor's perspective?

2. Who is the family that the Creature meets? 🌐

The Creature meets the De Lacey family. The family comprises:

- Felix, a young man
- Agatha, Felix's sister
- their father
- Safie, Felix's wife.

The family are French but have fled France for Germany, following political upset and the imprisonment (which the Creature tells Victor is unlawful) of the head of the family and Agatha.

Who is Safie? What is her story? ✍

Safie is the daughter of an Arab woman and a Turkish merchant, who is married to Felix. Her father betrayed the De Laceys, and she defies him by making her way to Germany to join her husband. It seems fitting that Safie arrives on a beautiful spring day, when, as the Creature notes, the land is now beginning to 'bloom with the most beautiful flowers and verdure' (Ch13).

PIT STOP ▼

S-T-R-E-T-C-H ✂

Safie's character provides an interesting addition to the characters with which Shelley has presented us so far. While she is an example of yet another woman who requires rescuing and who is vulnerable to the actions of men, she also represents the 'other' (much like the Creature). However, she differs from the Creature crucially in that she is considered beautiful. In being so, she may have been constructed by Shelley to highlight society's concern with physical beauty over the beauty of character and spirit.

When exploring Safie, learners may wish to:

- explore her in contrast to Agatha, Elizabeth and Caroline
- explore how she is viewed by the Creature
- Explore the family's reaction to Safie and her contributions to their family vs the Creature and his contributions
- explore the possible meaning in Safie's arrival in springtime, but the Creature's life beginning on a 'dreary day in November' (Ch5).

3. What does the Creature learn about humanity from books in this section? 🔍

In addition to learning how to speak, as the family teaches Safie to talk French, he also learns from the books that the family uses to teach her how to read French – namely Volney's *Ruins of Empires* (1791). From this book (which he admits that he understands primarily because Felix explains it in detail to Safie), the Creature learns about power, poverty and various races and their histories. In particular, he learns about social rank, property and how different areas of the world have different cultures and peoples who work together (for war or advancement).

How does the Creature respond to his new learning?

The learning that the Creature amasses via the De Laceys acts as a catalyst for self-reflection and analysis of his own position and place in the world. He realises that he has neither wealth nor property, and no rank or social standing. Moreover, he realises how alone he is in the world, both emotionally and physically, and questions 'What was I?' (Ch13), a sign that he recognises the difference between himself and others, and seeks knowledge of his identity.

4. What does the Creature think and feel about the family?

The Creature feels a number of emotions for the De Lacey family:

- He admires their kindness and support of one another.
- He delights in the music that they play.
- He finds joy in their familial relationship.
- He sympathises with their poverty and want.
- He envies their companionship.

These emotions are important for the Creature to feel, as they display his benevolent character and how, when given the right environment and nurture, he can be a positive contributor to society. For Shelley, this is important, as it allows her to emphasise that the Creature is far from the 'monster' that he appears to be.

PIT STOP ▼

Retrieval point ☁

When exploring the Creature's feelings for the De Laceys, Victor's feelings about his family and friends in Chapters 1 and 2 are a valuable point of comparison. Before exploring this chapter, teachers might choose to return to Victor's emotions to remind learners of these, to support them in developing an understanding of the connections between the Creature and Victor.

How?

Language 🔍 💡

Symbolism

Key quotation:

- 'I started up and beheld a radiant form rise from among the trees [the moon]. I gazed with a kind of wonder' (Ch11)

Very early in his 'life', the Creature sees and briefly fixates on the moon, which he describes as an 'orb' (Ch11). The moon has held rich symbolism for thousands of years and across many cultures around the world. In Western literature, the moon has been seen as feminine since ancient times, and it is easy to explore the meaning that this choice of symbol may have carried for the Creature. As a feminine symbol, it could symbolise the Creature's longing for a mother, or – as we see later in the novel – a female partner with whom to share his lot in the world. As a symbol of longing, it echoes this also, and perhaps foreshadows the Creature's passionate longing for companionship throughout the novel. Perhaps most well known by learners, the moon is a symbol associated with divine power and malicious intent (such as in relation to werewolves), and it is perhaps deliberate that Shelley chooses a full moon for the night on which the Creature is brought to life.

Use of the term 'wretch'

Key quotations:

- 'poor, helpless, insufficient wretch' (Ch11)
- 'Foolish wretch!' (Ch12)
- 'Miserable, unhappy wretch' (Ch14)

In Chapter 5 of the novel, Shelley has Victor repeatedly describe the Creature as 'the wretch': 'the wretch – the miserable monster', a 'wretch' who was more 'hideous' than a 'mummy endued with animation' – before he flees and 'sought to avoid the wretch' (Ch5).

The Oxford English Dictionary offers a range of definitions and uses for the word 'wretch', which have been in use since the thirteenth century. These include:

- one driven out of or away from his native country; a banished person; an exile
- one who is sunk in deep distress, sorrow, misfortune or poverty; a miserable, unhappy or unfortunate person; a poor or hapless being
- [a term] applied to animals, birds or insects
- a vile, sorry or despicable person; one of opprobrious or reprehensible character; a mean or contemptible creature.

Given the other language that Victor uses to describe the Creature, it is reasonable to assume that Victor's meaning is the latter. His actions also mean that the first definition is applicable to the Creature. However, Shelley does not limit her use of the word to Victor's narrative: the Creature frequently uses the word to describe himself too.

The Creature's intended meaning with the word is less clear than Victor's. In part, this is due to his narrative position: he tells his story knowing what he has suffered and what crimes he has committed. When he describes himself in Chapter 11 as a 'poor, helpless, insufficient wretch', he could mean that he is deeply sorrowful and miserable, but he could also be doing so in recognition of his position as a criminal and, in effect, exile. The meaning behind his use of the word, then, is ambiguous.

Character focus

The Creature

Key quotations:

- 'I was a poor, helpless, miserable wretch' (Ch11)
- 'How I was terrified when I viewed myself in a transparent pool!' (Ch12)
- 'I became fully convinced that I was in reality the monster that I am' (Ch12)
- 'I wished sometimes to shake off all thought and feeling' (Ch13)

In this section, the Creature changes drastically, from a naive and vulnerable creature to a grown 'man', who can understand, communicate and even philosophise. Initially, the Creature is childlike in much of his learning: he responds to light and sound, touches fire and experiments with foods. His childlike naivety and optimism contrast his clear intelligence and evoke readers' affection and sympathy.

The Creature has an enormous capacity to think and feel intensely and deeply. Josephine Johnston writes that it is this portrayal of the Creature as a 'sentient being – in particular one whose intellect and emotions rival or surpass those of her supposed protagonist' (Johnson, in Guston et al., 2017, p. 287) – that allows Shelley to offer clear critique on the behaviour of scientists and the 'responsibility that [they] owe to [their] creations' (Johnson, in Guston et al., 2017, p. 287).

The De Laceys

Key quotations:

- 'Nothing could exceed the love and respect which the younger cottagers exhibited towards their venerable companion' (Ch12)
- 'It was poverty, and they suffered that evil in a very distressing degree' (Ch12)
- '[De Lacey] was descended from a good family in France, where he had lived... in affluence, respected by his superiors and beloved by his equals' (Ch14)

The De Laceys almost function as one character unit in the novel: Shelley uses their family as an aspirational goal for the Creature. They are born into respectability and have maintained their virtuous characters through their mutual kindness and affections to one another, despite their poverty. From the perspective of the Creature (which is the only perspective that Shelley offers of the De Laceys), they are a perfect family unit, which has been made victims of the world and the sins of civilisation. They are learned and well-read (an important inclusion, as this allows the Creature to learn from them).

They are also portrayed as noble and self-sacrificing, Felix in particular. For example, Felix is so incensed by the injustice experienced by Safie's family that he takes risks for himself and his own family to seek resolution for this injustice. As a young man, he is portrayed as being well-educated, generous, loving and just.

Safie

Key quotations:

- 'I beheld a countenance of angelic beauty and expression' (Ch13)
- 'She was understood by, nor herself understood, by the cottagers' (Ch13)
- 'Lovely Arabian' (Ch14)
- 'She hesitated some time, but at length she formed her determination' (Ch14)

Safie's character is a useful plot device for Shelley (the Creature learns language from her and 'proves' his story via her letters), but her character also provides further critique on the place and role of women. She is portrayed as being in need of rescuing (like Elizabeth and Caroline, although she is perhaps more resourceful), and is idealised as one who brings joy and hope (again, like Elizabeth). Interestingly, she is not able to communicate verbally with the family until she learns their language – an occurrence that surely prompts questions about what Shelley wishes to convey about the voices of women and their validity in the eyes of men.

PIT STOP ▼

S-T-R-E-T-C-H

The Creature's admiration of Safie parallels Victor's admiration of Elizabeth, perhaps a device used by Shelley to convey the similarities between the Creature and Victor. Shelley includes several examples of parallels between Victor and the Creature in this section. Finding them and discussing their intended meaning could prove a valuable activity for learners.

Structure 🖥

Chapter 11 ⊗

Opening: 'It is with considerable difficulty that I remember the original era of my being; all the events of that period appear confused and indistinct'

Ending: 'The family, after having been thus occupied for a short time, extinguished their lights and retired, as I conjectured, to rest'

This chapter focuses throughout on the early days of the Creature's life in a chronological way, and the opening and closing of the chapter almost summarise the progress of these days, reflecting a shift from early confusion to finding some kind of sense of security and satisfaction. On the other hand, however, they do little to reveal the complexities of the Creature's development and the eloquent parallels of Shelley's multiple narratives.

It is important to note the stages of the Creature's development, but also the increments by which Shelley builds his interactions with mankind. At first, the Creature, like a newborn, does not even realise that he is in a room with a human (Victor). However, as he begins to recognise more about his existence in the world, Shelley introduces increasing numbers of people: a fire left by some departed beggars, a single man and then a village of people. By increasing the Creature's interactions by degrees, Shelley cleverly increases the intensity of the Creature's rejection. Here, she creates great contrast, as, up to this point, readers only know of the Creature's violence towards mankind, and not the violence that he suffers *because* of mankind.

At the end of the chapter, when the Creature finds the 'family' near whose cottage he will live, Shelley subtly contrasts the beginning of the chapter, where he experiences abandonment by his 'father', and cleverly hints that companionship is all that the Creature needs in order to be able to 'rest'.

Contrasting narratives

This chapter opens on a night already portrayed from Victor's perspective: one of horror and abject disgust. Victor's narrative is one that is driven by the knowledge that he is not the only living being in the room. In stark contrast, the Creature's perspective is one of perceived solitude. Interestingly, both perspectives contain fear and confusion. When Shelley shares the Creature's perspective on the 'dreary night', readers might ask: If the Creature is harmless, what is Victor so afraid of? This serves to sharpens Shelley's critique of Victor, and highlights his absolute prejudice based on physical appearance and his lack of consideration for the results of an experiment that he did not have the courage to face.

Chapter 12

Opening: 'I lay on my straw, but I could not sleep. I thought of the occurrences of the day. What chiefly struck me was the gentle manners of these people, and I longed to join them, but dared not'

Ending: 'the present was tranquil, and the future gilded by bright rays of hope and anticipations of joy'

There is little movement or action in this chapter; instead, it is dominated by admiration of the De Lacey family, and the Creature's maturation and learning as he begins to talk and learn language, and explores his own abilities. These are important, as Shelley utilises them in later chapters. Shelley also increasingly intertwines the Creature and the De Laceys: his feelings align with theirs; he stops stealing their food when he recognises that this leaves them hungry, he helps with their chores and he is even given a loose name of 'good spirit' by them (the closest to having a name that he will get in the novel).

Shelley punctuates the chapter with instances of the Creature's realisation of his difference from the family. The most important of these is in the central part of the chapter, when the Creature mentions how he admires the family's 'grace, beauty and delicate complexions', but is 'terrified' when he sees himself in a pool (Ch12). Shelley then includes a cataphoric reference to the coming events of the novel, when the Creature shares, 'Alas! I did not yet entirely know the fatal effects of this miserable deformity' (Ch12). These small cataphoric references (referring to events that appear later in the text) almost act to disrupt the readers' submersion in the Creature's narrative, and remind them that while the Creature appears to be increasingly integrating his life with that of the De Laceys, his fate remains as readers have seen: that of an unhappy murderer.

Chapter 13

Opening: 'I now hasten to the more moving part of my story'

Ending: 'allow me now to return to the cottagers, whose story excited in me such various feelings of indignation, delight, and wonder, but which all terminated in additional love and reverence for my protectors (for so I loved, in an innocent, half-painful self-deceit, to call them)'

In Chapter 13, Shelley shifts her tone and hints at what is to come. The first key shift in tone is Safie's entrance in springtime, which changes the tone of the Creature's descriptions of the cottage and also triggers the start of the Creature's education. Here, he crosses a threshold and becomes a being much more aware of the world and now able to be a part of it.

Halfway through the chapter, Shelley includes a pivotal moment in the novel, as she shifts the focus of her writing away from the family's new-found happiness onto the Creature's reflections on his learning about mankind and their virtues and vices. Here, Shelley provokes curious reflection in the Creature about his origins and his place in the world – a theme that will carry throughout the novel.

Cataphoric references and narrative bias

Shelley uses another cataphoric reference in this chapter: 'I will soon explain to what these feelings tended' (Ch13). This reminds readers again that the Creature's experiences will result in him murdering William (already shared in Victor's narrative). She also includes hints at his regret and longing for innocence, when the Creature describes that when he heard 'details of vice and bloodshed... [he] turned away with disgust and loathing' (Ch13). This contrasts the earlier portrayal that Victor provided of a creature whose instinct is to maim and kill.

Chapter 14

Opening: 'Some time elapsed before I learned the history of my friends'

Ending: 'the woman of the house in which they had lived took care that Safie should arrive in safety at the cottage of her lover'

This chapter differs from the others in the novel, as it focuses on a character other than its narrator. For this reason, and perhaps because it may be seen as superlative to an understanding of the main plot, teachers may be inclined to skip teaching it.

However, this chapter is structurally important, as it forms the central point of Shelley's concentric narratives: inside Walton's story lies Victor's tale, in which exists the Creature's tale and, at – approximately – the central point of the Creature's tale, is the tale of the De Laceys and Safie. Joyce Zoanna (1991) argues that it is Safie's letters that form the 'thematic and narrative centre of the novel'. This is interesting to note, especially as many teachers may skip Safie's narrative, seeing it as a diversion from Shelley's main plot. Furthermore, Shelley never provides the full details of Safie's story; it exists in her letters, which, copied by the Creature, pass to Victor and, eventually, Walton.

PIT STOP ▼

S-T-R-E-T-C-H

Safie's story has much in common with other stories in the novel, as, like the other female characters, her story is shared by a male voice, who relays it to another man. Shelley diminishes the role of Safie's narrative even more, as the letters from Safie that 'prove' the Creature's narrative are not only not shared with the reader but are also not even written by Safie herself, but by an old male servant of her father.

When exploring this, teachers may ask learners to discuss what Shelley may be reflecting about the voices and narratives of women, and who shapes and tells those narratives.

Extracts

Extract 1 (Ch11): How does Shelley use language to show the innocence and vulnerability of the Creature?

> '*I was still cold when under one of the trees I found a huge cloak, with which I covered myself, and sat down upon the ground. No distinct ideas occupied my mind; all was confused. I felt light, and hunger, and thirst, and darkness; innumerable sounds rang in my ears, and on all sides various scents saluted me; the only object that I could distinguish was the bright moon, and I fixed my eyes on that with pleasure.*'

In this extract, Shelley conveys the innocence of the Creature through his sense of awe in simple things – in particular, the moon. She writes that the Creature 'fixed his eyes' on it, which reflects his childlike amazement at things of which adults might be dismissive. His innocence is also revealed by his lack of thought and how 'all was confused' for him, suggesting that he doesn't understand things and can't make sense of them, just like a small child. Another way in which Shelley shows the Creature's innocence is by highlighting his vulnerability, as he is unable to help himself. He states, 'I felt light, and hunger, and thirst, and darkness', but instead of doing anything about these, he simply stares at the moon. By using a list, Shelley emphasises the Creature's vulnerability, as there are so many things that he feels that could lead him to become unwell.

Extract 2 (Ch12): How does Shelley use language to show the Creature's joy in Chapter 12?

'The pleasant showers and genial warmth of spring greatly altered the aspect of the earth... Happy, happy earth! Fit habitation for gods, which, so short a time before, was bleak, damp, and unwholesome. My spirits were elevated by the enchanting appearance of nature; the past was blotted from my memory, the present was tranquil, and the future gilded by bright rays of hope and anticipations of joy.'

In this extract, Shelley presents the Creature's joyful nature through positive descriptions of nature and several words related to happiness. Adjectives such as 'pleasant', 'genial' and 'tranquil' have clear connotations of happiness and joy, and suggest that the Creature is overwhelmingly happy and positive at this point in the novel. This is reinforced with the Creature's exclamative 'Happy, happy earth!', where Shelley's repetition of 'happy' emphasises his joy at finding earth restored to springtime. This is further emphasised by the exclamation mark, which suggests that the Creature is, like the leaves on the trees, bursting. Shelley builds on this sense of joy even further with the phrase 'Fit habitation of gods', which suggests that the Creature finds the environment in which he finds himself to be heavenly and suited for gods and angels. This in turn suggests that he feels that there is no better place on the planet, which reflects his utter delight in his current location.

Chapter 13: How does Shelley use language to convey the Creature's loneliness?

'But where were my friends and relations? No father had watched my infant days, no mother had blessed me with smiles and caresses; or if they had, all my past life was now a blot, a blind vacancy in which I distinguished nothing. From my earliest remembrance I had been as I then was in height and proportion. I had never yet seen a being resembling me or who claimed any intercourse with me. What was I? The question again recurred, to be answered only with groans.'

In this extract, Shelley creates a sense of the Creature's loneliness through her combination of questions and words related to not having something. In the opening of the extract, the question 'But where were my friends and relations?' reveals that the Creature has recognised the absence of these people and wishes others to consider this too. His repetition of the word 'no' before two separate examples of parents that he doesn't have also emphasises his loneliness, as it suggests that he is painfully aware of the intimate connections that he does not have. Shelley emphasises his lonely isolation even further when she has the Creature identify that he had 'never yet seen a being resembling [him] or who claimed any intercourse with me'. Here, the word 'never' highlights the clarity with which the Creature recognises his isolation and how distinct it is to him. His final question, 'What was I?', finally cements the readers' impressions of his lonely confusion, which is even further reinforced when this question is 'answered only with groans', as the Creature finds not only no one to answer him but also that he is unable to answer this for himself.

SECTION 8
LEARNING TO MAKE MISCHIEF (CHAPTERS 15–16)

At a glance

> **Summary quotation:** 'I am alone and miserable; man will not associate with me; but one as deformed and horrible as myself would not deny herself to me' (Ch16)

> **Big Question:** How does the Creature shift from benevolent to menacing?

> **Significant plot events**

Chapter 15:

- The Creature discovers a selection of books and reads them. He also reads Victor's lab notes and diary.

- The Creature decides that he will introduce himself to the De Laceys. He is anxious, but believes that they will welcome him. Initially, the father does.

- When the other De Laceys enter, they are horrified and beat the Creature, forcing him to flee.

Chapter 16:

- Dejected and furious, the Creature declares 'war' on mankind. He sets fire to the De Lacey cottage and sets out for Geneva to find Victor.

- He makes one last attempt at benevolence, but is rejected again.

- Near Geneva, the Creature meets young William Frankenstein and kills him. The Creature frames a young woman for the murder.

- Finally, the Creature reveals to Victor that he desires a mate.

> **Character focus:** the Creature

> **Key themes:**
- Family and companionship 👥
- Knowledge and discovery 🔍
- Death and grief ✝
- Revenge 🌸
- Power and responsibility 💡
- Rejection and its consequences ⊗

> **Handle with care:**

- These chapters contain several violent scenes, including the murder of a child.
- The Creature discusses a novel that features suicide.

Why?

- Why does the Creature hide and watch the De Laceys for so long?
- Why does the Creature finally introduce himself to the family?
- Why does Shelley have the Creature spend so long admiring the De Laceys?
- Why does the Creature seek revenge?

What?

What happens?

Chapter 15

In this chapter, the Creature evolves from a benevolent and innocent being to a knowledgeable but murderous monster. He shares the books that he has read and what he learned from them, and also shares that he has read Victor's notebook and is aware of his conscious creation and rejection. He has intense doubts but believes that he will be accepted by the De Laceys, and spends several months preparing himself for an introduction to them.

Initially, this introduction seems positive, as the Creature talks with the blind father under the guise of being a weary traveller. However, at the moment at which he reveals himself, Felix, Agatha and Safie enter. Shocked into terror and violence, the Creature is beaten and forced to flee the family that he has loved and admired for so long.

Chapter 16

Initially, the Creature is furious, so curses his creator for his existence and swears war on mankind. However, in the morning, he feels calmer and reflects that he needed to spend more time preparing the family for him. He returns to the cottage and sees that the cottagers are gone. He hears Felix tell the landlord that the family are in 'the greatest danger' so must leave immediately. In revenge, the Creature sets the cottage ablaze.

Now lacking purpose, the Creature heads for Geneva, hoping that Victor might take pity on him. His journey is difficult and takes many months, during which he tries to avoid mankind. When spring arrives, he crosses paths with a young couple and tries to save the woman after she falls into the river. Her partner is terrified, frantically pulls the girl away and flees. The Creature is 'inflamed by pain' and so once again vows 'eternal hatred' on mankind.

His hatred subsides over the coming weeks as he reaches Geneva. In a final attempt to bond with mankind, he approaches a 'beautiful child' in a bid to 'educate him as [his] companion'. However, when he learns that the child is the son of Frankenstein, he kills him. Having crossed a key threshold, he then frames a young woman for the murder, not because she *has* rejected him but because she *could*. Finally, the Creature talks directly to Victor to demand that Victor create a new creature for him – one of the 'same species' with the 'same defects' so that he is no longer alone.

Social and historical context

Historical context: The Creature's reading and its resonance

The idea that the Creature learns to read is one of wild improbability, and even Sir Walter Scott (in Bennett, 1999) commented on how deeply unlikely this was. However, like many other elements of the novel, this is one that readers must simply embrace and accept, as it is much more fruitful to explore the works and their meaning than the probability of the Creature being able to read them.

Shelley's choice of texts is one that has been written about in many ways by many critics. A summary of some of these texts and their key meaning to the Creature can be found below:

Milton's Paradise Lost (1667)

This is an epic poem about Adam and Eve's expulsion from the Garden of Eden and Satan's desire to disrupt mankind as an act of revenge on God. Blake republished the poem in 1807, making it popular with Romantic poets, which is likely how Shelley came to know it. With themes of rejection, the parallels with the Creature are clear, and it also contains themes of love and companionship, as well as of the 'fall' from acceptance after sin. Notably, not only is the Creature rejected *before* he commits any sins, but he also realises that even Satan 'had his companions, fellow devils, to admire and encourage him' (Ch15), whereas he is desperately solitary.

The Sorrows of Young Werther (von Goethe, 1774)

The Creature remarks that this book is 'simple and affecting', while also finding it a 'never-ending source of speculation and astonishment' (Ch15). The novel is an early example of Romanticism in literature and a staple of the German cannon. The story follows a young, artistic, middle-class man, who is charmed by country life and falls in love with a woman, Charlotte, whom he cannot have. After many trials and quiet rejections, he commits suicide, seeing his death as a sacrifice for her. The Creature 'wept, without precisely understanding' (Ch15) at this, a sign that his feelings resonated with that of the yearning, lonely Werther.

Plutarch's Lives (1470)

This work is a collection of biographies of 'great men' of ancient Greece and Rome, mostly historical, but some mythical. Arranged into pairs, Plutarch marries his chosen subjects for their common or contrasting moral virtues and failings. Like the book's pairings, Victor's virtues (his intelligence and determination) result in his vices: rejection and a lack of responsibility. Similarly, much like Plutarch's pairings, Victor and the Creature live parallel lives and are inescapably connected, living their narratives side by side and intertwined.

Historical context: Innocence and experience 🔍

Shelley was born at a time when great debates took place about what it was to be human and what the origins of mankind's corruption might be. Reflecting this, Romantic writers often featured children in their works to explore the nature of children and society's influence on them. This marked them as distinct from key Enlightenment figures before them, such as John Locke (1689), who suggested that children were neither sinful nor angelic, but were born as 'tabula rasa' (blank slates), who could be moulded and shaped by their education. Often, the Romantics idealised childhood as a time when human beings are at their most pure and as God intended. The theme of society corrupting children is explored heavily in Gothic and Romantic literature, and is present elsewhere in school curricula: Stevenson's *The Strange Case of Dr Jekyll and Mr Hyde*, Blake's poetry and even *Blood Brothers* explore similar ideas.

In this section of *Frankenstein*, Shelley explores the idea by portraying the Creature's evolution from a benevolent and innocent being to a knowledgeable but murderous monster. In many ways, Shelley presents us with a creature who follows Rousseau's concept of 'the child of nature' (Carpentier, 2020), who is essentially good and pure, and for whom civilisation is a damaging and corrupting force. Rousseau believes that the early days of mankind were a golden age when man was happy and free, and that it was with the advent of societies that mankind developed the traits of pride, jealousy and other vices. The Creature's contentment and resourcefulness in nature, and the cessation of this upon his introduction to society through literature, is a clear marker of Rousseau's influence on Shelley.

Literary context: What it is to be a monster

With her Creature, Shelley contributes to a vast literary history of creating 'monsters'. In many ways, she borrows archetypes formed thousands of years ago when creating her Creature but, in doing so, is able to subvert expectations and challenge what it is to be a monster. In order to explore how she does this, it is important for learners to recognise the archetypes of literary monsters with which Shelley plays and how she subverts these.

Traditional monsters

Like many traditional monsters, the Creature's physical form is one of abnormal assimilation and unusual traits, which surpass those of mankind. Chris Baldick (2011) notes that 'it is an almost obligatory feature of the monsters in classical mythology that they should be composed of ill-assorted parts, sometimes combined from different creatures'. Examples of this include the sphinx, the Minotaur and other ancient beasts. In this sense, the Creature has always been a 'monster'. Rather than having been born this way due to divine meddling, Shelley's Creature exists because of science – an act that she acknowledges in her alternative title, 'The Modern Prometheus'. Victor's fear of the Creature, despite him being a consciously constructed being, highlights Victor's lack of sympathy for his Creature.

Another aspect that frames the Creature as a monster is his power, both in body and in speech. Wallace and Smith (2009, p. 85) argue that Shelley's Creature follows a typically medieval tradition of monsters that hold a 'power and strangeness [that] point to and reveal (from *monstrare* – the Latin verb meaning "to show") the power and freedom of God'. In this vein, it is not only the Creature's physical capabilities and prowess that reflect his power, but his very existence is also a physical reflection of the power and wisdom (or, at least, capability) of his creator.

It is, of course, not enough for a monster just to be deformed in body and powerful; a true monster must be deformed in mind and use their power against others. Monsters such as Beelzebub and Satan are vengeful fiends who wish ill to others, and it is with this trait that Shelley plays in this section of the novel. Challenging mythical beasts who are tortured and torturous by birth or fate, it is the actions of mankind that provide motive for the monstrous descent of Shelley's Creature.

Shelley's subversion

In popular culture, the above ideas are those that have proved more powerful: the deformed and deranged monster who wishes to wreak vengeance on those who have harmed him. However, in making her Creature the more eloquent of her two central characters, Shelley is able to challenge her readers' – and Victor's – prejudices. Peter Brooks (1993) argues that, verbally, the Creature is 'the very opposite of monstrous' and is instead 'a sympathetic and persuasive participant in Western culture', which highlights that the Creature was not necessarily born to be a 'monster' but that society has made him so.

Vocabulary in context

Word	Quotation	Definition
virtue	'I felt the greatest ardour for virtue rise within me, and abhorrence for vice' (Ch15)	a good moral quality in a person or the general quality of being morally good
vice		a moral fault or weakness in someone's character; illegal and immoral activities
abhorrence		a feeling of hating something or someone
endured	'My travels were long and the sufferings I endured intense' (Ch16)	to suffer something difficult, unpleasant or painful
desolation	'I too can create desolation' (Ch16)	the state of a place that is empty or where everything has been destroyed

PIT STOP ⊕ ▼

Vocabulary builder

Many of these words can be applied to other events or characters within the novel. As a starter or retrieval activity, ask learners to use these words when discussing or writing about these other parts. For example:

- Walton and his crew endure difficult weather on their travels.
- Caroline Frankenstein is known for her benevolence.
- Victor brings the Creature to life during a tumultuous storm.

Plot and character development

1. What are the books that the Creature reads? What is their significance? 🔍

The Creature listens to and reads a number of books. These include:

- Milton's *Paradise Lost*
- *Plutarch's Lives*
- Von Goethe's *The Sorrows of Young Werther.*

The Creature has mixed feelings about these books. He says that 'The possession of these treasures gave me extreme delight' and that 'they produced in me an infinity of new images and feelings, that sometimes raised me to ecstasy, but more frequently sunk me into the lowest dejection' (Ch15).

The books allow a broader and deeper introduction to man than the Creature's first interactions, as he is exposed to texts that explore the contrasts in the achievements of mankind: great empires and art but also incredible suffering and conflict. This new knowledge heavily influences the Creature's thinking, and he evaluates his place and purpose. He questions, 'Who was I? What was I? Whence did I come? What was my destination?' and notes that while these questions 'continually reoccurred', he is 'unable to solve them' (Ch12), like a child requiring adult guidance and reassurance. Unlike Victor, who was given careful guidance and tuition when his self-created curriculum led him down the wrong path, the Creature has no parental or educational guidance, and so is left delighted but lost.

2. To whom is the Creature's narrative addressed? Who writes it?

This part of the narrative is a recording of what the Creature says to Victor Frankenstein when they meet in Geneva. This is the first time that they have seen each other since the night on which Victor brought the Creature to life. The Creature only directly refers to Victor once, when he mentions reading Victor's notes.

PIT STOP ▼

S-T-R-E-T-C-H

In the Creature's narrative, Shelley captures Victor's recalling of the Creature's tale, which he tells to Walton, which is then captured in Walton's writings to his sister. The readers also know that Victor's broken state has been brought about by the Creature, and that Walton is an admirer of Victor. Given this, it is worth asking learners to consider three questions:

- How reliable do we consider this narrative to be?

- What reason for bias might each narrator have?

- What does Shelley want us to feel about the Creature?

---

3. What impact does reading Victor's notes have on the Creature?

The Creature studies Victor's notes 'with diligence' (Ch15) and finds that they contain every detail of his creation (it is interesting to note at this point that the Creature describes himself to Victor as 'odious and loathsome' (Ch15). It is clear that he feels strong emotions about these, as he describes the 'circumstances' around his creation as 'disgusting' and notes that he 'sickened as [he] read' (Ch15). He also questions Victor directly, asking, 'why did you create a monster so hideous that even *you* turned from me in disgust?' (Ch15).

Perhaps most importantly for the plot, the reading of Victor's notebook provides the Creature with knowledge of his creator and, as a result, a focus for his anger and blame. As a device to impart knowledge and initiate a quest for vengeance, the reading of the notebook is arguably a key moment in the text.

4. What does the DeLaceys' rejection of the Creature reveal about them? How does the Creature respond? ⊗

The Creature sees the De Laceys as his saviours: a family that will welcome him despite his appearance and superhuman stature. Shelley cleverly blinds the patriarch of the family, freeing him from visual prejudice. In doing so, Shelley allows her Creature to be welcomed and to experience the 'first... voice of kindness directed towards me' (Ch15). Here, Shelley offers a glimpse of what the Creature's life could have been, and he is thankful and open to this.

However, Felix's response is aggressive rejection with 'supernatural force' (Ch15), which Benedetti suggests 'highlights the unnatural, inhumane nature of [Felix's] actions' (Benedetti, 2020, p. 4). Felix's actions seem even more violent because the Creature takes flight rather than fight back, despite being much stronger.

Confused and hurt, the Creature's initial response is typical for one who has been rejected: he questioned his existence, 'gave vent to [his] anguish in fearful howlings', (Ch16) vowed revenge against those who had hurt him and exhausted himself. We could interpret feeling such typical responses as highlighting the vulnerable and very human nature of the Creature at this point in the novel, a necessary characteristic for Shelley's demonstration of the corrupting force of society.

5. What events change the Creature's disposition?

There is not one single event that changes the Creature's disposition from naively hopeful to aggressively vicious. We could list them as follows:

- The Creature is rejected and abandoned by Victor at the moment of his 'birth'.
- The Creature is rejected by villagers when he is wandering around, trying to find a home.
- The Creature learns that mankind can be cruel.
- The Creature learns that he is the only one of his kind.
- The Creature is beaten by Felix.
- The Creature overhears Felix refusing to return to the cottage, as he fears that the Creature will return and cause them harm.
- The Creature tries to save a woman's life, but his good deed is mistaken for malice.
- The Creature is rejected by William.

PIT STOP ▼

An interesting point of discussion for learners would be which of these events they feel has the most impact on the Creature, and whether the Creature would not have become the way that he is were it for a different combination of events.

- Which of these events has the most impact on the Creature?
- Which event is the 'straw that breaks the camel's back'?
- Is Victor's abandonment of the Creature an event from which Shelley suggests that he cannot recover?
- Why do you think that Shelley chose to provide us with so many examples of the Creature experiencing rejection?

6. What is the significance of the Creature framing Justine?

We could argue that the murder of young William is the event that transforms the Creature into a monster. However, it could also be argued that the stealing and placement of the portrait is a more significant indicator of malice. Where the destruction of the De Lacey's cottage and the killing of William are motivated by intense rejection and hurt, the framing of Justine is more calculated: the Creature frames her because '[he is] for ever robbed of all she could give [him]' (Ch16), and he thus decides that she will suffer. It is this act of attacking before being rejected that marks his transgression into a life of revenge.

PIT STOP ▼

S-T-R-E-T-C-H
Why doesn't Shelley give her Creature a name?

Shelley has already introduced her readers to the Creature from Victor's perspective. In doing so, she has provided readers with a physical description of his grotesque and hideous appearance and his impressive stature. We have not, however, been given a name for him. Now in the hands of the Creature, Shelley still does not provide readers with a name for Victor's Creature. If we consider a name to be a sign of care, community and acceptance (as names are only required for interaction with others), the Creature's lack of a name is a clear reflection of society and of Victor's rejection of the Creature.

How?

Language

Negative adjectives

Key quotations:

- 'Everything is related in them which bears reference to my accursed origin'

- 'disgusting circumstances' (Ch15)

- 'my odious and loathsome person is given, in language which painted your own horrors and rendered mine indelible' (Ch16)

In Chapter 15, the Creature first shares the feelings that he holds for Victor and for his origins. In their negativity, they contrast his confused but largely admiring words about mankind. This is also the first time that the Creature is negative about himself.

Initially, Shelley has the Creature talk in a very objective and factual manner, reporting that the notes are filled with Victor's 'minutely described' preparations and experiments, which are 'mingled with accounts of domestic occurrences' (Ch15). Here, perhaps, Shelley hints at the Creature's interpretation that his creation was insignificant and mundane. His feeling are more clear when he describes 'the whole of that series of disgusting circumstances' that led to the creation of his 'odious and loathsome person' (Ch15). The power of these adjectives highlights the Creature's dislike of himself. This is reinforced when he describes that the notebook's passages 'painted [Victor's] own horrors and rendered mine indelible' (Ch15). The word 'indelible' reflects the depth and perceived permanence of the Creature's suffering, while Shelley provides the Creature with no comment on his longevity or the severity of Victor's 'horrors'. In doing so, Shelley hints at the pain of the inescapable ostracism that the Creature faces, while simultaneously indicating that the Creature ascribes the blame for this to Victor, planting a seed that is necessary for readers to fully grasp the depth of the Creature's hatred of Victor portrayed in Chapter 17.

Language to convey strong emotions

Key quotations:

- 'I gave vent to my anguish in fearful howlings' (Ch16)

- 'I was like a wild beast that had broken the toils, destroying the objects that obstructed me and ranging through the wood with a stag-like swiftness' (Ch16)

Throughout Chapter 16, Shelley portrays the Creature's pain and anger towards mankind as wild and uncontrollable, but later evolves these into contrived and menacing acts of revenge. In the first part of the chapter, Shelley uses words associated with animalistic and raw pain: 'fearful howlings', 'anguish', 'trembled violently' and 'a gush of tears'. These emphasise that here the Creature has little control over his emotions, and suggest that he is almost at the mercy of them. Initially, this pain is not directed at mankind. Instead, he wishes to 'tear up the trees… and then to have sat down and enjoyed the rain' (Ch16), suggesting that it is release from rejection that the Creature desires, rather than revenge. This anger is inconsistent and frantic, like the unmediated emotions of a child who has not yet learned to regulate their emotions and simply wishes to feel better. This is emphasised by Shelley's use of words that reveal his more timid and apprehensive side: 'soothed', 'crept' and 'waited anxiously' (Ch16).

Later in Chapter 16, Shelley's use of language changes as she portrays the erosive impact of the Creature's repeated exposure to rejection. As the year matures through summer, autumn and winter, the Creature matures too, moving from frantic child-like emotions to the focused and deliberate desires of an adult, whose anger has become part of their identity. The Creature states that his 'daily vows rose for revenge – a deep and deadly revenge' (Ch16). Here, the words 'deep and deadly' emphasise the intensity of his hatred, and the mention that they are 'daily vows' reveals the intention and almost religious observance of anger. Even the Creature's longing for William is intense and possessive: the word 'seize' appears twice in a short passage, in 'an idea seized me' and 'if I could seize [William]' (Ch16). In contrast to a word such as 'grab' or 'kidnap', the verb 'seize' has connotations of conscious and malicious choice and emphasises the strength of the Creature's malicious intentions.

Character focus

The Creature

Key quotations:

• 'As yet, I looked upon crime as a distant evil' (Ch15)

'I felt the greatest ardour for virtue rise with me, and abhorrence for vice' (Ch15)

'inflamed by pain, I vowed eternal hatred and vengeance to all mankind' (Ch16)

'I am alone and miserable; man will not associate with me, but one as deformed and horrible as myself would not deny herself to me' (Ch16)

This is arguably the section where the Creature's character develops the most, as he effectively comes of age. Shelley reveals his story through the different influences on him and their impact on his emotions and behaviour. In Chapter 15, he is exposed to sophisticated ideas and concepts that deepen and broaden his understanding of life, but he is still naive and childlike in his ambition to win over the De Laceys. Combined with the physical prowess and generous spirit that he has already displayed, the Creature's clear intelligence, diligence and openness to learn suggest that he would be a valuable companion.

However, instead of his benevolent potential being realised, he instead descends into bitter brutality. The repeated rejections through these chapters ensure that there is little chance that the Creature will be socialised in any behaviour beyond aggression, and we see his building resentment and lust for revenge build in bold fits and starts. Despite this, Shelley maintains an element of sympathy for her Creature, in that after seeing such callous actions against William and Justine, she has the Creature reveal his utter misery and loneliness to Victor. His call for a mate reveals that his nature is not that of a destroyer but that of someone who simply longs to feel mutual affection: a trait that renders him undeniably 'human'.

The De Lacey Family

Key quotations:

- 'They did not appear rich, but they were contented and happy' (Ch15)
- 'The hearts of men, when unprejudiced by any obvious self-interest, are full of brotherly love and charity' (Ch15)
- 'Felix darted forward, and with supernatural force tore me from his father' (Ch15)

In this section, the De Lacey family develops into embodiments of the ideas about which the Creature has read in his books. They feature little in Chapter 15, but their reactions to the Creature are important in both his development and Shelley's portrayal of mankind's responses to the Creature. In Felix and his father, Shelley provides us an echo of the key concepts of which the Creature has learned: that mankind can be virtuous but also cruel. The father of the family represents the virtue of those who act without prejudice and whose open heart we are led to admire. In contrast, Felix's brutality against the Creature highlights the worst of mankind, as his actions are prompted by prejudice and fear.

Structure

Chapter 15

Opening: 'Such was the history of my beloved cottagers'

Ending: 'I saw him on the point of repeating his blow, when, overcome by pain and anguish, I quitted the cottage, and in the general tumult escaped unperceived to my hovel'

Chapter 15 is effectively split into three separate sections. Each of these has a different impact on the Creature's development, and they are sequenced to support this.

Section 1

Shelley focuses on the books that the Creature reads and the Creature's expanding understanding of the world beyond the De Laceys. This shifts the Creature's views, as he sees the family as representations of wider mankind rather than a single family unit.

Section 2

The central part of the chapter is focused on the Creature's preparation and intentions to introduce himself to the family – his attempt to forge a place in the world.

Section 3

The Creature introduces himself to the De Laceys, which, in the final paragraph, results in a sudden violent rejection. As with several other chapters, this marks a threshold from which Shelley's characters cannot return. Despite being welcomed by the father, the horrified rejection of the Creature by the younger members of the family is a sharp shift, both in tone and also in the Creature's prospects, as his position as 'monster' becomes instantly concrete to him.

Chapter 16

Opening: 'Cursed, cursed creator! Why did I live?'

Ending: 'My companion must be of the same species and have the same defects. This being you must create.'

In this chapter, Shelley passes rapidly through time, place and emotion, as the Creature reaches the irrevocable change in his temperament that leads to the murder of William, and Shelley cements this beyond doubt with the framing of Justine. As such, these two quotations summarise this chapter succinctly.

Here, Shelley uses her structure to provide an impression of a creature who is wrestling with his nature, demonstrated in the central part of the chapter, as he attempts to rescue a young woman from drowning. However, both he and the readers learn that the prejudice against him is inescapable, from strangers (as in Chapter 11), from those who live near him (the De Laceys) and even from those who benefit from his actions (the De Laceys and the young couple). In bookending her chapter with the Creature alone and miserable, she envelops her Creature's experience in isolation and misery too.

Trials and tribulations

Like any bildungsroman (as explained earlier in this book, page 21) in which a young, naive character builds an understanding of the moral aspects of the world and their place in it through various trials, so too does the Creature.

It is notable that the Creature is rejected several times in several ways and goes back and forth in his feelings for mankind, as he makes several attempts to forge connections with them before finally rejecting them back. Here, Shelley suggests that ill meaning is not formed in the way in which Milton or other writers suggest, through immoral weakness or a single catastrophic moment, but through repeated exposures to inhumanity that are corrosive and lead to moral deprivation.

Without this collection of rejections, Shelley may have left readers wondering whether the Creature had an innate bias towards malice, but in offering so many examples of rejection, she solidifies for us the origin of his transgressions and bitterness, as he learns to echo the behaviours that he has experienced at the hands of man.

Extracts

Extract 1 (Ch15): How does the Creature feel about himself?

'And what was I? Of my creation and creator I was absolutely ignorant, but I knew that I possessed no money, no friends, no kind of property. I was, besides, endued with a figure hideously deformed and loathsome; I was not even of the same nature as man. I was more agile than they and could subsist upon coarser diet; I bore the extremes of heat and cold with less injury to my frame; my stature far exceeded theirs. When I looked around I saw and heard of none like me. Was I, then, a monster, a blot upon the earth, from which all men fled and whom all men disowned?'

Here, the Creature questions himself but also his worth in greater society. His readings have taught him that a man's worth is shaped by their status, property and social circle, which highlights to him the things that he lacks, emphasised by the repetition of 'no'. He also notes that he is 'not even of the same nature as man', displaying his self-awareness. Shelley reveals the Creature's confusion about his worth as he lists the assets that he has – agility, strength, resilience, adaptability and fortitude – but notes that rather than making him someone to be admired or praised, they instead make him an uncanny foreigner. Notably, this is the second time at which the Creature refers to himself as a 'monster', a suggestion that he is beginning to associate his difference with negativity and perceiving that instead of being the kind creature that he feels himself to be, he may actually be one destined to cause harm.

Extract 2 (Ch16): How does Shelley convey the changing power dynamic between the Creature and Victor?

> *'We may not part until you have promised to comply with my requisition. I am alone and miserable; man will not associate with me; but one as deformed and horrible as myself would not deny herself to me. My companion must be of the same species and have the same defects. This being you must create.'*

This extract marks a shift in the relationship between the Creature and Victor: no longer is Victor the authority figure, who can choose to run from or stay with his Creature. Instead, it is the Creature who now dictates that; despite Victor's attempt to sever his ties to the Creature, they are bound together. Here, Shelley demonstrates that in terms of understanding and managing human relationships, the Creature is actually more adept than his creator. Furthermore, where Victor has done little but forge his own path and remove himself from people, the Creature is his opposite in longing for companionship.

PIT STOP ▼

S-T-R-E-T-C-H

For those learners who have understood the objectification of Elizabeth, the Creature's perceptions of his future relationship with a mate are an interesting point of discussion. Shelley portrays Victor's possession of Elizabeth without noting her consent. Similarly, the Creature assumes that any creature created for him would instantly be his.

SECTION 9
THE SIGNIFICANCE OF THE MATE (CHAPTER 17)

At a glance

> **Summary quotation:** 'This you alone can do, and I demand it of you as a right for which you must not refuse to concede' (Ch17)

> **Big Questions:** What is the significance of the mate? How does this chapter change our views of Victor and the Creature?

> **Significant plot events:**

- The Creature continues to explain that if he had a mate, he would be content and no longer angry.

- Eventually, Victor agrees and the Creature leaves him, saying that he will return when the mate is created.

> **Character focus:** the Creature, Victor

> **Key themes:**

- Family and companionship 🖣
- Isolation and loneliness 🖣
- Power and responsibility 🖣
- Revenge 🖣
- Prejudice 🖣
- Narrator and narration **N**

Why?

- Why does the Creature want a mate?
- Why is Victor so torn about whether to create one?
- Why does Victor concede?
- Why does Shelley hand the narrative back to Victor at this point?

What?

What happens?

The narration is passed back to Victor, who relays the Creature's detailed explanations of his reasons for wanting a mate, emphasising how lonely and miserable he is and Victor's part in this. Victor's response to this wavers from anger to sympathy to disgust.

Eventually, Victor accepts that he is responsible for the Creature and also owes protection to mankind, so he vows to meet the Creature's request. At this, the Creature makes another final promise to uphold his end of the deal: a permanent exile from mankind. After telling Victor that he will watch over him, the Creature leaves. Victor follows him down the mountain, as night approaches and he realises the gravity of the bargain that he has made. Upon returning to his family in Geneva, he closes the chapter by expressing the weight that he feels about the 'abhorrent task' that he must undertake.

Social and historical context 🔅

Social context: Parental responsibilities 🔆

In 1818, when Shelley (then Godwin) published her first edition of *Frankenstein*, she had already held a number of roles in relation to parenting: daughter, motherless child, stepdaughter, mother of a living child and grieving mother. None of these roles had been easy. Her relationship with her father was often contrary and contradictory, and she felt enormous guilt for the death of her mother. She was deeply anxious about pregnancy, and understood 'how grief and guilt could torture a bereaved mother' (Gordon, 2015, p. 52). It is clear that Shelley had a sharp understanding of the concept of parental responsibilities and their impact.

Anne K. Mellor argues that *Frankenstein* reveals Shelley's fears about becoming a mother: 'What if my child is born deformed, a freak,... a "hideous" thing? Could I still love it, or would I be horrified and wish it were dead again?' (1988, p. 46) Mellor's interpretation resonates distinctly with the ideas in Chapter 17: can Victor be responsible to (and for) his creation despite its hideous appearance? Can he be a 'good' father?

As Shelley continues to explore the consequences of neglectful parenting for a child, the promise made in this chapter (which will, eventually, be violently destroyed) serves to highlight further the significance of sustained and consistent parental relationships and responsibilities.

PIT STOP ▼

Parenting and parental responsibility is a key theme throughout the novel, and one that is very specifically related to Shelley's biography. To support learners to develop their thinking around this theme (which can be a more abstract and demanding one), teachers may choose to use the following retrieval/development questions: ☁

- Who are the 'parent' figures in the novel? What are they like?

- What role do the different parent figures play? How do these differ?

- Which ones does Shelley use as examples (if any) or warnings?

- What impression of parenthood does Shelley perhaps wish to leave her readers with?

Literary context: 'The other' 🧑

In this chapter, Victor's revulsion at the Creature's physical appearance solidifies the Creature as a true 'other', a key feature of Gothic literature. Bienstock Anolik summarises that, 'traditionally, the Gothic represents the fearful unknown as the inhuman Other: the supernatural or monstrous manifestation' that 'symbolises all that is irrational, uncontrollable and incomprehensible' (2004, p. 1). Post-colonial critics have explored this in depth, particularly in relation to Orientalism (as explored earlier, page 115).

There are two angles from which to explore the Creature's 'othering': Shelley's presentation of the Creature as an 'other' and what Shelley intended to achieve through this.

The Creature is 'othered' through his physical characteristics: he is huge, strong and – Pinyerd suggests – has features often depicted on oriental figures: 'yellow' skin and dark hair (Pinyerd, 2016, p. 55). Shelley also frequently uses animal-related descriptions of his reactions and expressions.

In terms of what Shelley wishes to achieve through this othering, Malchow (1993) offers that the Creature serves to highlight the prejudice and wrongdoing suffered by those who are othered. Shelley leaves her readers in no doubt that had the Creature not been exposed so heavily to prejudice based on his physical appearance, his interactions with the world would have been vastly different. Indeed, while the Creature acknowledges his position as 'other' as early as Chapter 12 in the novel, it is only the repeated confirmation of this by mankind that leads him to develop the 'monstrous' side that he is suspected so strongly of having.

As such, by associating her Creature with physical characteristics of other races, Shelley evokes sentiments that align with her more explicitly political Romantic contemporaries, who championed a wider recognition of the humanity of 'other' races, not least in their drive towards the abolition of enslavement.

PIT STOP 👥

This is one of several examples of prejudice in the novel. In this case, Victor cannot move beyond the physical prejudice that he holds against the Creature. However, this is not the only case of prejudice in the novel. Key questions to support pupils in building understanding of this might be:

Which characters are prejudiced against? Why?

- What impact does this prejudice have on the characters' lives and/or actions?

- What might Shelley want readers to do, think or feel as a result of reading her novel?

- How does this relate to the key themes of Romantic writing?

Vocabulary in context

Word	Quotation	Definition
malicious	'I am malicious because I am miserable'	intended to harm or upset someone
passion	'This passion is detrimental to me'	a very powerful feeling

Plot and character development

1. What is decided at the end of the chapter? Why? Do we trust this decision? ☀

After much indecisiveness, Victor eventually vows to create a female mate for his Creature. When with the Creature, he suggests that this is because he owes the Creature a partner to save him from misery, but he later implies that his reason is the protection of his family. Through this contrast, Shelley emphasises again how much Victor has rejected the Creature, as even this act is not really for the Creature's benefit but for the benefit of Victor's preferred family.

Shelley reveals Victor's conflicted feelings on this through his internal thoughts and his dialogue with the Creature. Interestingly, as soon as Victor agrees, the Creature states that he will watch over Victor and then immediately leaves, implying that he fears another change in Victor's conviction. Victor also seems unsettled and unsure about his decision, stating that his 'sensations... weighed on [him] with a mountain's weight', suggesting that even contemplating the task has taken a toll on him.

S-T-R-E-T-C-H

Wallace and Smith argue that 'Victor's reconsideration of his promise to his creature in [Chapter 17] seems decidedly uncharacteristic given his past history' (2009, p. 197). A level learners may be invited to consider Victor's motivations and discuss the extent to which they agree with this interpretation.

2. Who does the Creature blame for his unhappiness?

The Creature undoubtedly places the blame for his unhappiness on Victor. In Chapter 15, the Creature blames Victor for his life and looks alone. However, perhaps symbolic of the Creature's now-comprehensive understanding of his life, in this chapter he definitively identifies Victor as the bearer of responsibility for his sorrows as well: 'This passion is detrimental to me, for you do not reflect that you are the cause of its excess.' (Ch17)

3. Why does the Creature want a mate?

The Creature believes that if he were given a mate, he could be content and his suffering could end. He accepts that he has no chance of companionship with mankind, so resorts to pleading for Victor to create another creature like himself, who he believes will not reject him. The Creature's only experiences of women have been those in the role of lover (Safie and the young woman whom he tries to rescue) or housemistress who serves men (Agatha and Justine). As his attempts at familial relationships have failed, he now seeks romantic companionship, in the naive optimism that this will provide him with the acceptance that he seeks.

4. What does the Creature promise Victor in return for the creation of a mate?

In return for Victor promising him a mate, the Creature vows that 'neither [Victor] nor any other human being shall ever see [him and his mate] again' (Ch17). Listing the practical consideration that he has given to this, the Creature explains that he and his mate will travel to 'the wilds of South America' and that the 'sun will shine on [them] as man' (Ch17). Here, Shelley reveals another of the Creature's desires: to experience life as man does.

5. How does the request for a mate influence the reader's feelings towards Victor?

Shelley shares the Creature's story through his words, providing insight that explains – though perhaps doesn't justify – the Creature's murderous actions, as she forces the reader to consider the events that led to these. In this way, we learn as Victor does: we know of the murderous behaviours of the Creature before beginning to understand the origins of them. Arguably, in tracing the story through the experience of Victor rather than the Creature, Shelley forces us to evaluate whether we would take the same path as Victor or another. It also highlights the contrast between the Creature's life and Victor's: the Creature is desperate for companionship, while Victor often appears to avoid his family and future wife.

6. What does the mate symbolise? 🙊

The Creature's desire for a mate 'of the same species' (Ch16) echoes a wider question that runs throughout the novel: what is it to be human? Wright (2016) questions: 'So is the monster human, or does he belong to "a new species"? And if so, what is that species? Do monsters constitute a separate species?' (p. 160) At a time when there was strong social and scientific debate about whether different races were, in fact, different species, she argues that Shelley plays with this idea, suggesting that 'blurring the lines between the monster and humanity adds to his monstrousness. He is a monster because he is not-human *and* because he is human.' (Wright, 2016, p. 160)

PIT STOP ▼

After finishing the novel, a common consolidation task for learners is the exploration of who the real 'monster' in the novel is. To prepare for this, teachers could use this chapter to explore what it is to be 'human' or what it is to have 'humanity'. This could include ideas such as wanting companionship, wanting to be able to connect with others and wanting to be able to empathise with others, among other ideas.

---

7. What does Victor's response to the Creature's request reveal about him?

This conflict reflects Victor's feelings of sympathy towards the Creature's plight and the rational promises of living in exile from mankind, which are contrasted with his repulsion at the Creature's horrific appearance and former acts of violence. Here, we could argue that Shelley encapsulates one of the key tensions of the novel, as Victor tries to navigate his relationship to a being that is similar to him in mind but crucially different in appearance and origin, and what that difference means for both the Creature and mankind.

How?

Language 🔍

Victor's contrasting feelings: Emotional language 👥

Within this chapter, Victor's feelings towards and about the Creature cover a wide spectrum of emotions. Across the chapter, Shelley portrays his responses as:

- 'Bewildered, perplexed and unable to arrange [his] ideas sufficiently to understand the... proposal'
- anger and determination to never consent
- 'Moved', with possibly a hint of admiration at the capability and sensibility of his creation
- curious, but resigned to his refusal to consent
- 'I compassionate him and sometimes felt a wish to console him'
- horrified at the Creature's appearance
- conflicted
- compelled to consent.

This chapter contains a lot of contrary emotions for such a short chapter, and it demands that learners have a mature appreciation for the complexities of human emotion. These emotions can be clearly examined in two parts – his speech and his thoughts – that display contrasting feelings.

Speech

Victor's speech is pragmatic and definite. He often speaks in clear terms: 'I do refuse it' and, later, 'I consent to your demand' (Ch17). In his other lines, he also questions the Creature and his intentions, suggesting outwardly that he is sceptical of the Creature's intentions and does not trust him. He even dismisses the Creature's plans, instead providing his own: 'you will... your evil passions will be' (Ch17). Victor's use of the modal verb 'will' reflects his self-righteous belief that his knowledge is superior, as he confidently purports to know the future actions of a creature with whom he has spent very little time.

Thoughts

Victor's internal thoughts (shared with Walton) reveal a different perspective, which Shelley is able to share by shifting the narrative back to Victor. On the one hand, Victor uses derogatory terms and repeatedly emphasises his revulsion at the Creature's appearance: 'fiend', 'filthy mass', 'too horrible for human eyes to behold' (Ch17). These serve to highlight Victor's fixation on the physical appearance of the Creature, aligning Victor with the other humans whom the Creature has met.

On the other hand, Victor acknowledges that the Creature is one of 'fine sensations' (Ch17), contrasting his previous perspective and almost acknowledging the Creature's humanity. Similarly, he calmly contemplates the responsibility that he owes the Creature as his creator: 'did [I] as his maker owe him all the portion of happiness that it was in my power to bestow?' (Ch17). He even goes so far as to 'sometimes [feel] a wish to console him' (Ch17), providing a fleeting demonstration of parental responsibility. By having Victor so swiftly shift away from this when he observes the 'filthy mass' of the Creature, Shelley utilises the juxtaposition of emotions to emphasise Victor's idolisation of 'beauty' at the expense of responsibility (Ch17).

PIT STOP ▼

The varied emotions of this chapter demand that learners have a sophisticated vocabulary with which to untangle and identify Victor's emotions. Providing them with a word bank and exploring these words before the chapter will enable learners to articulate their understanding, and will provide scaffolding with which they can map Victor's development as a character in this chapter.

Language to describe females 👥

Most of the women in the novel have been passive and/or only display influence in a domestic sphere, and even Mother Nature passively has her 'hiding places' (Ch3), pursued and invaded by Victor's scientific quests. In this chapter, Shelley continues to present this through the Creature's view of his female as he dictates how she lives: 'we shall be more attached to one another'; 'we shall be monsters' (Ch17). In a mere few sentences, the Creature demands that his female equivalent is created, moves her to South America, '[cuts]' her 'off from all the world', lists her diet and habitat, and declares that she will 'not be happy' but will live a life that is 'harmless and free from the misery [he feels]' (Ch17). On one hand, the inclusion of idealised imagery, such as 'the sun will shine on us as on man and will ripen our food', (Ch17) serves to reinforce this as a utopian imagining. However, it could also be argued that, for a woman who does not yet even exist, the Creature's authoritative voice on her future life and emotions continues the theme of passive women depicted elsewhere. Furthermore, as much of the debate around the mate is focused on whether or not she should exist at all, Shelley very much positions her as a possession – as she did Elizabeth for Victor.

Character focus

The Creature 👥

Key quotation:

- 'I am malicious because I am miserable' (Ch17)

In this chapter, Shelley offers us further dimensions to her already multifaceted Creature: we see him display power, authority, an ability to reason and a longing for affection in a way that we have not yet seen from him. In many ways, this concludes the maturation of the Creature, as he is no longer learning and finding his way but has reached 'adulthood' and holds his 'parent' to account, rather than being a subservient child. His maturation is also shown through his desire for a mate and his assertive attempts to realise this desire. Having twisted her reader's emotions back and forth with the Creature, Shelley continues to play with these through her complex layering of character traits.

Victor 🕷

Key quotations:

- 'But I was bewildered, perplexed, and unable to arrange my ideas sufficiently to understand the full extent of his proposition' (Ch17)

'Did I not as his maker owe him all the portion of happiness that it was in my power to bestow?' (Ch17)

While Shelley uses this chapter to deepen the portrayal of her Creature, so too does she do this with Victor. Hitherto, Victor's emotional connection with the Creature has been one of awe, horror, fear and hatred, but here we see a glimpse of the man that he might have been through flashes of empathy, guilt and paternal duty. Necessary though it may be to the development of the plot, this is arguably the first point in the story since the death of Caroline where readers might be inclined to feel a sense of affection for Victor, as his shallow revulsion is momentarily superseded by a sense of parental responsibility to his 'child'.

PIT STOP ▼

Shelley offers no commentary on Victor or guidance on how she wishes her readers to respond to him. In doing so, she allows readers to form their own views and judgements on him and his actions. During this chapter, those judgements are perhaps at their most complicated, making this a deep and interesting point at which to discuss with learners what their views on Victor are and how they have varied across the text.

Structure 🗂

Opening: 'The being finished speaking and fixed his looks upon me in the expectation of a reply'

Ending: 'The prospect of such an occupation made every other circumstance of existence pass before me like a dream, and that thought only had to me the reality of life'

Narrative shift to Victor

The reunion between Victor and his creation is a key moment in both of their lives, and signifies Shelley's reassertion of Victor's role as parent (albeit a neglectful one). By presenting us with so much dialogue – which reads much as the previous chapters of the Creature's narrative – but also Victor's internal thoughts, Shelley bridges the two narrators' input, simultaneously demanding that her reader process the perspectives of both. Gupta argues this is a moment where 'there are more questions asked than answers offered' (2007, p. xxv). These might include:

- What does Shelley want us to feel for her characters at this point?
- Why does Victor keep so much of his emotion hidden from the Creature?
- What are his true feelings?
- If there is such a contrast between what he says and what he feels, can we trust his narrative?

PIT STOP ▼

S-T-R-E-T-C-H

Chapter 17 resumes Victor's narration, which ended in Chapter 10. Given the deep emotions of the Creature's story, it would be reasonable to expect Victor's position and perspective to have changed. However, both chapters contain a similarly juxtaposed mix of curiosity, admiration, revulsion and compassion. This may be an interesting point to explore with higher-prior-attaining learners: how much does the Creature's narrative impact on Victor?

Shelley's use of direct speech 🔍 Ⓝ

Chapter 17 is over 1,200 words shorter than the one before it and almost 1,000 words shorter than the next. The chapter's word count can be divided as follows:

- total word count: 1,915 words
- total words of speech: 1,067 words
- Creature's speech: 833 words
- Victor's speech: 234 words.

This raises two interesting points of discussion:

1. In terms of speech, the Creature dominates this chapter. In this way, Shelley challenges the usual position of authority held by the narrator. This poses a question about which of the two characters holds authority and superiority.

2. Shelley's authorial decision to hand the narration back to Victor is enabled by the sophisticated articulation and openness of the Creature. Despite the narrative not being in his control, Shelley still provides her readers with great insight into her Creature's emotions, through both his dialogue and Victor's description of the Creature's physical expression of feeling.

S-T-R-E-T-C-H ▼

As an additional challenge, particularly for A level learners, teachers may pose the question as to whether this chapter would work as well if Shelley had not transferred the narrative back to Victor. Given the strong contrast between Victor's thoughts versus what he says, arguably this chapter would provide a very different perspective for readers if Shelley had not done so.

Extracts

Extract 1 (Ch17): How does Shelley use language to present Victor's feelings towards the Creature?

"'I do refuse it," I replied; "and no torture shall ever extort a consent from me. You may render me the most miserable of men, but you shall never make me base in my own eyes. Shall I create another like yourself, whose joint wickedness might desolate the world. Begone! I have answered you; you may torture me, but I will never consent."' (Ch17)

In this extract, Shelley has Victor repeatedly refuse to consent to the Creature's demands, providing examples of how much he would suffer while still refusing. The phase 'no torture shall ever extort a consent from me' highlights his steadfast conviction, with the word 'torture' revealing how much he would suffer in order to maintain this stance. His repeated statements of refusal also serve to highlight his determination, and the word 'Begone!', emphasised with an exclamation mark, clearly demonstrates his feeling of authority in this situation, as he orders the Creature to leave – further implying that there is nothing that the Creature could say that would convince him. He also repeats his early suggestion that even torture would not persuade him – 'you may torture me, but I will never consent' – which cements the impression of his determination.

Extract 2 (Ch17): How does Shelley's Creature use language to appeal to Victor?

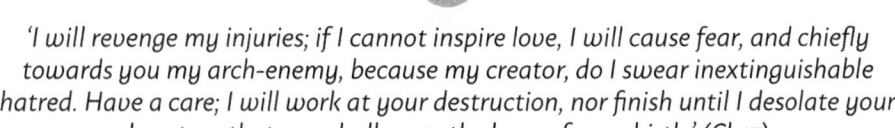

'I will revenge my injuries; if I cannot inspire love, I will cause fear, and chiefly towards you my arch-enemy, because my creator, do I swear inextinguishable hatred. Have a care; I will work at your destruction, nor finish until I desolate your heart, so that you shall curse the hour of your birth.' (Ch17)

In this chapter, the Creature uses a range of strategies to appeal to Victor. The most clear of these is the use of threats. For example, he says 'if [he] cannot inspire love', then 'towards [Victor]... do I swear inextinguishable hatred'. The word 'inexhaustible' emphasises how intensely the Creature hates Victor, as he suggests that his 'hatred' will never diminish. Furthermore, the line 'nor finish until I desolate your heart' highlights how determined the Creature is to cause Victor pain. The verb 'desolate' emphasises how much the Creature wishes to destroy Victor's life through suffering. In describing that he will do this to Victor's 'heart', he implies that it won't simply be Victor who suffers but those he loves too, causing greater suffering than if he attacked Victor physically. Here, Shelley is able to make utterly clear to the reader how desperate and determined the Creature is by utilising such a brutal threat to Victor as an act of persuasion.

At a glance

> **Summary quotation:** 'If I were alone, would he not at times force his abhorred presence on me, to remind me of my task, or to contemplate its progress?' (Ch18)

> **Big Question:** How does Shelley use journeys?

> **Significant plot events:**

Chapter 18:

- Victor has returned to Geneva.

- Victor's health has improved but he his unable to consider the creation of a mate for the Creature.

- He enjoys the solitude of sailing on the lake.

- His father talks of the marriage to Elizabeth, but Victor needs to delay this because of his promise to the Creature.

- Victor leaves for England with Henry Clerval, travelling across Europe.

- Victor retrospectively reflects on the qualities of his beloved friend, Clerval.

Chapter 19:

- Victor spends time in London with Clerval, and then they set off on a tour of England, heading for Scotland.

- Victor is suffering from the 'blight' of depression and does not enjoy company, despite what he learns from it.

- They continue to travel north to Scotland.

- Victor leaves Clerval to set up a laboratory in the Orkneys.

- He works on the 'filthy process' of creating a mate, understanding the horror of the process that he had previously ignored.

- Victor feels a sense of foreboding.

> **Character focus:** Victor Frankenstein, Alphonse Frankenstein, Henry Clerval

> **Key themes:**
  - Family and companionship &
  - Knowledge and discovery 🔍
  - Death and grief ✝
  - Society and social class ✂
  - Prejudice 👥
  - Power and responsibility 💡

> **Handle with care:**
  - Victor's psychological health is described.
  - Colonisation is referenced.

Why?

- Why do Victor and Clerval travel from Geneva to Scotland?
- Why does Victor compare Clerval to his former self?

S-T-R-E-T-C-H questions

- Why does Victor choose a 'barren' place in which to work on creating a new life?
- Why is the landscape important?
- Why is Victor's past significant?

What?

What happens?

Chapter 18

Victor returns to Geneva to recover, but not sufficiently to begin a second creation. He considers travelling to England to do this. His father suggests that he brings marriage to Elizabeth forward, to assuage Victor's 'misery'. There is a discussion about how marriage might bring happiness. Victor cannot 'allow himself' to 'enjoy the delight of a union from which [he] expected peace' until the mate is created.

He cannot tell his father the true reason for his proposed journey, which is to learn from English philosophers and create the mate. His 'insurmountable aversion' to creating a laboratory in his father's house is understandable, keeping this unnatural process away from his life with his family and Elizabeth. Alphonse agrees to the visit to England, hoping that it will raise his son's spirits, with the agreement that the marriage happens on his return. Victor hopes that the Creature will follow him, thus protecting his family in Geneva.

Victor eventually begins his journey, meeting Clerval at Strasburgh, where Shelley creates a contrast between their moods; Victor is despondent but Clerval is joyful. They proceed, observing the landscape in detail. The chapter ends with their arrival in London.

Chapter 19 🔍

Victor and Clerval make London 'a point of rest', with Victor meeting 'distinguished natural philosophers'. He does not find fulfilment in company, haunted by the memories of the deaths of William and Justine. He appears to envy Clerval's enjoyment of the people that they meet. Clerval is eager to gain 'experience and instruction' about the European colonisation of India to expand his knowledge, whereas Victor retreats to spend time alone, to gather materials in preparation for his second act of creation.

They are invited to Perth, and Victor desires to see mountains and streams again, rather than people. They embark upon a meandering journey, with Victor reflecting upon the history of the places that they encounter. Time passes and Victor is concerned that he has not kept his promise to the 'daemon', and he is afraid of the consequences for Clerval, for his family and for Elizabeth if the Creature has stayed in Switzerland. Despite this fear, Victor parts company from Clerval, travelling further north to create a mate for the Creature.

In the Orkneys, Victor establishes a place in which to live, as well as his laboratory. While he engages with the landscape and the sea, he becomes increasingly disgusted with his labours of creation. He is fearful of both the Creature and the mate that he is creating. The chapter ends with Victor feeling a mixture of hope (to be free of the Creature) and 'forebodings of evil'.

Social and historical context ⚙️

Historical context: Travel in Georgian England ⚗️

Travel in Georgian England was not uncommon for young, wealthy men. Beginning as a trend in the sixteenth century, the 'Grand Tour' was a journey undertaken by young English aristocrats, travelling from England to Paris and then onto other European cities, seeing classical ruins, reading Greek and Latin texts and viewing Renaissance art. This is not dissimilar to the journey taken by Victor and Clerval, who travel in Europe and then to England in a reverse of the Grand Tour, with a macabre focus for Victor. It is notable that, as was common at the time, it is only the male characters who travel (including the Creature), as the female characters remain in their domestic spheres, restricted by adoption, employment or marriage. This is in contrast to the mobility of Shelley, although her travels were dominated by men. It is useful to think about Shelley's travel books based on her journals – for example, *History of a Six Weeks' Tour* (1817).

Travel is used as a prominent motif in the novel; Quinn (2024) states, 'Shelley placed her work within the larger pattern of travel as a motif in literature throughout history and in her own time.' (p. 38) Travels are significant to the novel's narrative structure, developing both plot and character. Lanone (2016) comments that journeys create 'kinetic suspense' through the concept of a chase; Victor and the Creature are constantly moving in pursuit of each other. Dekker (2004) says, 'Travel takes many forms and has many purposes in *Frankenstein* beginning with the explorer Walton setting out by dog-sled from St Petersburgh to Archangel and concluding with the creature's departure from Walton's ship on an ice-floe raft.' (p. 209) He outlines the various forms of transport used, reflecting those available to the eighteenth-century traveller. The Creature can only travel on foot, yet his giant size and strength afford him the ability to travel great distances at speed, thus creating this kinetic suspense.

Literary context: Intertextuality and contemporary writers

Journeys are important in the novel as a structural feature but also as part of the novel's linguistic style. Significant parts of the novel echo the travel genre, so it is important to consider Shelley's travel writing, e.g. *History of a Six Weeks' Tour* (1817); understanding the basic elements of the genre is useful in deconstructing the novel. The novel's journeys and landscapes directly relate to Shelley's experiences of travel.

Intertextual use of poetry is also significant. Many critics explore the importance of allusion to *Paradise Lost* in the structures, imagery and events of the novel. Reference to and quotation of the poetry of the Romantic poets is also significant, but not surprising.

Shelley quotes from Wordsworth's *Lines Written a Few Miles above Tintern Abbey*, similar to her use of *The Rime of the Ancient Mariner*. Shelley was familiar with the work of both poets and heard Coleridge recite *Rime* at her father's house, from which Victor quotes from at the end of Chapter 18, addressing Clerval in his thoughts – 'Clerval! beloved friend!' – commenting on his emotions and qualities and his love of nature. Clerval's joyful perception of nature – 'a childlike love and trust' – runs through the chapter. Brooks (1978, p. 600) says, 'The novel dissents from the optimistic assumption that nature is support and comfort and source of right moral feeling... This dissent is suggested most forcefully through... Clerval who balances Victor's pursuit of science with the study of poets.' But nature does not protect Clerval from 'the malignant possibilities of nature itself', as manifested by the monster (ibid, p. 601).

Vocabulary in context

Word	Quotation	Definition
sentiments	'The expression of your sentiments of this subject' (Ch18)	a thought, opinion or feeling about a situation
dilatory	'The latter method of obtaining the desired intelligence was dilatory and unsatisfactory' (Ch18)	slow and likely to cause a delay
machinations	'exempt my family from the danger of his machinations' (Ch18)	complicated and secret plans
picturesque	'The course of the Rhine below Mayence becomes much more picturesque' (Ch18)	attractive in appearance, especially in an old-fashioned way (in relation to a place)
irksome	'Company was irksome to me' (Ch19)	annoying
abhorred	'although I abhorred society' (Ch19)	to hate something or someone

Plot and character development

1. What type of journeys do the characters go on? (Symbolism)

- **physical:** travelling towards and away from specific places
- **psychological:** emotional changes within (some of the) characters
- **intellectual:** searching for education and enlightenment.

PIT STOP ▼

A blank or partially filled table could be given to learners to complete, supporting their review and consolidation of the topic of journeys (see the teaching resources).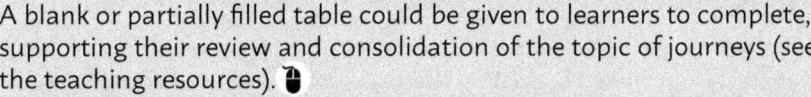

Journeys	Victor	Clerval
Physical	From Geneva to the Orkneys (see the list below)	From Geneva to Perth and then later to Ireland (Ch21)
Where do Victor and Clerval travel to?	Chapter 18: • Geneva to Strasburgh, where Victor meets Henry Clerval • Strasburgh to Rotterdam, sailing along the Rhine • A day in Mannheim • Then to Mayence • Cologne to the plains of Holland • Rotterdam to Tilbury Fort, Gravesend, Woolwich and Greenwich, and then St Paul's Chapter 19: • London, staying several months • In March, north to Edinburgh, travelling via Windsor, Oxford, Matlock, Derby and the Cumberland lakes • Then Edinburgh, Coupar, St Andrew's, along the banks of the Tay, to Perth • Victor travels alone to the north of Scotland and then the Orkneys, where he establishes his laboratory	
Psychological	• His father worries about Victor's 'melancholy, which every now and then would return by fits, and with a devouring blackness overcast the approaching sunshine'. (Ch18) • Victor is burdened by his promise to the Creature. He worries that he is being pursued by the Creature. • First-person narrative allows us to understand how travelling affects his thoughts and feelings. • Victor travels away from marriage to Elizabeth. • He travels to fulfil his promise to the Creature, but also to draw the Creature away from Elizabeth and his family in order to address his worries about their safety.	• Clerval is enlivened by the landscape. • Victor reflects on Clerval's nature and personality. • First-person narrative precludes understanding of Clerval's psychological development.
Intellectual	Victor wants to learn more from an English philosopher about the creation of life.	Clerval has 'his mind expanded in the company of men of talent' (Ch19). He seeks to learn more about the European colonisation, with the intention of visiting India.

2. How does Shelley use the journey through England to Scotland to build up to the creation of the female Creature?

In Chapter 18, Victor prepares for another journey – 'I expressed a wish to visit England' – but he is 'concealing the true reasons of this request'. He hides the true reason for travelling from his father, who 'Without previously communicating', has arranged with Elizabeth that 'Clerval should join' (Ch18) him, complicating this journey of concealment and potential creation. The physical journey leads to psychological and emotional consequences: 'my present sensations strongly intimated that the fiend would follow me' – which he indeed does. This act of destruction links the Creature with Clerval, Victor's true friend.

3. How is Clerval presented in this section?

Clerval delights in travel and nature – 'He was alive to every new scene' (Ch18) – and shows us his elevated feelings: 'He felt as if he had been transported to Fairy-land, and enjoyed a happiness seldom tasted by man' (Ch18). In Chapter 19, Clerval appears to have agency and pursues his interests, separating from Victor. However, Victor contrasts himself with Clerval, as we see him from Victor's narrative viewpoint. Shelley shows Clerval flourishing in the company of clever men, wanting to understand the colonial administration of India – an acceptable form of intellectual development. Clerval's inquisitive nature should benefit him, in contrast to Victor's intellectual path. Ultimately, we know that Victor's pursuits lead to Clerval's death.

How?

Literary methods

What do journeys symbolise in the novel?

- physical (moving away from and towards places)

- psychological (emotional changes within (some of the) characters)

- intellectual (searching for education and enlightenment).

Here Victor's travel begins in earnest, accompanied by Clerval. This journey takes two years, moving across Europe to the isolated Orkneys, where he creates another creature.

Quinn (2024) argues that 'travel is the vehicle which proves Victor's total alienation from the world, both nature and humanity'. We see this alienation on his journey to England; he is 'careless of what was passing around' during the first stage and he ignores the delight of the landscape, while his 'eyes were fixed and unobserving' (Ch18). Dekker (2005, p. 27) discusses Schiller's (1795–6) portrait of the modern man as a sentimental character who is alienated from their own nature and seeks 'wholeness and harmony in...

non-human nature or other ("naïve") individuals'; the alienated man finds expression in 'troubled and restless heroes… [such] as Shelley's Frankenstein'. We see this restlessness in Victor's constant travelling and his unsuccessful search for intellectual fulfilment and peace. Victor's local travels become international travels, so that he can study and practise scientific explorations. While Victor may learn intellectually at university and in England, his emotional development is static, seen in his attitude and language to the Creature later in Chapter 20, his journeys away from his family and his encouragement of Walton to travel further into danger to kill the Creature. Jarvis (2005, quoted in Quinn, 2024) comments that 'travel as the compulsive antidote to personal sorrow' is common in Romantic literature, and we see that Victor is compelled to travel, that travel is used to heal at times and that he suffers much personal sorrow and loss.

Chapter 18 brings us to the consequences of the encounter with the Creature in the Mer de Glace. Victor's exterior and interior journeys relating to the creation of a mate are significant. Victor places greater weight on fulfilling his promise to the Creature than on his marriage to Elizabeth. Travel appears to be a means of avoiding consummating his relationship with Elizabeth, under the guise of the Creature's threat. Chapter 18 shows us both his thoughts (interior journey) and the physical, exterior journey to his destiny. Victor chooses to travel to a barren island, where he begins to create a new life – ultimately destroyed – rather than immediate marriage to Elizabeth.

Why are letters important in this chapter?

Letters are used as a narrative intervention. The Creature's threat left Victor static on the island, and now he has reason to travel. Clerval requests Victor's presence, and Victor is 'determined to quit my island at the expiration of two days' (Ch20). He casts evidence of his work into the sea, under darkness. The sea takes matters into its own hands and the boat drifts to unknown shores, where Victor becomes a villain, 'but is the custom of the Irish to hate villains' (Ch20). The reader is interested, as Victor has always travelled as a privileged young man. He must 'give an account of… the gentleman who was found murdered here last night' (Ch20) to the magistrate. This unexpected journey has led to death, just as his journey into the mysteries of creation led to William's murder, Justine's death and then to the death of Clerval. The narrative device of the letter is a key driver in the plot.

Language 🔍

Chapter 18

Victor's emotions: Revulsion

Victor's thoughts and dialogue centre on his disgust for the Creature and the creation of a mate:

- 'I was unable to overcome my repugnance to the task' (Ch18)
- 'Alas! to me the idea of an immediate union with my Elizabeth was one of horror and dismay' (Ch18)
- 'I had an insurmountable aversion to the idea of engaging myself in my loathsome task in my father's house'

The motif of revulsion, using abstract nouns, occurs throughout the novel, but here it is Victor's revulsion to the second act of creation that is the focus. This is overt in terms of the Creature and the mate, but it is a subtext related to marriage to Elizabeth.

The position of 'horror and dismay' could be read as pertaining to the marriage, and not just the 'solemn promise' (Ch18) that he has made to the Creature. Six years have passed since he left for Ingolstadt, leaving Elizabeth behind. He describes their prospective marriage as 'this deadly weight' (Ch18), alluding to the Mariner's albatross. Reader privilege means that we are aware that he is referring to the Creature.

PIT STOP ▼

Learners can identify other emotions (abstract nouns) as motifs, categorise them and then write an analysis: e.g. anguish, misery, self-pity or fear.

Character focus

Victor Frankenstein

Key quotations:

- 'I feared the vengeance of the disappointed fiend' (Ch18)
- 'I am happy to remark, my dear son... And yet you are still unhappy, and still avoid our society' (Ch18)
- 'my heart often sickened at the work of my hand' (Ch19)

Shelley focuses on Victor's thoughts and feelings about his promise to create a mate for the Creature. Here, he feels revulsed and 'sickened' by what he has to do. His hubris is diminished because he has suffered the consequence of his challenge to God and to nurture. He is no longer blind to the 'horror of my employment' and there will be no procreation in the 'barren' (Ch19) womb of the island.

Alphonse ✳

Key quotations:

- 'I am happy to remark, my dear son, that you have resumed your former pleasures' (Ch18)
- 'I have always looked forward to your marriage with our dear Elizabeth as the tie of our domestic comfort' (Ch18)
- 'Do not suppose, however, that I wish to dictate happiness to you' (Ch18)

Alphonse revisits his paternal role, nurturing Victor back to health, which he will do in Chapter 21. As a father, he focuses on Victor's marriage to Elizabeth, which has been assumed since his mother's death – 'the tie of our domestic comfort'. In the 1831 edition, Elizabeth is adopted rather than being a cousin, to avoid accusations of incest. Alphonse acknowledges the closeness of their bond and wonders whether this is a barrier to marriage. He does not know the real reason for Victor's hesitation. However, while Alphonse wants happiness for his son and Elizabeth, he is understanding and not dictatorial: 'Do not suppose'. The peace that he seeks for his son, and which his son wants – 'enjoy the delight of a union from which I expected peace' (Ch18) – cannot be achieved until the promise to the Creature is kept.

Clerval 🐚

Key quotations:

- '"This is what it is to live," he cried, "now I enjoy existence!"' (Ch18)
- 'his friendship was of that devoted and wondrous nature' (Ch18)
- 'Is this gentle and lovely being lost for ever?' (Ch18)

Clerval is Victor's loyal and longstanding friend, chosen to accompany him to England and Scotland: 'Clerval should join me at Strasburgh' (Ch18). Although Victor prefers solitude, he knows the value of Clerval's friendship and companionship. Chapter 18 shows the reader Clerval's pleasure in their journey: 'Clerval, who observed the scenery with an eye of feeling and delight'. He is light-hearted and carefree, unburdened by the knowledge of Victor's mission. Clerval is a developmentally static character, whose narrative purpose is as foil to Victor. Victor's narrative juxtaposes his dark feelings as a 'miserable wretch' (Ch21) with Clerval's enjoyment of life. The Creature recognises that Clerval is a precious companion to Victor, which marks him as a victim. In Chapter 19, Clerval and Victor's journeys diverge, but we see Clerval's love for Victor clearly expressed: 'hasten then, my dear friend, to return, that I may again feel myself somewhat at home, which I cannot do in your absence'. He does not wish to be parted for long, which the reader has seen from the beginning of their friendship. He sees Victor as 'home'. We feel anticipatory sympathy for Clerval, as we are aware that he will die. This love makes Clerval a target of the Creature's desire for revenge, leading to further distress for Victor – the Creature's intention.

Structure 🗂

Chapter 18 🔍

Opening: 'Day after day, week after week,... I feared the vengeance of the disappointed fiend, yet I was unable to overcome my repugnance to the task which was enjoined me'

Ending: 'At length we saw the numerous steeples of London, St. Paul's towering above all, and the Tower famed in English history'

Chapter 19

Opening: 'London was our present point of rest; we determined to remain several months in this wonderful and celebrated city'

Ending: 'I looked towards its completion with a tremulous and eager hope, which I dared not trust myself to question, but which was intermixed with obscure forebodings of evil, that made my heart sicken in my bosom'

The journey from Geneva to Scotland acts as the structural device of this section, linked with Victor's promise to create a mate in the distant islands of the Orkneys, with his attendant horror of the process and his fears for the consequences. Students can track the pattern of emotions, perhaps making a table of contrasts and tracking the intensity of the emotions.

The start of Chapter 18 shows us Victor at home with his family, with his vow to the Creature looming in his mind. The first-person narrative allows us to see his preoccupation with another unholy act of creation. Shelley creates tension between the knowledge that we have as readers – the Creature's existence and murderous intentions – with the limited knowledge of the family. His father worries about Victor's state of being and revisits the idea of marriage to Elizabeth. However, Victor cannot explain the true reason behind his state of mind and has to find a way to go to England to fulfil his promise, so that 'the monster would depart for ever' (Ch18). Shelley constructs the journey to isolation over two chapters, to build worry, anticipation and tension. Yet this is built slowly, with the journey in stages and over approximately two years. However, Shelley proceeds to one of the most significant events: the destruction of the mate (Ch20) and the impact of this on Clerval, Elizabeth and himself.

Extracts

Extract 1 (Ch18): How does Shelley use language to present the character of Clerval?

'After some days spent in listless indolence, during which I traversed many leagues, I arrived at Strasburgh, where I waited two days for Clerval. He came. Alas, how great was the contrast between us!... In truth, I was occupied by gloomy thoughts, and neither saw the descent of the evening star, nor the golden sunrise reflected in the Rhine. – And you, my friend, would be far more amused with the journal of Clerval, who observed the scenery with an eye of feeling and delight, than in listening to my reflections. I, a miserable wretch, haunted by a curse that shut up every avenue to enjoyment.' (The full extract can be found in the teaching resources.)

This section begins a focus on time, using a temporal adverbial to show time passing on the journey. Time continues to move forward, even though Victor is static. Shelley then contrasts Victor's 'indolence' with Clerval being 'alive to every new scene' (Ch18). This reflects their different reasons for travel and their previous emotional experiences. Clerval's dialogue highlights their differences further, through Clerval's descriptive declarative and his question to his friend, 'wherefore are you desponding and sorrowful!' (Ch18). Throughout this section, Shelley focuses on the characters' emotions, ending with the phrase 'miserable wretch' – both words that are repeated throughout the wider text, linking Victor with the Creature.

Extract 2 (Ch18): How is Victor Frankenstein's retrospective grief conveyed? †

'And where does he now exist? Is this gentle and lovely being lost forever? Has this mind, so replete with ideas, imaginations fanciful and magnificent, which formed a world, whose existence depended on the life of its creator; –... overflowing with the anguish which his remembrance creates. I will proceed with my tale.' (The full extract can be found in the teaching resources.)

Before Victor's narrative reaches Clerval's death chronologically, he uses a question, both cataphorically and anaphorically: 'And, where does he now exist?' Shelley's complex narrative form places us as listeners at the end of the story on Walton's ship, but simultaneously takes us through the story as Walton writes to his sister. This prepares the reader for the death of Clerval, but we have to read the next chapter to find out how he dies: 'I will proceed with my tale.' Victor's language is reflective and mournful, using a series of questions – epiplexis – to elicit our emotions. Shelley also uses religious references – 'creator', 'divinely wrought' and 'spirit' (Ch18) – which reminds us of Victor's usurpation of God as creator, in contrast to the natural creation, within God's laws, of his closest friend. Victor's grief, sorrow and regret are paramount in this extract and prepare the reader for what is an inevitable outcome of Victor's broken covenant.

Extract 3 (Ch19): How is Victor Frankenstein's view of the island and its inhabitants conveyed?

'On the whole island there were but three miserable huts, and one of these was vacant when I arrived. This I hired. It contained but two rooms, and these exhibited all the squalidness of the most miserable penury... As it was, I lived ungazed at and unmolested, hardly thanked for the pittance of food and clothes which I gave; so much does suffering blunt even the coarsest sensations of men.' (The full extract can be found in the teaching resources.)

From the northern Highlands, Victor travels to the remotest of the Orkneys. Here, he seems to be punishing himself by residing in misery: 'three miserable huts'. However, his viewpoint must be interrogated, as he is dismissive of the life of the inhabitants – 'benumbed by want and poverty' (Ch19) – from his position of wealth and privilege. He seems to seek self-punishment by living in a place of hardship and degradation, seeing only 'squalidness' and 'squalid poverty' (Ch19). The repetition of 'squalid' emphasises the extreme unpleasantness and dirtiness, further enhanced by the superlative 'most miserable penury'. He commands the repairs to be completed, demonstrating his superior and temporary status, and is critical of the lack of thanks, observing that suffering blunts the feelings of the destitute. However, he is satisfied that he is now 'ungazed at and unmolested' so that he can proceed with the creation of the mate.

SECTION 11
DESTRUCTION AND DEATH (CHAPTERS 20-21)

At a glance

> **Summary quotation:** 'a truce was established between the present hour and the irresistible, disastrous future' (Ch21)

> **Big Question:** What is the impact of the destruction of the female Creature?

> **Significant plot events:**

Chapter 20:

- Victor reflects on his creation of a mate for the Creature and destroys her while the Creature looks on.

- The Creature visits Frankenstein to threaten that he will make Victor utterly miserable and will be with Victor on his wedding night.

- Victor leaves and sets sail, dropping the remains of the female creature into the sea. The boat drifts and he arrives in Ireland.

- He is then taken to a magistrate by the local people.

Chapter 21:

- Victor meets the magistrate and is told his supposed crime: the murder of a gentleman (Clerval).

- Victor succumbs to a fever and is ill for two months.

- When recovered, the magistrate shows him great kindness and writes to Victor's father.

- Alphonse arrives in Ireland and Victor is soon acquitted of the murder.

- Victor urges his father to take him home to Geneva, thinking that the Creature will go there next.

- Frankenstein takes laudanum, but this does not stop him from having nightmares.

- Frankenstein realises that the Creature is not on the boat and thinks that 'truce was established between the present hour and the irresistible, disastrous future'.

> **Character focus:**

- Chapter 20: Victor Frankenstein, the Creature
- Chapter 21: Victor Frankenstein, Mr Kirwan (the magistrate)

> **Key themes:**

- Family and companionship 🫂
- Death and grief ✝
- Society and social class ✄
- Betrayal and guilt 🐍
- Crime and justice ⚔
- Isolation and loneliness 🧎
- Revenge 🔁
- Power and responsibility 💡
- Prejudice 👥

Why?

Chapter 20

- Why does Frankenstein reflect on his creation of a mate for the Creature?
- Why does Frankenstein destroy the female creature? What reasons does he give?
- Why does he do this with the Creature watching?
- What are the consequences of the destruction of the female creature?

Chapter 21

- Why does the opening focus on the 'calm and mild manners' of the magistrate?
- Why do we hear so many witness statements about the discovery of the body?
- Why does Frankenstein develop a fever?

S-T-R-E-T-C-H questions

What is the importance of setting in Chapter 20?

- What is further revealed about the relationship between Frankenstein and the Creature from each of their perspectives?
- Why does Shelley focus on the interrogation and imprisonment of Frankenstein?

What?

What happens?

Chapter 20

Victor destroys the mate after considering the potential consequences of creating another creature. The Creature sees this destruction and despairs. In an act of revenge, he threatens Victor and flees. Letters arrive from Clerval (a narrative device). Victor clears his 'odious work' and then gets rid of the female creature's remains. He leaves when the moon rises and falls asleep, meaning that the boat drifts off course – another narrative device.

The boat drifts to Ireland, where Victor is arrested and seen as a 'villain'. Both the reader and Victor are perplexed by this and by the 'mixture of curiosity and anger' from the local people. He is taken to the magistrate, who takes Victor's account of the 'death of a gentleman'. The chapter ends with Victor preparing 'to recall the memory of the frightful events', which leads the reader to the next chapter.

Chapter 21

Victor meets Mr Kirwan, the magistrate. A body has been found, and Victor is accused of murder and attempting to sail away. He is shown the body and is devastated to see that it is Clerval, with the Creature's handprint. He succumbs to a fever and, while ill, is visited by Mr Kirwan who contacts Alphonse. When Alphonse arrives, Victor is terrified that he is the Creature.

Eventually, Victor is freed, but he is still deeply unhappy. He begins taking laundanum, but is haunted by dreams of the 'fiend'. Finally, his father wakes him, bringing him a sense of security.

Social and historical context

Historical context: Laudanum

'Victor Frankenstein, who incidentally was a medical student and not a doctor, was very disturbed when the creature he created killed his friend Henry Clerval. Unable to sleep, he dosed himself with laudanum... Laudanum was a 10 percent solution of opium powder in alcohol, widely used to treat everything from pain and insomnia to female disorders. It was even used to quiet crying babies.'
(Schwarcz, 2015)

Dr Joseph Crawford, author of the chapter 'Opium and gender in Romantic literature' in Psychopharmacology in British Literature, looks at how both male and female writers used laudanum, detailed in a news article for the University of Exeter (2018). For example, Coleridge, notably for Xanadu, and De Quincey, detailed in *Confessions of an English Opium Eater*, took the drug as a stimulant and to seek inspiration, but women, such as Sara Coleridge and Elizabeth Barret Browning, often took it to distract from the drudgery and hardships of everyday life. Shelley was familiar with a number of poets who took opium or laudanum, such as Byron, Coleridge and Percy Shelley. She was also familiar with the harm caused by the drug, with her half-sister Fanny Imlay dying from a deliberately fatal dose of laudanum.

Vocabulary in context

Word	Quotation	Definition
malignant	'she might become ten thousand times more malignant than her mate' (Ch20)	having a wish to do harm (evil)
countenance	'his countenance expressed the utmost extent of malice and treachery' (Ch20)	the appearance or expression of someone's face
malice		the wish to harm or upset people
treachery		behaviour that deceives or is not loyal to someone who trusts you
presentiment	'I felt a presentiment of who it was' (Ch20)	a feeling that something, especially something unpleasant, is going to happen
spectre	'walked about the isle like a restless spectre' (Ch20)	ghost
odious	'the scene of my odious work' (Ch20)	extremely unpleasant and causing or deserving hate
deposed	'A woman deposed' (Ch21)	gave a statement

Plot and character development

1. How does Victor feel about creating the mate in this chapter? ☀

In Chapter 20, we see Frankenstein's stillness as he reflects on the potential of a new creation for the Creature, who may leave his control and then 'inhabit the deserts of the new world', creating a race of 'devils' (Ch20), which may spread across the world. Victor's focus is on the potential future generations, for which he now feels a sense of guilt: 'Had I right, for my own benefit, to inflict this curse upon everlasting generations?' (Ch20). The reflective question and the weighted word 'curse' reveal more about his shift in thinking. He is more conscious of his selfish motives and his responsibility for what he has unleashed. However, his reflection does not extend to the reason for his culpability: his abandonment of the Creature. Here, the reader sees him blame the Creature for the ills that have taken and could take place.

PIT STOP ▼

Explore the Creature's dialogue. Look at:

- the language that the Creature and Victor use to refer to each other
- the pattern of imperatives, exhortations and exclamatory sentences

---

2. How does Victor act in this section?

Positioning Victor on an island looking out to sea shows Victor's isolation. 'I was alone; none were near me to dissipate the gloom' (Ch20). However, despite this, the Creature visits Victor at his laboratory and then his apartment. 'I felt the silence... until my ear was suddenly arrested by the paddling of oars near the shore, and a person landed close to my house' (Ch20). Earlier, Victor had destroyed the half-finished mate, feeling 'a sensation of madness' (Ch20) and thus ending the Creature's happiness and sealing the destruction of Elizabeth. He shows a fear and awareness that he did not have before in his Promethean hubris. Yet, in dialogue with the Creature, he tries to be superior: 'be sure that you are yourself safe' (Ch20).

3. How does the Creature react to Victor's destruction of his mate? Why? ✝

The chapter shows the Creature's anger and despair at the cruel destruction of his future. He has been searching for companionship on his physical journey, and his developing intellectual understanding has shown him his loneliness. He needs someone like himself. When Victor destroys the mate, we see that this is deeply painful. The Creature promises revenge by also destroying what Frankenstein most values – Elizabeth: 'I shall be with you on your wedding-night' (Ch20).

Brooks (1978, p. 598) argues that 'The destruction of the monsteress marks the doom of any hope that the Monster might gain access to a signifying chain of existence'. It is this desire for existence and recognition, and the breaking of this 'covenant' (Brooks, 1978, p. 597), that drives the Creature to threaten Victor. The series of modal verbs shows his desperation for revenge and his willingness to continue to pursue Victor, ending with the ominous threat to destroy the most precious person in Victor's life: his future wife. If the Creature cannot have a companion, he will make sure that Victor cannot either.

During a reading of Chapter 20, ask learners to gather examples of the negative language used by Victor about the Creature and to divide these into categories, e.g. disgust or evil, and to consider how these: a) show Victor's viewpoint; and b) influence the reader.

4. How does Victor react to Clerval's murder?

Victor describes the murder of Clerval as part of a series of 'frightful events', and he is 'startled' when told that a man has been murdered (Ch20). He does not yet know that this is Clerval, but he knows who the murderer could be. The detail of 'black mark of fingers' causes him to be 'agitated' and for his body to respond physically: 'my limbs trembled, and a mist came over my eyes' (Ch21). A more intense reaction comes when Victor actually sees the body, with him gasping for breath and throwing himself on Clerval's body. He is in agony when he realises that the murdered man is Clerval. The loss of his friend is too much, and he is 'carried out of the room in strong convulsions' (Ch21). Victor becomes very ill and he spends 'two months on the point of death' (Ch21). This is a typical response from Victor, but this is also the third loss of someone dear to him, through his own making, and his illness is a symptom of both guilt and grief.

5. Who is Mr Kirwan?

He is a magistrate in Ireland and a compassionate and benevolent man, yet severe when he meets a potential criminal. The townspeople respect him, as Victor is taken to him straight away. He tests Victor by taking him to see the body of the victim. He shows 'extreme kindness' to Victor and ensures that he is taken care of. He also finds out who Victor is and where he is from, so that he can write to Victor's family and reunite him with them. He investigates the murder and finds out that Victor is innocent, so he can return to Geneva with his father.

6. What is Victor's response to being freed from prison?

Despite being freed, Victor is cast into the depths of despair, with 'the cup of life being poisoned forever' (Ch21). Dark thoughts haunt him as he reflects on his actions and their consequences, calling 'to mind the night in which he first lived. I was unable to pursue the train of thought; a thousand feelings pressed upon me, and I wept bitterly' (Ch21). To calm himself, Victor begins taking laudanum. However, despite the soporific effects of the drug, Victor is haunted by dreams of the 'fiend'. His father wakes him and the chapter ends with him feeling 'a sense of security' (Ch21).

How?

Language

Modal verbs and the subjunctive mood

Victor speculates about the potential actions of a mate, evident in Shelley's use of modal verbs in the first paragraph. The verb 'might' carries the weight of ideas, as Victor does not know what the consequences will be. He can only judge from the Creature's behaviour – for which he is responsible. Victor's suppositions stem from his fear of the female: 'Even if they were to leave Europe... race of devils would be propagated' (Ch20). The subjunctive mood is used to introduce this key idea and brings to the fore Victor's fear of an act of creation outside his power: the natural power of the female form.

Victor's focus on the maliciousness of his Creature, and the assumed malice of the mate, show that Victor has never fully understood his creation. Even after listening to the Creature's narrative of cruel treatment by the human race, Victor does not comprehend that the Creature's fall from grace was the product of the treatment by himself and other humans. His creation has never been treated with kindness. It is this that destroyed the Creature's innocence and eagerness to become part of the human race and turned it into a malevolent force. Victor's assumption that his creation is innately evil (based purely on his appearance) leads Victor to misconstrue the Creature's actions repeatedly: from the outstretched hand at the moment of the Creature's birth to the Creature's threat of 'I will be with you on your wedding night' (Ch20). This failed understanding of his own creation has fatal consequences for his family and his beloved Clerval.

Literary methods

Use of landscape and seascape 🔍 💡

Chrzanowska-Kluczewska (in Quinn, 2024) explains how the landscapes in the novel 'represent the inner landscape of Victor Frankenstein':

The laboratory

We see Victor in the laboratory when 'the sun had set, and the moon was just rising from the sea' (Ch20); he does not have enough light to work but there is enough light to see. This laboratory echoes his first: 'Three years before I was engaged in the same manner' (Ch20). It symbolises his reflection on the consequences of his actions: 'the wickedness of my promise burst upon me' (Ch20). At this realisation, the laboratory becomes a place of destruction, echoed by the 'barren soil' of Chapter 19. There will be no race of devils to inhabit the new world.

The island and the sea

Victor watches the sea. It is 'motionless' and 'the winds were hushed, and all nature reposed under the eye of the quiet moon' (Ch20). This sense of stillness should convey peace and tranquillity, but the reader knows that the Creature has witnessed the destruction of his dream. This calmness is a moment of stillness that anticipates the later disruption of the Creature's return – the 'creaking' of the door and the 'sound of footsteps' (Ch20), which are in contrast to the repose of nature. Victor briefly considers a desire to stay on the island, regarding the sea 'as an insuperable barrier between me and my fellow-creatures' (Ch20). He wanders like a 'restless spectre' (Ch20) until he succumbs to sleep. Yet the sea is not insuperable, despite what Victor may crave, and he awakes to find a fishing boat with a delivery of letters, one of which is from Clerval asking to join him. Even in the perceived isolation of an island in the Orkneys, Victor is not alone. The barren landscape is a symbol of his inability to escape his deeds.

The sea

The sea is a means of both escape and entry. The Creature escapes from the island and 'was soon lost amidst the waves' (Ch20), foreshadowing the ending of the novel, where the Creature is borne away by the waves and is 'lost in darkness and distance' (Ch20). The fishing boat is a sign of human habitation even in this distant place, also delivering letters. Victor unintentionally leaves the island by his small boat and uses the depths of the sea to hide evidence of his second ungodly act, 'determined to throw them into the sea that very night' (Ch20).

The sea has agency in the narrative: 'the murmur lulled me, and in a short time I slept soundly' (Ch20). Sleep allows the sea to take the boat to another shore, 'when suddenly I saw a line of high land towards the south' (Ch20), bringing Victor to his experience of the justice system – this time in Ireland.

The prison

As soon as Victor lands, he is taken prisoner, to be spoken to as villain. He is unaware of the death of Clerval and the finding of his body on the shore earlier. He awakes from a fever some months later to find himself 'in a prison, stretched on a wretched bed, surrounded by gaolers, turnkeys, bolts, and all the miserable apparatus of a dungeon' (Ch21). The prison symbolises the justice system, to which earlier he condemned Justine. This reminds us of Justine's innocence. Here, Victor comes to reflect on his silence, which condemned her. Victor is lucky and, despite the 'carelessness' and 'brutality' of the old woman who watches over him, he experiences the kindness of the 'benevolent' Mr Kirwan (Ch21). Victor is saved by his class status, evidenced in his clothing and his documents. He is found to be innocent, as 'Mr Kirwin charged himself with every care of collecting witnesses, and arranging my defence' (Ch21). Victor is rescued by his father and returns to Geneva. This is in stark contrast to Justine's treatment. As a servant, she is not privileged in this way and is lost to the momentum of the justice system, with a conviction prioritised over proving her innocence.

Character focus

Victor ☀

Key quotations:

- 'Three years before I was engaged in the same manner, and had created a fiend' (Ch20)

- 'Begone! I do break my promise; never will I create another like yourself, equal in deformity and wickedness' (Ch20)

- 'But sleep did not afford me respite from thought and misery; my dreams presented a thousand objects that scared me' (Ch21)

In this section, Victor reflects on the creation of the mate and how he perceives his original creation: 'created a fiend whose unparalleled barbarity had desolated my heart' (Ch20). Victor's narcissism, however, makes him focus on his own feelings not those of the Creature, whom he rejected. Victor's ignorance prevents him from understanding that the 'fiend' is of his own making, having never shown the Creature the love and affection from which Victor has benefited from his birth. Victor's scorn and derision are carefully contrasted with the paternal love and care that he receives when his father arrives. We also see Victor neglect the significance of the Creature's threat to be with him on his wedding night.

We have one small glimpse of Victor's potential humanity and sympathy ,when he 'almost felt as if I had mangled the living flesh of a human being' (Ch20). This does not last very long, and soon he reverts to introspection and self-absorption. His egotism returns in Chapter 21, when he compares his condition with all humanity: 'More miserable than man ever was before, why did I not sink into forgetfulness and rest?' Victor falls into a fever, demonstrating that his emotional and physical resources are once again depleted, but this is his own doing.

PIT STOP ▼

Does the reader feel sympathy for Victor? Students could use think-pair-share to explore this question.

Mr Kirwan ✄

Key quotations:

- 'I was soon introduced into the presence of the magistrate, an old benevolent man, with calm and mild manners. He looked upon me, however, with some degree of severity' (Ch21)

- 'I soon learned that Mr. Kirwin had shown me extreme kindness' (Ch21)

- 'I instantly wrote to Geneva' (Ch21)

Mr Kirwan begins as a symbol of the justice system in Chapter 20, but he becomes a quasi-paternal figure in Chapter 21. We can see some conflict in these two roles. Mr Kirwan appears to respect Victor because of his evident high social standing, even though Victor is a potential murderer. Mr Kirwan has a key role to play in the narrative here: he is deliberately crafted as a good and kind character, so that he can ensure that Victor is not a victim of the justice system, in contrast to lower-class Justine. At first, Mr Kirwan looks with 'severity' at Victor, as he is suspected of murder, but despite this initial encounter, Victor finds that Mr Kirwan has ensured that he has been cared for until his recovery, even assigning him 'the best room' (Ch21) in the prison. He shows 'sympathy and compassion' (Ch21) and contacts Victor's father to take Victor home. He gathers evidence to show that Victor is not guilty and even makes sure that Victor 'was spared the disgrace of appearing publicly as a criminal' (Ch21). This reminds us that Justine was convicted in a public trial. Shelley uses Mr Kirwan to make clear links and contrasts throughout the novel.

Alphonse 🕯 ⚙

Key quotations:

- 'Nothing, at this moment, could have given me greater pleasure than the arrival of my father' (Ch21)
- 'My father tried to awaken in me the feelings of affection' (Ch21)
- 'My father, who was watching over me' (Ch21)

Alphonse's role in Chapter 21 is to rescue Victor and return him to the comforts of home. When Victor realises that it is his father and not the Creature, he behaves once again in a selfish manner: 'But where is he, why does he not hasten to me? (Ch21). Alphonse's reaction is selfless, worrying immediately about his son's health. However, when Victor sees his father, he is relieved that his father is safe, as well as Ernest and Elizabeth. Alphonse is now a symbol of home and comfort; he takes responsibility for their safe repatriation, but considers a delay to ensure that his son is completely recovered. His father watches over Victor, possibly going without sleep to protect him from his nightmares.

Structure 🗂

Chapter 20

Opening: 'I sat one evening in my laboratory; the sun had set, and the moon was just rising from the sea; I had not sufficient light for my employment, and I remained idle'

Ending: 'I must pause here; for it requires all my fortitude to recall the memory of the frightful events which I am about to relate, in proper detail, to my recollection'

At the start of this chapter, Shelley foregrounds a recurring theme of the procrastination of Victor while making the Creature's mate. Whereas in Chapter 4 he is obsessed and relentless in his commitment to the creation of the Creature, his reluctance to complete the female is visible with every plodding, reluctant step towards it.

By the end of this chapter, Victor has aborted the mate in what could best be described as a fit of pique, without thought for the consequences of doing so. Therefore, Shelley ends the chapter by foreshadowing the death of Clerval *and* the rest of his family. Once again, Victor's lack of foresight has fatal consequences for other characters.

Chapter 21

Opening: 'I was soon introduced into the presence of the magistrate, an old benevolent man, with calm and mild manners'

Ending: 'truce was established between the present hour and the irresistible, disastrous future, imparted to me a kind of calm forgetfulness, of which the human mind is by its structure peculiarly susceptible'

Chapter 21 is structured around the aftermath of the murder. The evidence is given against Victor as the murderer of an unknown man. Shelley deliberately delays the revelation about who the deceased gentleman is. In the previous chapter, the reader knows that Frankenstein has received letters from Henry Clerval, who is wanting to rejoin Victor. The description of the 'black mark' (Ch21) causes Frankenstein to think back to the murder of his brother, William. Victor has already prepared the reader for Clerval's death in his role of narrator. Later, Frankenstein thinks of Justine, 'less innocent than poor Justine had been' (Ch21), making a clear link to earlier in the novel.

Following a fever, Victor's acquittal leads to his return home in the company of his father. At the end of the chapter, the sea acts as a space in which for Victor to reflect on Clerval's death and his 'whole life'. Shelley uses the very end of Chapter 21 to make Victor and the reader think of 'the irresistible, disastrous future'.

Section

This section – Chapters 20 and 21 – is linked by the use of sea as a device to move the plot forward. It brings the Creature to the island but also allows him to leave. Victor is also transported by the sea, albeit accidentally, taking him to Ireland, where he faces trial. Then he travels by sea, with his father, back to Europe.

Once again, we have a chapter (Ch20) structured around an encounter between the Creature and Victor. This is preceded by Victor's reflection on his actions, which almost seems to prompt the arrival of the Creature. The Creature witnesses the destruction of his mate, which leads to his return to argue and threaten vengeance. This then drives Victor to dismantle his laboratory and hide the evidence of the second creature at sea. The sea is then used as a means by which to remove Victor from the island and place him in danger of imprisonment. Shelley makes a deliberate link between the end of Chapter 20, introducing the name of Mr Kirwan, the magistrate, and opening Chapter 21 with Victor meeting him to hear the evidence against him regarding a murder.

PIT STOP ▼

How does the beginning of Chapter 20 link to the end of Chapter 19?

Why is this important?

Why does Shelley have Frankenstein reflect on the potential personality of the mate ('was now about to form another being, of whose dispositions I was alike ignorant')? (Ch20)

PIT STOP ▼

S-T-R-E-T-C-H

How is place used as a structural device?

Extracts

Extract 1 (Ch20): How does Shelley present Victor's response to seeing the Creature? 🔬

---- 66 ----

'As I looked on him, his countenance expressed the utmost extent of malice and treachery. I thought with a sensation of madness on my promise of creating another like to him, and trembling with passion, tore to pieces the thing on which I was engaged. The wretch saw me destroy the creature on whose future existence he depended for happiness, and, with a howl of devilish despair and revenge, withdrew.'

---- 99 ----

In this extract, Victor's response to the Creature is utter hatred and fear. The words 'utmost extent of malice and treachery' reveal that Victor sees the Creature as the most dangerous creature that could exist, with the words 'malice' highlighting that he considers the Creature to be pure evil. Victor's response is also reflective, though, as he thinks about his own promise and actions. The words 'sensation of madness' suggest that Victor now thinks that he was out of his mind to make such a promise to the Creature, and the words 'trembling with passion' further emphasise that Victor is so consumed by his fear and hatred that he almost can't control himself when he is around the Creature. Even though Victor acknowledges that the mate is the thing on which the Creature 'depended for happiness', Shelley hints that Victor still cannot see the Creature as having a human side. The words 'devilish despair and revenge' suggest that, in Victor's eyes, even when hurt, the Creature is still a fiend.

Extract 2 (Ch21): How does Shelley demonstrate Victor's prejudice against social class and appearance?

> 66
>
> 'This sound disturbed an old woman who was sleeping in a chair beside me. She was a hired nurse, the wife of one of the turnkeys, and her countenance expressed all those bad qualities which often characterise that class. The lines of her face were hard and rude, like that of persons accustomed to see without sympathising in sights of misery. Her tone expressed her entire indifference; she addressed me in English, and the voice struck me as one that I had heard during my sufferings.'
>
> 99

Shelley shows us Frankenstein's view of women and class. He is shown to have a condescending view, seeing her only as 'an old woman' and focusing on her physical features as symbolising only bad qualities, 'which often characterise that class'. He describes the hardness and rudeness (roughness) of her features. Shortly after this extract, Victor demonstrates his ignorance and self-importance: 'I turned with loathing from the woman who could utter so unfeeling a speech to a person just saved, on the very edge of death' (Ch21). He is unable to understand that she sees him as a murderer. He expresses disgust, both for her appearance and for her character, not understanding that these result from her poverty and low social status.

Extract 3 (Ch20): How does Shelley present Victor's fear of the female?

> 66
>
> 'she might become ten thousand times more malignant than her mate, and delight, for its own sake, in murder and wretchedness'
>
> 99

This is a motif throughout the novel. In this section, Victor is afraid that if he creates a mate, the pair of creatures will procreate. Victor will no longer be solely in charge of the creation of new life. He considers that the female will be more evil than the male Creature. He does not consider that their companionship could be the solution to the Creature's unhappiness and loneliness. It is interesting to reflect that Victor's fear of the female is evident from the beginning of the novel in his creation of a male being. Mellor (1988,

p. 119) asserts that he is afraid of independent female will and that she may demand her 'evolutionary right to determine her own existence'. Mellor discusses that Victor may also be afraid that the mate will find the Creature too ugly and want to mate with human males, and also that the mate will be uglier than the Creature and that he will refuse to have her as a mate. Mellor tells us that Victor 'truly fears female sexuality' and that he 'violently reasserts male control over a female body' (ibid, p120). The reader can link this with the presentation of the other female characters in the novel.

Extract 4 (Ch20): How does Shelley convey how strongly the Creature wants revenge?

'Man! you may hate; but beware! your hours will pass in dread and misery, and soon the bolt will fall which must ravish from you your happiness for ever. Are you to be happy, while I grovel in the intensity of my wretchedness? You can blast my other passions; but revenge remains – revenge, henceforth dearer than light or food! I may die; but first you, my tyrant and tormentor, shall curse the sun that gazes on your misery. Beware; for I am fearless, and therefore powerful. I will watch with the wiliness of a snake, that I may sting with its venom. Man, you shall repent of the injuries you inflict.'

The confrontation between the Creature and Victor is central to this section of the novel. The Creature expresses his anger, anguish and frustration in a series of questions and direct address. He understands the depth of feeling that Victor has towards him – 'you may hate' – and warns him to 'beware!'. The Creature threatens that Victor will feel the same as him as he continues to exact revenge. He contrasts his 'wretchedness' with Victor's 'happiness'. This includes the famous line 'Beware; for I am fearless, and therefore powerful.' The Creature has nothing more to lose, as he has already lost the affection of his creator and the affection of old De Lacey; he is rejected by all and now has no companionship to which to look forward. Therefore, the Creature will exact the cruellest form of revenge, which Victor cannot imagine: the murder of Elizabeth.

SECTION 12
THE LOSS OF LOVE
(CHAPTERS 22–23)

At a glance

> **Summary quotation:** 'I devote myself, either in my life of death, to his destruction' (Ch23)

> **Big Question:** What is the impact of the loss of love?

> **Significant plot events:**

Chapter 22:

- Victor and his father make their journey home from Ireland to Geneva.

- Elizabeth worries that Victor loves another, but is reassured by him.

- The two are married and set off for Villa Lavenza, their honeymoon destination.

Chapter 23:

- Elizabeth is murdered.

- The search for the Creature is unsuccessful.

- In shock, Alphonse dies of a stroke.

- Victor confesses his story to a magistrate.

- Victor vows to seek out and destroy the Creature.

> **Character focus:** Victor, Elizabeth, Alphonse

> **Key themes:**

- Family and companionship 🐾
- Death and grief ✝
- Revenge 🐾
- Crime and justice ✎
- Betrayal and guilt ♡
- Society and social class �֍
- Obsession 🧠
- Narrator and narration **N**

> **Handle with care:**

- traits of a toxic relationship between Victor and Elizabeth
- the murder of Elizabeth

Why?

- Why does Shelley have Victor return to Geneva for his wedding?
- Why does Victor wish to get married soon?
- Why is Elizabeth murdered?
- Why does Victor vow revenge on the Creature?

S-T-R-E-T-C-H questions

- Why do so many of Shelley's female characters die?
- Why does Shelley have Victor confess his story?

What? ▣

What happens?

Chapter 22

Victor and Alphonse continue their journey home via Paris. Alphonse is keen for Victor to socialise, believing that it will make him feel better, but Victor struggles with this. Desperate, he confesses his responsibility for the deaths of William, Justine and Clerval. Alphonse is confused and insists that Victor is innocent. A letter from Elizabeth arrives: she doubts their engagement, as she feels that Victor might love another. Remembering the Creature's threat to be with Victor on his wedding night, Victor decides that the marriage should take place as soon as possible. Victor and Alphonse arrive home and set a date for the wedding. Victor is increasingly anxious and begins to carry pistols. Elizabeth is 'melancholic', but the two are married and they set off for their honeymoon.

Chapter 23 ✎

Victor and Elizabeth arrive at Villa Lavenza for their honeymoon. Victor is fearful and unsettled, but tries to reassure Elizabeth. He arms himself, leaves Elizabeth to rest, and searches for the Creature, vowing to kill or be killed. Suddenly, he hears a scream. Elizabeth is murdered. On her neck is the same mark found on the necks of William and Clerval, telling Victor that the Creature is the murderer. He faints, and then feebly tries to help local men in boats search for the murderer. After failing to find the Creature, Victor returns to Geneva to protect the rest of the family. Alphonse grieves heavily and soon dies. Now desperate, Victor turns to a Genevan magistrate and confesses everything. To his surprise, the magistrate believes him, but says that searching for such a powerful and resourceful creature would be futile. Fuelled by anger and heartbreak, Victor vows that he alone will seek out and destroy the Creature.

Social and historical context

Historical context: Marriage

There were many conventions and expectations around marriage in Georgian England. Despite herself having a marriage that bucked many of these, Shelley echoes a number of them with the marriage of Victor and Elizabeth.

Many marriages in the Georgian era were transactional and an arrangement of convenience. Echoing this, Elizabeth and Victor's is arranged by family. While the age of consent was in the early teens, many couples did not marry until they had greater financial stability, in their mid-twenties – just as Elizabeth and Victor do not marry before his education is complete. However, their courtship differs from many of the time. The era's increasing use of love tokens, Valentine's cards and lengthy letters testify to the importance of courtship at the time, yet Victor and Elizabeth's relationship is far from this, with its long periods without communication. Much has been written about Victor's avoidance of the marriage, from explorations into queer theory, including Victor's repeated delay of a sexual union with a woman, to psychological explorations into Victor's obsession with the 'child' that he created without a woman, which forms a barrier against his marrying.

By the point of their wedding, the marriage between Victor and Elizabeth has become little more than a mutually beneficial alliance. Their union serves to fulfil their shared promise to Caroline and provide a perceived sense of security for Elizabeth. It is also a source of moral respite for Victor, although his reason for needing this is far from the mistress-related profanities of many Georgian men. His sudden drive to marry quickly once the threat from his Creature intensifies would echo this Georgian sentiment, while also serving as a way for Shelley to repeat once again the role that Elizabeth (and perhaps all women) have in providing moral and spiritual solace.

Interestingly, Shelley has Victor mention that, prior to the wedding, Alphonse ensures that Elizabeth's inheritance is 'restored to her by the Austrian government' (Ch23). This may seem insignificant to modern readers, but to Shelley's contemporaries this would be a key enabler of the marriage, as a woman like Elizabeth would be expected to have a dowry. Given Elizabeth's unconventional origins, asserting her lineage and inheritance before the marriage would avoid any potential questions or embarrassment for the Frankensteins (it is interesting to note here that in the 1818 edition, the house is purchased for them, rather than being part of Elizabeth's inheritance).

Given Shelley's unconventional romance and subsequent marriage, perhaps this inclusion serves to comment on social expectations around marriage.

Victor and Elizabeth's is a marriage that follows social conventions and yet is woefully doomed, so is Shelley reflecting her thoughts about the perfunctory nature of those social conventions?

Vocabulary in context

Word	Quotation	Definition
Chapter 22		
imperious	'I curbed the imperious voice of wretchedness'	unpleasantly proud; expecting to be obeyed
invincible	'I should almost regard him as invincible'	impossible to defeat or prevent from doing what is intended
Chapter 23		
incredulous	'Appeared at first incredulous'	not wanting to believe something, and usually showing this
proportionate	'He shall suffer punishment proportionate to his crimes'	an appropriate amount
transitory	'enjoying the transitory light'	temporary; not permanent

PIT STOP ⚐

To develop learners' understanding of the word 'incredulous' and other useful vocabulary for this chapter, teachers could utilise these words for retrieval practice. Learners could be asked to list events that are incredulous, relationships or emotions that are transitory, or times where characters have been imperious.

Plot and character development

1. What are the reasons for Victor's marriage to Elizabeth? ⚙

In Elizabeth's letter to Victor, she reminds him that their marriage is Caroline's dying wish: 'our union had been the favourite plan of your parents' (Ch22). However, instead of focusing on his mother's wishes, Victor's focus is the Creature and his threat about Victor's wedding night. Beyond simply seeing the marriage as a means with which to bring 'of my father's happiness' (Ch22), he also wishes to marry to bring the conflict with his Creature to an end.

2. How does Victor feel about the marriage?

At times, Shelley implies that Victor carries affection for Elizabeth, his 'beloved girl' (Ch22) He also states to his father that 'I love Elizabeth and look forward to our union with delight' (Ch22). However, within a few lines of this he also states, 'I would rather have... wandered a friendless outcast over the earth than consented to this miserable marriage' (Ch22). Shelley focuses his narrative more on what the marriage will mean for the Creature. From this, it can be inferred that despite writing positively about Elizabeth, she is not his priority.

As the wedding approaches, Shelley ensures that Victor's uncertainty is clear, as he becomes very contrary, sometimes talking about arming himself with pistols, but also saying that the wedding talk focused him on the 'happiness [he] hoped' (Ch22). Finally, when the ceremony has taken place and he and Elizabeth set off to cross Lake Como, he describes this as the 'last moments' (Ch22) in which he enjoys happiness. In a reversal of usual behaviour, he notes that Elizabeth is sorrowful, and asks her to 'endeavour to let [him] taste the quiet and freedom from despair' (Ch22). As her emotions have been so influenced by his, this perhaps suggests that his happiness is stronger in memory than it was at the time.

3. What impact does Victor have on Elizabeth?

Shelley echoes a similar sense of uncertainty through Elizabeth, who also seems more unsettled in this chapter than she has in previous chapters. Victor describes that she views the coming marriage with 'placid contentment, not unmingled with a little fear' and that, on their wedding day, she was 'melancholy' (Ch22), very different to how brides may be expected to feel.

PIT STOP

There are many ways in which the relationship between Victor and Elizabeth is not a healthy one; it could even be described as a 'toxic' relationship. There are several points here that should be considered when exploring the relationship with learners:

- Victor has talked about Elizabeth as an object several times throughout the novel.

- Elizabeth feels obliged to marry Victor due to an old agreement; he does not appear to feel this same obligation.

- Elizabeth has deep emotional ties to Victor, although these do not appear to be reciprocated.

- He tells her that he has a 'dreadful' secret, but will not share it with her until she has married him.

- When Elizabeth is unhappy, Victor does not seek to cheer her but appreciates this, as it better suits his current mood.

While this is a fictional relationship, the relationship traits exist in real relationships, and teachers have a duty to challenge them and make it clear to learners that these are not acceptable.

---

4. Where do Victor and Elizabeth go for their honeymoon?

Victor and Elizabeth plan to honeymoon in Villa Lavenza, her family seat in Austria. It is, perhaps, ironic that she should be reunited with her ancestral property at the time when she becomes a married woman (traditionally a time of shift away from her biological family) and, in quick succession, loses her life.

5. How does Elizabeth die? ✏

Much like William and Clerval, Elizabeth dies at the hands of the Creature. Just like them, he leaves a mark on her neck so that there is no doubt as to who the murderer is.

6. What is the impact of Elizabeth's death on Victor? ✝

Initially, Victor 'faints' at the sight of Elizabeth's murder. Later, after failing to help local men search for the murderer, he walks 'like a drunken man' as his 'head whirled round' and he falls again in a 'state of utter exhaustion' (Ch23). His mourning is intense and sharp, as he 'crawl[s]' into the room of the murder and 'reflects confusedly on [his] misfortunes' (Ch23). This sadness is briefly lived, however, and he soon sets off to hunt down the Creature.

In the remainder of the section, Victor's anger and determination to seek vengeance grow, as he quickly moves from sadness to aggression.

7. What is the impact of Elizabeth's death on Victor's father? ✝

The impact of Elizabeth's death on Alphonse Frankenstein is succinctly described by Victor. Alphonse's eyes 'lost their charm and delight' and 'the springs of existence suddenly gave way' (Ch23) and, in a few days, Alphonse dies in Victor's arms.

PIT STOP ▼

S-T-R-E-T-C-H

The death of Elizabeth is not the first time that Alphonse has experienced grief: he has grieved for his close friend, his wife and his son, as well as supporting Victor through his troubles. It could, then, be discussed as to why Shelley chooses the death of Elizabeth as the final blow that causes Alphonse's death: is it to compound Victor's suffering or is there another motive here?

---

8. What does Victor do next?

At first, Victor seeks the support of the conventional systems of justice and seeks out a Genevan magistrate. Despite the portrayed flaws of formal justice in the novel so far (the wrongful conviction of Justine and Victor's accusation as Clerval's murderer), Victor's faith in social institutions is still strong and he confides his story to the magistrate to bid for manpower and support.

PIT STOP

S-T-R-E-T-C-H

Victor's reflections on his own storytelling abilities here are an interesting avenue to explore with learners. He remarks that he 'was impressive but calm' and that he relays his story with 'firmness and precision... never deviating into inventive or exclamation' (Ch23). Given the obscure timeline, and Victor's relatively frequent self-indulgence, it would be interesting to discuss the extent to which learners agree with Victor's perspective on his own storytelling abilities. Do they believe that Victor is capable of a 'brief' and objective report on the events related to his life?

9. What is the magistrate's response to Victor's story?

Victor provides us with his perspective on the magistrate's response to his story. At first, he describes the magistrate as 'perfectly incredulous', but then he becomes 'more attentive and interested' and occasionally 'shudder[ed] with horror' (Ch23). While the magistrate is in disbelief at the take, he acknowledges its truth but also the 'impracticable' (Ch23) nature of the quest. Here, Shelley is ambiguous as to whether the magistrate truly believes Victor or whether he is entertaining it due to Victor's situation and aristocratic standing.

10. What does Victor vow to do next?

Enraged by the response of the magistrate that the quest to find and bring the Creature to justice will be almost impossible, Victor vows to seek the Creature himself and destroy him. With little left to lose, Victor aims to 'devote' his life – or death – to the 'destruction' (Ch23) of the Creature.

How?

Language

Shelley's use of settings

Key quotations:

- 'the sun was hot, but we were sheltered from its rays by a kind of canopy while we enjoyed the beauty of the scene' (Ch22)
- 'the clouds swept across it swifter than the flight of the vulture and dimmed her rays' (Ch23)
- 'Suddenly, a heavy storm of rain descended' (Ch23)

Often in the novel, Shelley utilises settings to reflect, embody or foreshadow other elements: the storm in Chapter 5, for example. In this section, too, Shelley utilises her setting to frame the events of these chapters. In Chapter 22, the joyful weather of the ceremony and wedding breakfast is described by Elizabeth as 'divine'. She even describes how the clouds sometimes 'obscure' parts of their view, but that this made the 'scene of beauty still more interesting', again revealing her optimistic and joyful character. Like the clouds, Victor notes that Elizabeth's 'temper was fluctuating', an example of Shelley reinforcing the connection between Elizabeth and nature by echoing her emotions in the day's weather. As the chapter nears its end – along with their wedding day – the sun sets and the wind drops, perhaps foreshadowing the ending to come.

When they reach the shore, the 'sun sank beneath the horizon', prompting Victor's 'cares and fears [to] revive' (Ch22), a clear parallel between the end of the day and the end of Victor's temporary happiness. As is conventional in Gothic fiction, darkness is an enabler of fear, but also the time at which the most violent events take place. By ending her chapter with the onset of night, Shelley skilfully marks the ushering in of a darker atmosphere for the harrowing and climactic events of Chapter 23.

Not content with having marked this change, Shelley softens her tone in the opening of Chapter 23, providing the readers with a moment of calm and enabling her to build a greater crescendo. Victor describes how they enjoyed 'the transitory light' and 'the lovely scene', while Shelley also provides a juxtaposition, in that the lovely scene is 'obscured in darkness', suggesting that the scene has faded to a memory, with faded clarity and tangibility – much like the chance of happiness has for the Frankensteins.

Shelley conducts a crescendo for Victor, as the wind 'rose with great violence in the west', the clouds 'swept across [the moon]' and a sudden 'heavy storm of rain descended' (Ch23). In doing so, Shelley simultaneously ensures that senses and clarity are obscured, both in vision and in sound, with a pounding storm and the erasure of even the moon's light, effectively drawing a curtain on Elizabeth's life and Victor's final source of solace.

Character focus

Victor

Key quotations:

- 'Could I behold this and live? Alas, life is obstinate and clings closest where it is most hated' (Ch23)

'I devote myself, either in life or death, to his destruction' (Ch23)

This section sees a continuation of Victor's previous character development as an increasingly emotional and unstable man. He sways manically between melancholy, rage, solace, contentment, delirium and abject fear. As his emotions and the peril that he faces increase, his behaviour becomes more desperate. His confessions to Alphonse and the magistrate – and his promised confession to Elizabeth – highlight his growing inability to contain his fears and protect others. While he was once content with limited company, this need for contact and communication is a lasting example of the parallels between him and his creation, which also serves to highlight Victor's stark inability to offer sympathy.

S-T-R-E-T-C-H

Sha alludes to this section being the peak of Shelley's critique of Victor, exploring his 'total narcissism' and asking 'How could he possibly know that out of all mortals, he is the most miserable?' (2021, p. 56). In stating that 'I would die to make her happy', Sha suggests that here Shelley reveals the 'strength of [Victor's] egotism' and that his lack of recognition that 'there is no scenario under which his death could make [Elizabeth] happy' (2021, p. 56) reveals his failure to understand Elizabeth at all.

Alphonse ✝

Key quotations:

- 'My father's care and attentions were indefatigable' (Ch22)

- 'My father yielding at length my desire to avoid society and strove by various arguments to banish my despair' (Ch22)

- 'I intreat you never to make such an assertion again' (Ch22)

This section sees the pinnacle of Alphonse's lack of understanding of his son, as he tries in vain to help Victor, first by encouraging him to be social and by shutting down Victor's pleading confession. This is the final in a series of emotional rejections from Alphonse to Victor: he swiftly sends Victor off to university after Caroline's death, and warns him against 'excessive sorrow' when William dies (Ch9). Ultimately, he also fails to support Victor in his grief for Elizabeth, as he is consumed by his own sorrow and dies of a stress-induced stroke.

Alphonse's name comes from *alpha*, meaning first, perhaps reflecting that he is the most senior of the Frankenstein men. It could also suggest that he is the origin of Victor (and the Creature's) unhappiness.

Debating how much Alphonse's parenting could be to blame for Victor's unhappiness and neglect may facilitate valuable critical thinking. Teachers could pose questions such as:

- Do you feel that Alphonse is a good father?

- How much do you think that Alphonse really understands Victor?

- Do you think that Victor feels safe and happy around his father?

- Do you think that Alphonse has been a good parental role model for Victor?

The Creature ⚜

Key quotation:

- 'A grin was on the face of the monster, he seemed to jeer, as with his fiendish finger he pointed to the corpse of my wife' (Ch23)

In this section, the character becomes his most powerful, despite having no dialogue. In killing Elizabeth, the Creature fulfils his threat to Victor and crosses a threshold in their relationship. By leaving a 'murderous mark' (Ch23) on Elizabeth's neck, he overtly seeks Victor's attention, and furthers this by 'point[ing]' (Ch23) to Elizabeth through the window, with an expression that Victor interprets as jeering. David Clark argues that these marks are symbolic of the Creature's desire to communicate with Victor, stating, 'like speech, these killings seek and elicit a response' (2021, p. 24). The Creature is resourceful and, as his verbal communication with Victor failed, killing Elizabeth becomes his communication method. The fact that Victor had misinterpreted the Creature's threat as one to himself, rather than to his wife, further exemplifies how little he understands the Creature.

Elizabeth

Key quotations:

- 'I hope to see peace in your countenance and to find that our heart is not totally void of comfort and tranquillity' (Ch22)

- 'Happy and serene all nature appears!' (Ch22)

- 'Elizabeth observed my agitation for some time in timid and fearful silence' (Ch23)

In this section, Shelley reveals for the first time the impact that Victor has on Elizabeth. In Chapter 22, she is 'thinner', has 'lost much of that heavenly vivacity' and seems on edge, being described as 'ever-watchful'. While she is 'melancholy', she still finds joy in nature when on the lake, suggesting that her joyous side is not entirely lost.

Shelley also portrays Elizabeth as perhaps having strong intuition, as she watches Victor in 'timid and fearful silence' and 'tremble[s]' (Ch23), suggesting that she knows that something is wrong.

Far from the joyful and effervescent young woman that she was early in the novel, here the negative impact that Victor has on Elizabeth is clear to see. The greatest impact, however, comes in the form of Victor's naive assumption that the Creature will kill him, neglecting to consider Elizabeth's vulnerability. As such, he leaves her alone, only for her to be murdered moments afterwards.

Structure 🗂

Chapter 22

Opening: 'The voyage came to an end'

Ending: 'The sun sank beneath the horizon as we landed, and as I touched the shore I felt those cares and fears revive which soon were to clasp me and cling to me for ever'

Chapter 23

Opening: 'It was eight o'clock when we landed; we walked for a short time on the shore, enjoying the transitory light, and then retired to the inn and contemplated the lovely scene of waters, woods, and mountains, obscured in darkness, yet still displaying their black outlines'

Ending: 'I broke from the house angry and disturbed and retired to meditate on some other mode of action'

Section

These chapters see the peak of Victor's emotional outpouring and outrage. This section is, in many ways, a section of beginnings and endings, such as:

- the end of Victor's silence over his scientific endeavours
- the beginning (and end) of Victor and Elizabeth's marriage
- the end of the threat made by the Creature
- the end of Victor's naive belief that the Creature's ultimate aim is to kill him
- the beginning of Victor's pursuit of the Creature in a bid for revenge.

In this way, Shelley plays with her structure, shifting Victor across locations but almost as swiftly shifting him across different emotional plains.

Victor's perspective vs the Creature's

Throughout the novel, Victor and his Creature have often mirrored each other to echo their intrinsic connection; often, the Creature serves to represent Victor's fears, shortcomings and psychological instability. As with many other themes in the novel, in this section the parallels between the two characters reach their pinnacle.

Victor's destruction of the Creature's mate sends him to absolute rage. Similarly, it is the Creature's destruction of Victor's wife that sends Victor to his. Both cut off from usual forms of justice (the Creature because he is not human and Victor because his story is so wild), vengeance is the only route that remains for each of them, and they begin to mirror each other's anger. Shelley has portrayed her Creature as losing rationality when society – and, ultimately, Victor – fails to embrace him; so too does Victor lose not only the rationality of a scientist but also the decent and civilised response of a feeling human.

PIT STOP ▼

As within earlier chapters, mapping the parallels and similarities in the journeys of the Creature and Victor can be a rich foundation for debate and discussion among learners. Teachers may wish to focus on their similarities or differences in key themes too. For example:

- How do Victor and the Creature respond to grief?

- What do Victor and the Creature do to seek revenge?

- How do Victor and the Creature seek justice? Where have we seen them do this earlier in the text?

Extracts

Extract 1 (Ch22): How does Shelley portray Victor's guilt?

———————— 66 ————————

"'I am not mad," I cried energetically; "the sun and the heavens, who have viewed my operations, can bear witness of my truth. I am the assassin of those most innocent victims; they died by my machinations. A thousand times would I have shed my own blood, drop by drop, to have saved their lives; but I could not, my father, indeed I could not sacrifice the whole human race."'

———————— 99 ————————

This extract follows Alphonse's comment that Victor should 'never' again talk of his guilt for the deaths of his family. Here, we see the intensity of Victor's guilt, but also how much he longs to share his burden of knowledge. In stating that 'I could not sacrifice the whole human race' (a confession that his father cannot possibly understand), he reveals how much his mind has been focused on the conflicting responsibilities that he feels to his Creature and to the human race, as he is responsible both to and for the Creature. The hyperbolic language stresses how great Victor feels that his guilt is: the 'whole human race' would unlikely have been impacted, and he could not 'shed [his] blood... a thousand times'. In addition to this, in Victor's declaration of the Creature as 'the assassin', he promotes the status of the victims (only substantial figures are 'assassinated') and claims agency over their killing, despite having no direct involvement. Shelley uses this hyperbole to emphasise the magnifying power that Victor's guilt has over his emotions and his interpretation of events. Here, she leaves us in no doubt as to the pervasive nature of his guilt, which she implies has ballooned in his imagination to an almost delusional degree.

PIT STOP ▼

How guilty is Victor? ✏

In this extract, Victor confesses his guilt to his father. This contributes to one of several overarching questions that Shelley explores throughout the novel: how much are parents responsible for the actions of their children, and how much blame should they shoulder for those actions? Here is a good opportunity to discuss this question, exploring the different parts of the novel that raise the question and developing learners' understanding of the question by debating it.

Extract 2 (Ch23): How does Shelley present Victor's determination to destroy the Creature? 💬 ⚙

❝

'My revenge is of no moment to you; yet, while I allow it to be a vice, I confess that it is the devouring and only passion of my soul. My rage is unspeakable when I reflect that the murderer, whom I have turned loose upon society, still exists. You refuse my just demand; I have but one resource, and I devote myself, either in my life or death, to his destruction.'

❞

This extract follows the magistrate's explanation of how difficult he believes that it would be to capture the Creature. Here, Victor responds by emphatically declaring his determination to bring about the Creature's destruction and describing the depth of his anger. In describing his rage as 'the devouring and only passion of my soul', Shelley reveals how Victor feels that he has nothing left in his life but anger and that his anger is all-consuming. In this quotation, he continues his recent thread of ascribing responsibility for the Creature's actions to himself, referring to the 'murderer whom I have turned loose upon society'. It is interesting to note that Shelley has Victor refer to the Creature simply as 'the murderer', unlike his previous references to the 'wretch', 'daemon' and 'monster', among other terms, as 'murderer' is a term that arguably carries fewer connotations of horror and which defines the Creature by his actions rather than his creation. This perhaps further reflects Victor's desire to reprimand the Creature, as he is explicitly framing him as monstrous due to his actions, rather than monstrous due to his being. In the final line of the extract, Victor's determination to destroy the Creature is clear in Shelley's phrasing: in writing 'I devote myself', rather than 'I am devoted', she positions Victor's statement as a determined vow, a pledge that cements his determination to end the life of his Creature.

SECTION 13
THE JOURNEY'S END
(CHAPTER 24)

At a glance

> **Summary quotation:** 'My spirit will sleep in peace, or if it thinks, it will not surely think thus' (Ch24)

> **Big Question:** What ideas of legacy does Shelley leave us with?

> **Significant plot events:**
>   - Victor's tale ends.
>   - Walton turns away from his quest.
>   - The Creature kills Victor before disappearing over the ice.

> **Character focus:** Victor, the Creature, Walton

> **Key themes:**
>   - Death and grief ✝
>   - Ambition and legacy 🏆
>   - Obsession 🎧
>   - Prejudice 👥
>   - Destiny and fate 🧬
>   - Rejection and its consequences ⊗
>   - Power and responsibility 💡
>   - Narrator and narration Ⓝ
>   - Betrayal and guilt 🫴

> **Handle with care:**
>   - the murder of Victor
>   - the Creature's suicide

Why?

- Why does Victor wish Walton to continue?
- Why does Walton turn home?
- Why does Walton not sympathise with the Creature?
- Why is the Creature so heartbroken by Victor's death?

S-T-R-E-T-C-H questions

- Why does Shelley have Walton turn home?
- Why does Shelley give the final part of the tale to the Creature?

What?

What happens?

This chapter opens with Victor's immediate thoughts and actions after leaving the magistrate. He visits the cemetery where William and Justine are buried and resolves to bring unimaginable suffering to the Creature. Having followed him, the Creature laughs at this, says that he is satisfied by Victor's suffering and then disappears. Victor leaves Geneva and begins an epic quest to find the Creature, who leaves him messages and food. When Victor eventually comes within close reach of the Creature in the icy Arctic, he is separated from him by broken ice. It is then that Walton's crew find him.

The narrative shifts back to Walton. He summarises Victor's expressions and animation while relaying his tale, and writes that Victor provides proof of the tale's truth through Safie and Felix's letters and by reading through and amending his notes. Walton conveys his admiration for Victor and provides Margaret with a brief overview of the conversations that he holds with Victor about ambition and regret.

In his next letter, Walton despairs at his ship being trapped in the ice. Despite this, a few days later, when it appears likely that the ship will be freed, he struggles with the idea of turning home and away from their mission. At this, Victor rouses and urges the men to continue on their mission. Two days later, Walton concedes to return home if they manage to break free.

In his final letter, Walton shares the story of three days as they turn back towards England. At first, Walton describes the breaking up of the ice that frees the ship, enabling it to turn home. Victor, however, will not give up on his quest, and – despite his severe weakness – determines to stay and find the Creature. While Walton contemplates the loss of his newfound friend, he hears noises from Victor's cabin.

In the cabin, Walton finds the Creature weeping over Victor's dead body, repenting his actions and sharing more of his tale. While Walton is briefly sympathetic, he quickly prompts the Creature to share a final reflection on his fall from virtue to sin, and the irreconcilable tension between his rage and his grief. Finally, the Creature declares his intentions to die and throws himself into the sea.

Social and historical context ⚙

Literary context: The Creature's final act

As with many of the key events in the novel, much has been written about the Creature's final actions and how they can be interpreted. After hundreds of pages of detailed narration on the Creature's few years of existence (including some actions that Shelley offers twice, through her different narrators), Shelley gives her readers an ambiguous ending: does the Creature in fact survive or does he – as he desires – find a final comfort in his solitary death? Naturally, the ambiguity of this has led to various rewritings and sequels, where fans of the novel try to imagine what futures the Creature may have found for himself. Despite this, the majority of academics accept the interpretation that the Creature plans and enacts his suicide.

One interpretation is that the Creature's act is driven by his desire for justice for his actions. Erin M. Goss (2021) argues that the Creature is excluded not only from a social world, but also from a legal one, resulting in him having no options but to bring justice to himself by committing suicide. Goss highlights that by the end of the novel, the Creature's options are limited: he has failed to find a place in the world or in Victor's affections, and both have failed to bring him to the justice that he deserves for his murderous acts. With nowhere to turn, Goss argues that both the plot and the logic of the novel 'require' the Creature's suicide (2021, p. 188).

Vocabulary in context

Word	Quotation	Definition
pilgrimage	'My tedious toil and torturous pilgrimage'	a visit to a place that is considered special, or a journey undertaken by a pilgrim

Plot and character development

1. What motivates Victor to pursue the Creature? ⊙

By this point in the novel, Victor has been intermittently ill for a period of several years and has travelled extensively. He is worn and weary, and even states, 'How I have lived I hardly know' (Ch24). However, he tells Walton that 'revenge kept [him] alive' and, more than that, allowed him to be 'calm' or 'calculated' in order to keep going in a quest to achieve his aim.

2. What landscapes does Victor travel through?

At first, Victor finds himself very close to home and simply in the cemetery of Geneva, where his family are buried. After this, he travels through a number of landscapes across Europe. He mentions that he travels through the Rhone Valley and to the Mediterranean, but also that he crosses the Black Sea into Russia and into the Arctic. It is interesting to note that Victor mentions that sometimes he travels by river and through cities, where the Creature does not tend to go. Despite this, Victor appears to be able (or, at least, suggests that he is able) to follow the Creature as he traverses the continent.

3. What does Victor dream about?

Despite being so desperately unhappy and enraged during the day, Victor's dreams offer him great comfort and '[lull] him even to rapture' (Ch24). He dreams of his father, William, Clerval and Elizabeth, and describes seeing them with 'agonising fondness' and how he found himself 'clinging' to them, suggesting that he does not wish to wake. Moreover, sometimes he feels that he almost persuades himself that they are still alive, echoing his great sense of longing and loss.

PIT STOP ▼

S-T-R-E-T-C-H

Victor's dreams do not simply offer him comfort, but also provide him with great motivation. He describes that he sees his 'path' to destroying the Creature as one 'enjoyed by heaven' (Ch24), suggesting that he sees it almost as a divine duty that is his to fulfil. Learners may benefit from discussing this suggestion within a wider context of Victor's character, exploring how Victor has seen himself and his wider duties at different times throughout the novel.

---

4. How does Victor keep track of the Creature?

Like many other chapters, this one requires readers to suspend their disbelief. At times, Victor's pursuit may seem plausible, but at others it seems wholly unlikely without aid. Victor mentions that he is 'guided by a slight clue', has a sighting of 'strange chance' and spots the Creature's 'print' (Ch24), which provides him with guidance. Add the fact that Victor states that, wherever possible, he follows the courses of rivers that the 'daemon generally avoided' (Ch24), and it soon becomes clear that Victor is not always the follower in his travels. It seems far more reasonable to consider that, rather than the Creature being pursued like prey, the two of them are engaged in gameplay. The Creature even deliberately entices Victor, forging trails for him to follow and even leaving food to ensure that the game continues.

5. What happens to Walton's ship?

Walton is in the Arctic Ocean, around northern Russia. The voyage has been fraught with trials, as he is aiming to venture on a passage not yet explored. In this chapter, Walton finds his ship trapped in ice and unable to move – a situation that could prove deadly. His shipmates look to him for aid, but he knows that he 'has none to bestow' (Ch24). Walton appears well aware of the danger that potentially awaits him, and that if the ship cannot be released, then will all be lost. He even writes to his sister, 'Years will pass, and you will have visitings of despair and yet be tortured by hope' (Ch24), suggesting that he acknowledges that they are so remote from civilisation that no one will even know of their demise.

Thankfully, the ice begins to melt and, despite some debate about whether or not to continue, Walton takes the decision to return home to England.

6. What does Victor want Walton to do? ♣

When Walton's crew appeals to him to turn the ship homeward if they get the opportunity to do so, Walton appears to be unconvinced by this. However, while he considers his response to his crew, Victor interjects with a speech about how important it is that they continue on their quest. He suggests that the men should not have called the mission 'glorious' if they are now to give up on it, and that they should wear the 'stigma of disgrace' (Ch24) if they do.

PIT STOP ▼

S-T-R-E-T-C-H

Walton's narratives can, to some learners, seem unnecessary and an added confusion to the text. However, in this example, Shelley cleverly uses Walton's situation to highlight Victor's lack of foresight and ability to learn from his own experiences. Here, Walton has a chance to save his crew from likely death, yet, in Victor's eyes, this is a worthwhile risk. Deadly or not, it is the glory of the undertaking that matters to Victor. Teachers may wish to contrast Walton and Victor's attitudes and explore other examples of where Victor has been bold – or reckless – in his pursuits.

---

7. What is Walton's response to Victor's tale?

As with earlier in the novel, Walton admires Victor and sees his tale as one of victimhood. He recognises that the story is 'strange and terrific' and also one that can make 'blood congeal with horror' (Ch24). Perhaps most revealing of the similarities between Walton and Victor, Shelley has Walton press Victor for 'the particulars of the Creature's formations' – a request to which Victor responds by accusing Walton of possessing 'senseless curiosity' and asking, 'Are you mad, my friend?' (Ch24). Nonetheless, Walton continues to admire Victor, describing that his 'eloquence is forcible and touching' and again describing that he is 'noble and godlike' (Ch24).

Walton's opinions of Victor appear to differ little between the letters before Victor's tale and now after them. However, he does appear to have altered in his determination to continue with his exploration. It would be interesting to debate with learners why this might be and what Shelley wishes us to think of Walton, and how his character contributes to our wider understanding of Victor and of the messages of the novel.

How?

Language 🔍 💡

Language of prejudice 👥

Key quotations:

- 'Never did I behold a vision so horrible as his face, of such loathsome yet appalling hideousness' (Ch24)

- 'there was something so scaring and unearthly in his ugliness' (Ch24)

Walton is the only living human who knows the Creature's story, with all its complexities. As such, Shelley is able to utilise Walton's response to the Creature to summarise the Creature's potential future: if Walton is able to overcome his horror at the Creature's appearance, then perhaps this would suggest that mankind is not as prejudiced and unforgiving as they may seem.

Walton's first sight of the Creature immediately tells us otherwise, though, as Shelley reminds us of mankind's fixation with physical humanity. Walton describes the Creature as 'gigantic in stature, yet uncouth and distorted', with skin having 'the appearance of a mummy' and a face that is 'loathsome yet appallingly hideous' (Ch24). The adjective 'uncouth' serves to emphasise Walton's blindness to the Creature's sophisticated sentiments when faced with his appearance. Further on, Walton also refers to the Creature as having 'something scaring and unearthly', suggesting again that the 'monster' (as Walton refers to him) could not possibly be from the same earth as mankind, despite knowing his origin story.

Here, Shelley is able to tap into the Romantic exploration of what it is to be human, as Walton's understanding of the Creature's sentience and intelligence fails to override his repulsion at the Creature's appearance. Andrew Griffin (1979) argues that 'either from Mary Shelley's or from Victor's perspective, Walton looks naive and superficial'. Knowing more than any other human – bar Victor – about the Creature, and being in a landscape offering unique opportunities for privacy, Walton's failure to acknowledge the Creature is arguably Shelley's ultimate comment on society's struggles to move beyond ignorance to accept those who are different to themselves.

Character focus

Victor

Key quotations:

- 'Revenge kept me alive' (Ch24)
- 'Like the archangel who aspired to omnipotence, I am chained in an eternal hell' (Ch24)
- 'Do not return to your families with the stigma of disgrace marked on your brows' (Ch24)

Victor's character is varied and contradictory in this chapter. He is both fractious and restless, yet sometimes focused and astute: Walton describes that Victor has periods of 'unbounded knowledge and a quick and piercing appreciation' (Ch24). Shelley continues to portray him as unwaveringly obsessive in his pursuits. For the first time, though, Victor is also troubled by this, and Shelley cleverly uses the dual narration of the chapter to share how Victor only seems at peace in his sleep when he dreams of his dead companions.

Most telling are his responses to Walton's consideration of turning home. At this, Victor is 'roused' to comment with 'vigour' that Walton should not, stating that he should be 'steady in his purpose' and continue to pursue a 'glorious' outcome (Ch24). Here, Shelley makes clear for her readers that, despite seeing the devastating results of his thoughtless pursuits, Victor has ultimately learned nothing from the consequences of these. As a final critique of character, Shelley leaves her readers in no doubt that Victor is a character whom they should not strive to emulate.

The Creature

Key quotations:

- 'You live and I am satisfied' (Ch24)
- 'You will find near this place... a dead hare, eat and be refreshed' (Ch24)
- 'Now this crime has degraded me beneath the meanest animal' (Ch24)
- 'You hate me, but your abhorrence cannot equal that with which I regard myself' (Ch24)

The Creature also continues to be intense and contrary in this chapter. Early in Chapter 24, he appears taunting and menacing when he offers Victor a 'loud and fiendish laugh' and tells Victor that he is 'satisfied' that Victor is alive: an ambiguous statement that could suggest that he is happy to see Victor suffering in life *or* that he is happy that Victor is still alive. Later, his teasing becomes clearer, as he leads Victor through presents and clues (which, arrogantly, Victor believes to be good luck), in gameplay reminiscent of a child vying for their parents' attention.

Ultimately, the Creature is unable to regulate his emotions when he kills Victor. Now lost and alone, his intelligence means that he recognises that he now has no chance of acceptance, but also that he has committed a mortal sin in killing his creator. Being ever self-reflective, the Creature recognises the significance of the killing of his creator, seeing it as a mortal sin, which, he perceives, should bring about his final condemnation and death (or, rather, suicide) on the funeral pyre he vows to build for himself.

Walton

Key quotations:

- 'Yet, could I, in justice, or even possibility, refuse the demand?' (Ch24)
- 'It is well that you come here to whine over the desolation that you have made' (Ch24)

Walton is used in this chapter to offer final comments and perspectives to Shelley's readers. Initially, Walton seems to have learned little from the tale; he even presses Victor for details about the Creature's creation. However, when surrounded by ice and trapped, he shows glimpses of responsibility to his men that serve as a foil to Victor's lack of responsibility to the Creature. The destructive conflict between responsibility to others and individual glory is cleverly highlighted by Shelley here, through Walton's admittance that he would rather die than return home a failure, but also through his final decision to return home.

Structure 🖧

Victor's narrative

Opening: 'My present situation was one in which all voluntary thought was swallowed up and lost'

Ending: 'Hear him not; call on the names of William, Justine, Clerval, Elizabeth, my father, and of the wretched Victor, and thrust your sword into his heart. I will hover near and direct the steel aright'

Walton's narrative

Opening: 'You have read this strange and terrific story, Margaret; and do you not feel your blood congeal with horror, like that which even now curdles mine?'

Ending: 'He was soon borne away by the waves and lost in darkness and distance'

Conflicting narrators Ⓝ

In this section, Victor's story is told directly from two narrators: Victor and Walton. Furthermore, the chapter ends with a large section of the Creature's speech, creating a sense of all three narrative voices converging. This is also the first chapter in which Shelley includes mention of all three and in which the three characters are aware of each other's existence.

Dunn (1974) argues that, despite their common journeys and shared stories, Shelley's three narrators 'remain strangers' to one another', even in this final chapter. This is clear when Walton and Victor clash strongly on the matter of the expedition's future, and when the Creature and Walton are conflicted in their values and motives. More significantly, Shelley denies her readers access to the final words between Victor and the Creature, choosing instead to culminate their relationship in a final act of violent, vengeful communication: murder.

Walton's letters

In the first letters in this chapter, Shelley echoes the earlier letters in the novel: Walton addresses his sister, beginning some with 'My beloved sister' (Ch24). However, by the third letter, Walton explicitly recognises that these 'letters' may never reach Margaret. Here, Shelley begins to shift the structure and tone of Walton's writings to more like those of a diary that he is driven to write, stating he 'cannot forbear recording' the events (Ch24). This need to record becomes even more evident, as Shelley briefly has Walton shift the narrative to present tense as the Creature enters the ship: 'I am interrupted. What do these sounds portend?... I must arise and examine.' (Ch24)

At this point, Shelley shifts to an almost play-like quality, where – much like in Chapter 17 – she uses the balance and structure of her dialogue to reflect the power dynamic of her characters. After describing the Creature's appearance, Walton talks to the Creature to comment, 'If you had listened to the voice of conscience and heeded the stings of remorse... Frankenstein would have yet lived.' (Ch24) Here, Shelley perhaps channels the irony that had Victor listened to a 'voice of conscience', then perhaps he would not have brought the Creature to life in the first place. Importantly, Shelley silences Walton and drowns out his judgement with an extended speech delivered by the Creature, which dominates the final pages of her novel and leaves readers with no doubt as to which character our reflections should focus on.

This is further emphasised as Shelley breaks the pattern with which she has ended Walton's previous contributions. In all of his other letters, Walton ends his communication with a personal reflection or statement about himself in either the penultimate or final sentence: 'I love...' (Letter 2), 'I must...' (Letter 3), 'I possess...' (7 September). However, in his final letter (the final words of the novel), Walton's commentary captures the Creature's movements away and into the ocean, with no offering of perspective or commentary but allowing us, like Walton, to remain in stunned silence at the story of the Creature and his suicidal anguish.

Extracts

Extract 1 (Ch24): How does Shelley use language to present the Creature's pain? ⊗ ⅌

"'Do you think that I was then dead to agony and remorse? He," he continued, pointing to the corpse, "he suffered not in the consummation of the deed. Oh! Not the ten-thousandth portion of the anguish that was mine during the lingering detail of its execution. A frightful selfishness hurried me on, while my heart was poisoned with remorse. Think you that the groans of Clerval were music to my ears? My heart was fashioned to be susceptible of love and sympathy, and when wrenched by misery to vice and hatred, it did not endure the violence of the change without torture such as you cannot even imagine."'

In this extract, Shelley makes it clear that the Creature feels that his pain is grossly underestimated by others. The question 'Do you think that I was then dead to agony and remorse?' reveals that the Creature believes that Walton thinks him to be as inhuman in emotion as he is physically, and the use of the question suggests that he wants to provoke Walton to reflect on this misconception. His frustration at this is also revealed through Shelley's use of the exclamative 'Oh!', which serves to emphasise the Creature's annoyance and serves also as a volta, where Shelley shifts the focus onto the Creature's actual experience rather than Walton's perception of it.

Shelley emphasises the Creature's pain through his comparison of his pain and Victor's: 'not the ten-thousandth portion of the anguish that was mine'. Here, Shelley is able to reflect the Creature's level of suffering but also hint at the resentment that he holds towards the idea that Victor suffered more. The word 'anguish' suggests that the pain was intense and inescapable, while the hyperbolic 'ten-thousandth' highlights how the Creature is utterly incredulous that Victor could possibly have suffered something similar to his level of pain. By twice mentioning the Creature's heart and his past experiences, Shelley is able to emphasise the Creature's pain through the contrast between his potential and his current circumstances. Notably, the Creature describes how his heart was 'susceptible to love and sympathy', but that it has been 'poisoned' by his own acts (specifically the murder of Clerval) and 'wrenched by misery'. The verb 'wrenched' has connotations of force and aggression, while 'poison' has connotations of contamination and visceral pain. These two combine cleverly to emphasise the variety of torturous sufferings that the Creature has suffered, and by including mention of suffering from others and from himself, Shelley reinforces this suffering even further.

Extract 2 (Ch24): How does Shelley use language to reveal Walton's feelings towards the Creature?

"'Wretch!" I said. "It is well that you come here to whine over the desolation that you have made. You throw a torch into a pile of buildings, and when they are consumed, you sit among the ruins and lament the fall. Hypocritical fiend! If he whom you mourn still lived, still would he be the object, again would he become the prey, of your accursed vengeance. It is not pity that you feel; you lament only because the victim of your malignity is withdrawn from your power."'

Shelley's opening of this passage with the word 'wretch!' is a clear indication of Walton's feelings towards the Creature. The word 'wretch' suggests that Walton thinks little of the Creature and believes that he is an awful being. The exclamation mark further emphasises this. Shelley also makes it clear that Walton has very little sympathy for the Creature: 'you come here to whine over the desolation you have made'. The verb 'whine' suggests that Walton sees the Creature's behaviour as childish and attention-seeking. This is reinforced when Walton comments that he thinks that the Creature 'throws a torch into a pile of buildings' and then 'sit[s] amongst the runs and lament[s] the fall'. This comment neglects to consider the Creature's experiences of violence and harm against him, and suggests that Walton sees the Creature as a bringer of suffering to others, rather than as a victim. This is emphasised even further in the use of the word 'prey' to describe Victor, as this positions the Creature as an aggressive predator (and, in contrast, positions Victor as a victim).

Shelley further builds on the impression that Walton sees the Creature in this way in the sentence 'Hypocritical fiend!'. Here, the word 'fiend' highlights that Walton sees the Creature as a devilish demon and a great sinner. The words 'accursed vengeance' and 'malignity' suggest that Walton believes that the Creature and his actions are damned and that he is a truly evil being.

CONCLUSION

Final reflections

When learners reach the end of the novel, they may be left with more questions than answers. To help them bring their understanding together, learners may be asked to consider these different points.

Why does Shelley end her novel ambiguously?

Shelley offers no clear ending for the Creature and no clear direction as to how the reader should feel. Instead, she creates an ambiguous ending and a juxtaposition of violence and vulnerability for the Creature. Learners could be asked to consider why this is. What does Shelley want us to believe happens next? Will the Creature go through with his funeral pyre plans? Why does she leave us guessing?

Could the Creature have found a place in the world?

Learners might be invited to explore whether the Creature ending his life is as necessary as the Creature believes it to be. Does Shelley provide hints that another life may have been possible? If not, at which point did the Creature's life become irredeemable and beyond hope?

Who is the real monster?

By the end of the novel, both Victor and the Creature have committed awful acts. The justification and legitimacy of these is a topic of ripe debate, along with which of them is the greater monster. While the Creature causes more direct death, are Victor's crimes of neglect and deception of equal monstrosity?

Is the Creature worthy of our sympathy?

Finally, readers might be asked to consider how Shelley wishes us to feel about the Creature. Is he a victim worthy of our sympathy or not? If not, who does deserve our sympathy?

PIT STOP ▼

S-T-R-E-T-C-H

More able learners may be asked to consider these questions:

- To what extent are women portrayed as passive victims in Frankenstein?

- Shelley's portrayal of women is complicated: they fulfil the role of saviour and are clearly influential, and yet they each succumb to a tragic downfall, often as a result of a man's actions. What might Shelley wish us to think or feel about women in the story, and how does this influence what we think about the male characters?

- What does Shelley wish us to think about science? Is it science alone that is the concern, or is it science without conscience and feeling that is the worry?

- What does Shelley wish her readers to feel about nature and its influence? What relationship can mankind have with nature?

Tracking themes

Even though lesson time demands that the novel be taught in chunks, learners still need to view the text as a whole. The following tasks will enable them to track key themes and the overarching big idea in the text, *and* their own responses to it.

- Before reading: 'Monsters are made and not born.' To what extent do you agree with this statement?

After reading about Victor's childhood in Chapters 1 to 3: Now that you have read about Victor's childhood, do you still agree with what you initially wrote in response to 'Monsters are made and not born'? Why? Why not?

After reading Chapter 5: Taking into account what you have read so far about Victor and the Creature in Chapter 5, to what extent do you agree with the statement 'Monsters are made and not born'?

After reading all of the Creature's narration: What do you now think in response to the statement 'Monsters are made and not born'?

A similar approach can be adopted when considering reader positioning and where our sympathies are meant to lie at different parts of the novel. This is especially useful and enlightening as the Creature's violence against the Frankenstein family escalates.

A level language and literature

Below is a typical question style for AQA's A level language and literature course:

Read the extract printed below. This is from the section of the novel just before Victor leaves Clerval to work on the Creature's mate in Orkney.

Start of extract: 'But in Clerval I saw the image of my former self'

End of extract: 'it caused my lips to quiver, and my heart to palpitate' (Ch19)

Explore the significance of the character of Clerval in the novel. You should consider:

- the presentation of his character in this extract and other parts of the novel

- the use of fantasy elements in constructing the fictional world.

REFERENCES

AQA (n.d.), 'AQA set text editions', www.aqa.org.uk/subjects/english/gcse/english-8702/specification/subject-content/shakespeare-and-the-19th-century-novel [accessed 2 February 2025].

Baldick, C. (2011). *In Frankenstein's Shadow: Myth, Monstrosity, and Nineteenth-Century Writing*. Oxford: Oxford University Press.

BBC Sounds (2016). '200 years of Frankenstein', *The Infinite Monkey Cage*, series 14, first aired 1 August 2016.

Benedetti, C. (2020). 'The misunderstood monstrous: An analysis of the word "monster" in Mary Shelley's *Frankenstein*'. *The Yale Undergraduate Research Journal*, 1(1), article 15, https://elischolar.library.yale.edu/yurj/vol1/iss1/15 [accessed 13 January 2025].

Bennett, B.T. (ed) (1995). *Selected Letters of Mary Wollstonecraft Shelley*. Baltimore and London: The John Hopkins University Press.

Bennett B.T. (1999). *Lives of the Great Romantics III, Volume 3*. London: Pickering & Chatto.

Bienstock Anolik, R. (2004). 'Introduction: The dark unknown'. In: Bienstock Anolik, R. and Howard, D.L. (eds), *The Gothic Other: Racial and Social Constructions in the Literary Imagination*. London: McFarlane and Company, pp. 1–16.

Blackstone, W. (1765). Blackstone's Commentaries on the Laws of England Book the Fourth, https://avalon.law.yale.edu/18th_century/blackstone_bk4ch27.asp?utm_source=chatgpt.com [accessed 20 January 2025]

Botting, F. (ed.) (1995). *Frankenstein: A New Casebook*. Basingstoke: Macmillan.

Brennan, M.C. (1988). 'The landscape of grief in Mary Shelley's *Frankenstein*'. *Studies in the Humanities*, 15(1), p. 33–44.

Britannica (2024). 'Hubris', www.britannica.com/topic/hubris [accessed 5 November 2024].

Brooks, P. (1978). 'Godlike science/unhallowed arts: Language and monstrosity in *Frankenstein*'. *New Literary History*, 9(3), pp. 591–605.

Brooks, P. (1993). 'What is a monster?' In: *Body Work*. Cambridge: Harvard University Press, pp. 199–220. Accessed at https://knarf.english.upenn.edu/Articles/brooks2.html [accessed 2 February 2025]

Burke, E. (1757). *A Philosophical Enquiry into the Origin of Our Ideas of the Sublime and Beautiful*. London: R. and J. Dodsley.

Cambridge Dictionary (n.d.), 'Hubris', https://dictionary.cambridge.org/dictionary/english/hubris [accessed 7 January 2025].

Carpentier, J. (2020). *Rousseau: The Child of Nature*. London: Routledge.

Clark, D.L. (2021). 'Last words; voice, gesture, and the remains of *Frankenstein*'. In: Wang, O.N.C. (ed.), Frankenstein *in Theory: A Critical Anatomy*. London: Bloomsbury Academic, pp. 13–32.

Clark, R.C., Lyons, C. and Hoover, L. (2004). 'Graphics for learning: Proven guidelines for planning, designing, and evaluating visuals in training materials'. *Performance Improvement*, 43(10), pp. 45–7.

Coleridge, S.T. (1798). *The Rime of the Ancient Mariner*. Great Britain: J. & A. Arch.

Dawley, J.S. (1910). *Frankenstein*, Thomas Edison Films, YouTube, www.youtube.com/watch?v=9LQj68W7O9Q [accessed 23 November 2024].

De Hart, S.D. (2013). *Shelley Unbound: Discovering Frankenstein's true creator*. New York: Feral House.

Dekker, G. (2004). *The Fictions of Romantic Tourism: Radcliffe, Scott, and Mary Shelley*. Stanford, CA: Stanford University Press.

Dunn, R.J. (1974). 'Narrative distance in *Frankenstein*', *Studies in the Novel*, 6, pp. 408–17, https://knarf.english.upenn.edu/Articles/dunn.html [accessed 17 January 2025].

Fishelov, D. (2016). 'The indirect path to the literary canon exemplified by Shelley's Frankenstein'. *CLCWeb: Comparative Literature and Culture*, 18(2), article 6, doi. org/10.7771/1481-4374.2847

Gilbert, S. and Gubar, S. (1979). *The Madwoman in the Attic*. New Haven, CT: Yale University Press.

Gordon, C. (2015). *Romantic Outlaws: The Extraordinary Lives of Mary Wollstonecraft & Mary Shelley*. New York: Random House.

Goss, E.M. (2021). 'The smiles that one is owed: Justice, Justine, and sympathy for a wretch'. In: Wang, O.N.C. (ed.), Frankenstein *in Theory: A Critical Anatomy*. London: Bloomsbury Academic, pp. 185–98.

Griffin, A. (1979). 'Fire and ice in *Frankenstein*'. In: Levine, G. and Knoepflmacher, U.C. (eds), *The Endurance of 'Frankenstein': Essays on Mary Shelley's Novel*. Berkeley, Los Angeles and London: University of California Press, https://knarf.english.upenn.edu/Articles/griffin.html [accessed 23 November 2024].

Gupta, N. (2007). *Frankenstein*. Delhi: Dorling Kindersley.

Guston, D.H., Finn, E. and Robert, J. S. (eds) (2017). *Frankenstein: Annotated for Scientists, Engineers, and Creators of All Kinds*. London: The MIT Press.

Harding, D.W. (1957). 'The character of literature from Blake to Byron', in Ford, B. (ed.), *Volume 5 of The Pelican Guide to Literature*. Harmondsworth: Penguin Books, pp. 33–64.

Hogg, T.J. (1858). *The Life of Percy Bysshe Shelley*, Volume I. London: E. Moxon.

Lanone, C. (2016). 'Context of the novel'. In: Smith, A. (ed.), *Cambridge Companion to Frankenstein*. Cambridge: Cambridge University Press, pp. 56–69.

Locke, J. (1689). 'An Essay Concerning Human Understanding', Project Gutenberg eBook #10615, www.gutenberg.org/files/10615/10615-h/10615-h.htm [accessed 25 January 2025].

Malchow, H.L. (1993). '*Frankenstein*'s monster and images of race in nineteenth-century Britain'. *Past & Present*, 139(1), 1993, pp. 90–130.

Marquette University (n.d.), 'Glossary of the Gothic: Byronic hero', https://epublications.marquette.edu/gothic_byronichero [accessed 29 July 2024].

McCormack, M. (2005). *The Independent Man: Citizenship and Gender Politics in Georgian England*. Manchester: Manchester University Press.

Mellor, A.K. (1988). 'Making a monster'. In: *Mary Shelley: Her Life, Her Fiction, Her Monsters.* New York: Methuen, pp. 38–51.

Mercer A. (2015). 'On this day in 1815: The Shelleys and "mutability"', *BARS Blog*, www.bars.ac.uk/blog/?p=966 [accessed 10 January 2025].

Milton, J. (1667, Reiss. 1968). *Paradise Lost.* London: Penguin Classics.

Moers, E. (1978). *Literary Women.* London: The Women's Press.

Murray, C. (2016). '*Frankenstein* in comics and graphic novels'. In: Smith, A. (ed.), *The Cambridge Companion to Frankenstein.* Cambridge: Cambridge University Press, pp. 219–40.

O'Brien, R. (n.d.), *The Rocky Horror Picture Show*, https://rockyhorror.co.uk [accessed 12 October 2024].

Offord, S. (2018), 'Frankenstein on stage', *V&A Blog*, www.vam.ac.uk/blog/museum-life/frankenstein-on-stage [accessed 23 November 2024].

O'Flinn, P. (1995). 'Production and reproduction: The case of "Frankenstein"', in Botting, F. (ed.), *Frankenstein: A New Casebook.* Basingstoke: Macmillan.

Oxford English Dictionary (n.d.), 'wretch (noun & adjective)', www.oed.com/dictionary/wretch_n [accessed September 2024].

Oxford Reference (n.d.), 'Byronic', www.oxfordreference.com/display/10.1093/oi/authority.20110803095539831 [accessed 29 July 2024].

Paivio, A. (1969). 'Mental imagery in associative learning and memory'. *Psychological Review*, 76(3), pp. 241–63.

Pinyerd, T. (2016). 'The other: Orientalism in *Frankenstein*', *Hohonu*, 14, pp. 55–6.

Plutarch (1470). *Plutarch's Lives* (trans. 1899 by Stewart, A. and Long, G.). London: George Bell & Sons. Project Gutenberg eBook #14114,www.gutenberg.org/files/14114/14114-h/14114-h.htm [accessed 13 January 2025].

Polidori, J. (1819). 'The Vampyre'. *The New Monthly Magazine and Universal Register*, 1(63), pp. 195–206.

Quinn, E.G. (2024). 'Beyond "his native town": Travel and alienation in Mary Shelley's *Frankenstein*'. *Criterion: A Journal of Literary Criticism*, 16(2), article 5, https://scholarsarchive.byu.edu/criterion/vol16/iss2/5 [accessed 15 January 2025].

Richardson, S. (1740). *Pamela; or Virtue Rewarded.* Project Gutenberg eBook #6124 (2002), www.gutenberg.org/files/6124/6124-h/6124-h.htm [accessed 13 January 2025].

Said, E. (1978). *Orientalism.* New York: Vintage Books.

Schoene-Harwood, B. (2000). *Writing Men: Literary Masculinities from Frankenstein to the New Man.* Edinburgh: Edinburgh University Press.

Schwarcz, J. (2015). 'Opium and laudanum history's wonder drugs', Chemical Institute of Canada, www.cheminst.ca/magazine/article/opium-and-laudanum-historys-wonder-drugs/#:~:text=Victor%20Frankenstein%2C%20who%20incidentally%20was,Victorian%20era's%20most%20popular%20medicine [accessed 16 January 2025].

Sha, R.C. (2021). '*Frankenstein*'s embodied imagination: Or, the limits of embodied cognition'. In: Wang, O.N.C. (ed.), Frankenstein *in Theory: A Critical Anatomy.* London: Bloomsbury Academic, pp. 47–64.

Shah, Z. and Kurczij, K. (2024). *Bloomsbury Teacher Guide: Anita and Me.* London: Bloomsbury.

Shelley, M. with Shelley, P.(1817). *History of a Six Weeks' Tour*. London: T. Hookham and C. and J. Ollier.

Shelley, M. with Shelley, P. (1818). *The Original Frankenstein: Two New Versions: Mary Shelley's Earliest Draft and Percy Shelley's Revised Text*. Robinson, C.E. (ed.) (2009), New York: Vintage Books.

Shelley, M. (1831). *Frankenstein: or, The Modern Prometheus*. London: Henry Colburn and Richard Bentley. Project Gutenberg eBook # 84, www.gutenberg.org/files/84/84-h/84-h.htm [accessed 23 November 2024].

Spark, M. (2013). *Mary Shelley*. Manchester: Carcanet.

Stevenson, R.L. (1886, reiss. 2018). *The Strange Case of Dr Jekyll and Mr Hyde*. Bristol: Peripeteia Press.

Stoker, B. (1897, reiss. 2021). *Dracula*. New York: HarperCollins.

The Student Voice Network (n.d.), 'Adapting "Frankenstein" through the 19th and 20th Centuries', https://thestudentvoicenetwork.com/2176/news/adapting-frankenstein-through-the-19th-and-20th-centuries [accessed 23 November 2024].

Todorov, T. (1971). 'The 2 Principles of Narrative', *Diacritics*, 1(1), Autumn, pp. 37-44.

Tosh, J. (2005). 'Masculinities in an industrializing society: Britain, 1800–1914'. *Journal of British Studies* 44(2): 330–342.

University of Exeter (2018). 'The female Romantic poets who use opium for its "tranquilising power"', Featured news, https://news-archive.exeter.ac.uk/featurednews/title_645441_en.html [accessed 18 December 2024].

von Goethe, J.W. (1774). *The Sorrows of Young Werther*. Project Gutenberg eBook #2527 (2001), www.gutenberg.org/cache/epub/2527/pg2527-images.html [accessed 24 November 2024].

Wallace, D. and Smith, A. (2009). *The Female Gothic: New Directions*. Basingstoke: Palgrave Macmillan.

Walpole, H. (1764; reiss. 2001). *The Castle of Otranto*. London: Penguin Classics.

Watts, D. (n.d.), 'Burden and standard of proof', Ministry of Injustice, https://ministryofinjustice.co.uk/burden-and-standard-of-proof/#:~:text=In%20criminal%20cases%2C%20the%20prosecution,to%20as%20the%2099%25%20test [accessed 9 January 2025].

Weissman, J. (1976). 'A reading of *Frankenstein* as the complaint of a political wife'. *Colby Library Quarterly*, 12: 171–180, https://knarf.english.upenn.edu/Articles/weissma2.html [accessed 23 November 2024].

Wollstonecraft, M. (1792), *A Vindication of the Rights of Woman: With Strictures on Political and Moral Subjects*. London: J. Johnson.

Wordsworth, W. (1798). *Lines Written a Few Miles above Tintern Abbey*.

Wright, A. (2016). 'The female Gothic'. In: Smith, A. (ed.), *The Cambridge Companion to Frankenstein*. Cambridge: Cambridge University Press, pp. 99–172.

Zoanna, J. (1991). '"They will prove the truth of my tale": Safie's letters as the feminist core of Mary Shelley's *Frankenstein*'. *Journal of Narrative Technique*, 21(2), pp. 170–84.

FURTHER READING

- *How to Teach Grammar* by B. Aarts, B., I. Cushing and R. Hudson.
- *Teaching English Language and Literature 16–19* by F. Ahmen, M. Giovanelli, M. Mansworth and F. Titjen.
- *Mary Shelley and the Rights of the Child* by E.H. Botting.
- *Explicit and Direct Instruction: An Evidence-Informed Guide for Teachers* by A. Boxer.
- 'Prometheus' by Britannica, www.britannica.com/topic/Prometheus-Greek-god
- 'Mary Shelley, Frankenstein and the Villa Diodati' by G. Buzwell.
- 'Tales of terror and wonder – a Gothic legacy' by G. Buzwell.
- 'The sea of ice and the icy sea: The Arctic frame of *Frankenstein*' by J. Cavell.
- *Gothic Literature: Texts, Contexts, Connections* by S. Chaplin.
- *Exploring Language and Literature* by S. Croft and R. Myers.
- *The Rhetoric of Romanticism* by P. De Man.
- *Grotesque: The New Critical Idiom* by J.D. Edwards and R. Grauland.
- *The Elements of Eloquence: How to Turn the Perfect English Phrase* by M. Forsyth.
- *Narrative* by M. Giovanelli.
- *Cognitive Grammar in Stylistics: A Practical Guide* by M. Giovanelli and C. Harrison.
- *The Language of Literature* by M. Giovanelli and J. Mason.
- *A History of Natural Philosophy* by E. Grant.
- '*Frankenstein*: The horrifying otherness of family' by J. Hall.
- *Making the Monster: The Science Behind Mary Shelley's Frankenstein* by K. Harkup.
- 'The history of masculinity, circa 1650–1800' by K. Harvey.
- *The Writing Revolution* by J.C. Hochman and N. Wexler.
- *The Game of Love in Georgian England* by S. Holloway.
- *Mary Shelley's Frankenstein, the 1818 Text: Contexts and Criticism* by P.J. Hunter.
- *Language and Power* by G. Ives and R. Rana.
- 'Is there a woman in this text?' by M. Jacobus.
- 'Changes between the 1818 and 1831 editions of *Frankenstein*' by E. James.
- 'Mary Shelley's *Frankenstein* and Milton's monstrous myth' by J.B. Lamb.
- *The Voyage of Italy* by R. Lassels.
- *The Life and Letters of Mary Wollstonecraft Shelley* by F.A. Marshall.
- 'Choosing a text of "Frankenstein" to teach' by A.K. Mellor.
- '*Frankenstein*: Gender, and mother nature' by A.K. Mellor.
- *The Bakhtin Reader: Selected Writings of Bakhtin, Medvedev, Volosshinov* by P. Morris.
- *The Mad Woman in the Attic* by J. Mortimore.
- 'Making up Universal's Frankenstein' in *Monsters of Make Up*, by L. Munson.
- *Women and Marriage in Nineteenth-Century England* by J. Perkin.
- '"A paradise of my own creation": Frankenstein and the improbable romance of polar exploration' by J. Richard.
- 'Introduction' in *Frankenstein: Annotated* by C.E. Robinson.
- *Mary Shelley* by M. Seymour.
- *Child of Light: A Reassessment of Mary Shelley* by M. Spark.
- 'Three women's texts and a critique of imperialism' by G.C. Spivak.
- *I May Be Some Time: Ice and the English Imagination* by F. Spufford.
- 'How Frankenstein became a literary classic' by C. Suciu.
- 'Body snatchers: What led to the Anatomy Act of 1832?' by The National Archives.
- '200 years of Frankenstein on stage and onscreen' by I.A. Veysey.
- 'Innocent until proven guilty' by D. Watts.
- *African American Gothic: Screams from Shadowed Places* by M. Wester.

INDEX